JAZZ

For most of his adult life, John Chilton has divided his time between playing jazz, writing about it and collecting records. He has worked with many groups with varying jazz styles and companied several great jazz men, including Buc Coleman, Milt Buckner, Matty Matlock, Shavers and Ben Webster. During th band, 'The Feetwarmers', worked in the UK and on the Continent, an at the Newport Jazz Festival.

John Chilton's books include *Who's Louis – The Louis Armstrong Story*, with *Music.*

TEACH YOURSELF BOOKS

JAZZ

John Chilton

Foreword by George Melly

TEACH YOURSELF BOOKS
Hodder and Stoughton

First Impression 1979

British Library C.I.P.
Chilton, John
Jazz. – (Teach yourself books).
1. Jazz music
I. Title II. Series
785.4'2 ML3561.J3

ISBN 0–340–23847–X

Printed and bound in Great Britain for
Hodder and Stoughton Paperbacks, a Division of Hodder and
Stoughton Ltd, Mill Road, Dunton Green, Sevenoaks, Kent,
(Editorial Office: 47 Bedford Square, London WC1 3DP)
by Richard Clay (The Chaucer Press) Ltd,
Bungay, Suffolk

Published in the USA by David McKay & Co. Inc.,
750 Third Avenue, New York, NY 10017 USA

Contents

To Brian Peerless,
for all the hundreds of pleasurable hours
that we have spent discussing jazz.

Acknowledgements

The author and publisher would like to thank The Melody Maker for permission to reproduce photographs of Sidney Bechet, Jelly Roll Morton, Louis Armstrong, Edward (Duke) Ellington, William (Count) Basie, Benny Goodman, Leon Bix Beiderbecke, Billie Holiday, Thomas (Fats) Waller, Bessie Smith, Coleman Hawkins, Django Reinhardt, Lionel Hampton, Weldon (Jack) Teagarden, George Lewis, Charlie (Yardbird) Parker, William (Bunk) Johnson, Roy Eldridge, Theodore (Sonny) Rollins, Lee Knoitz, Thelonious Monk, John (Dizzy) Gillespie, Gerry Mulligan, Lester Young, Miles Davis, Dave Brubeck, Sun Ra (ne Herman Blount), John Coltrane and Ornette Coleman. Thanks also to Mrs T Chilton for use of the photograph of Earl Hines.

Foreword

If I get up from the motel dressing-table where I am writing these words and look obliquely through the window into an identical room set at a right-angle to this one, I can see John Chilton adding the final touches to this book. Last night, we played a concert here in Cwmbran, a new industrial town in South Wales. Tonight it's Swindon. We've spent about five years together, playing an average of twenty gigs a month, the majority of them one-night stands. It's a very public life. We travel together, eat together, laugh together, occasionally quarrel with each other, and, of course, perform on the same stages in front of the same audiences, but, as writers, we retire monk-like into our anonymous cells to work. What follows is the result of over a year of distillation and research on John's part. It is I believe the best introduction to the history, practice and meaning of jazz music to date.

John Chilton is among the leading jazz historians of the world, but he wears his learning lightly. If his subject were Sanskrit, or the Industrial Revolution, he would no doubt hold the chair at a university. As it is jazz, this option is not yet open. He is in the happy position of practising what he preaches, living out what he writes about. It gives his work an objective–subjective approach almost unique among historians; a built-in empathy for the jazz musician, the life he lives and the music he creates.

He is, however, well aware of jazz musicians' love of myth-making, their tendency to tell the researcher what he wants to hear, and their mischievous propensity to see what Paul Bunyan-like absurdities they can get away with. John checks and double-checks everything, conducts an enormous correspondence with practitioners, both famous and obscure, has accumulated vast files, read everything on the subject, including the most transitory magazines and the most tentatively relevant books. His memory is phenomenal but he never trusts it. He is, when it comes to jazz history, and in the best sense of the word, an academic.

This is not a long book nor, of necessity, a very detailed one. It could have been a superficial book. It is not superficial because, behind its lucid and even prose, it encapsulates a life-time of study. It reveals too an open-minded approach to the whole history of the music, unusual in a musician who plays in the style of a particular era. The only area for which John had to do much new research was in avant-garde jazz of the last decade. It is not a music for which he felt, initially, much sympathy, but, typically, by listening and studying, he emerged with a new understanding and respect. Jazz is a country of fiercely divided factions. Chilton is able to perceive and clarify what joins and relates one development of the music to another. He is committed to breaking down those prejudices which have always diverted so much energy in the long history of jazz. Excellence and honesty of intention are his criteria. His enthusiasm is the equal of his scholarship.

George Melly

Introduction

This book deals with jazz in two ways: it presents a summary of its history, and it also outlines the methods that jazz improvisers use.

Most of the book is concerned with the evolution of jazz, but three chapters, six, ten and thirteen, are on technical aspects of jazz creation. They are a listener's guide rather than a performer's treatise, and are intended as much for those who do not read music as for those who do.

At the conclusion of each chapter there is a list of recommended books dealing with each specific era discussed. At the end of the book there are suggestions for further reading, lists of reference books, and recommended jazz periodicals, and an alphabetical glossary of jazz terms. A selection of recordings, from 1917 to 1977, is given, and, wherever possible, the most recent issue number is included; most of the records are available at the time of writing.

John Chilton
February 1978

1 The ancestry of jazz

An outline of African music-making; how slaves brought some of those sounds to America; the growth of organised music-making among the deprived blacks of the Southern states of America; the linking of various musical cultures within the city of New Orleans, Louisiana; after the Civil War new opportunities for black musicians occur; the beginnings of ragtime.

Anyone can enjoy a jazz performance without knowing the names of the participating musicians or any aspect of jazz history. However, listening pleasure can be greatly increased by acquiring knowledge of the history of the music and its performers.

Do not be deterred by the layer of mystique that some jazz lovers attempt to put around the music. Years ago, jazz fans developed a sort of snobbery whereby anyone who said they liked jazz was expected to know by heart the entire personnel of dozens of recording bands. Fortunately, that attitude is fast disappearing. Today, it is realised that the most important aspect of jazz appreciation concerns the sound of the music and not its statistics.

Paradoxically, an all-round knowledge of the music is gained by delving into an era from which no sounds have survived, and learning something of the musical developments that took place in North America during the two-hundred-year period that preceded the first gramophone recordings.

Jazz had been played for some years before the Original Dixieland Jazz Band (a five-piece band from New Orleans, Louisiana) became the first band to record the music in January 1917. Many of the ingredients in the music that the ODJB featured were centuries old, but the manner of their presentation seemed new. The band's cornet-playing leader, Dominic La Rocca, spent much of his later life repeating the preposterous claim that he had invented jazz.

There are two certainties about jazz: firstly, no one man invented it and secondly, it originated in North America – a fusion of several cultures brought to that continent, the most important being the music imported with African slaves.

It is usual for non-Africans to think of Africa as a vast homogeneous continent wherein all native people follow comparable life-styles and have similar customs. In reality, it is a conglomeration of different peoples, speaking different languages, many of them having dissimilar traditions and religions. The area from which most of the American slaves originated (that bite of West Africa stretching from Dakar across to Lake Chad and down again to the coast) covers almost two million square miles, and contains many disparate tribes living in differing climates. What all these tribes have in common is an important regard for music in their everyday lives, each possessing songs and dances appropriate to local customs and ceremonies. A close analysis of these various musical styles might reveal the ancestry of certain jazz rhythms and phrases but no single example of pure African music could be called jazz. In North America, African music underwent two hundred years of miscegenation with music of Spanish, English and French origin before the first notes of jazz were heard. These outside influences shaped the harmonies and melodies of early jazz but its rhythm and timbre hail from Africa.

It has been said that drumming is the very heart of all African music and initially the slaves' main instrument was the drum. Few slaves were allowed to take possessions to America, so the expatriate musicians had to do the best they could to make instruments similar to those that they had known in their homelands.

Besides many types of drum, the slave would also have been aware of other African instruments: stringed instruments similar to primitive banjos, single-stringed lyres, harps, and many varieties of gong, marimba and xylophone. Flutes, horns, pipes and one-stringed violins also existed, but the sound most commonly heard in African music, alongside the drums and hand-clapping, is the human voice.

In describing the 'full ensemble' of African music, A. M. Jones (in *African Native Music*) wrote: 'this consists of the instruments of the orchestra, the hand-clapping, the song and the dance. All these four ingredients combine to form the central act of African music.' Chapter six which is devoted to musical theory will show how these ingredients percolated into jazz. However, an extensive study of the myriad intricacies of African music is not essential for someone wishing to understand jazz. Time will be better spent finding out what happened to the slaves after they reached their enforced destination in the New World.

The first African slaves brought to North America were landed in 1619. The consignment arrived in a Dutch ship and was sold to a settler in the English colony of Virginia. Five years later, in the same locale, the first Negro born in the English colonies was baptised in Jamestown. Slavery was gradually introduced into other States, either by direct importation from Africa, or by purchasing African slaves who had previously served in the West Indies. At first, the landings were in low figures. Thirty years after the initial importation there were only 300 slaves in Virginia, many of them indentured servants able to buy land after their term of service had ended.

The mood of tolerant integration did not last. The need for a huge, cheap workforce, combined with the greed of the slave-traders, caused the influx to increase rapidly. Countless Africans died *en route* to America as European slavers packed their holds with human cargo. The hardship, vile food and enforced squalor brought diseases that killed many of the captives long before the ships reached America, but the lost lives meant little to traders working on vast profit margins.

By 1700, there were about 28 000 slaves in the North American British Colonies, of which about 6000 were in the North, and 22 000 in the South. By 1750, the overall figure had increased to about 236 000, with 200 000 in the South. As the numbers increased so did the restrictions, injustices and atrocities.

In the early days of slavery, most of the owners were small-holding farmers or tradesmen, and few of them owned more than two slaves. The slaves worked and lived close by their owners, and gradually discarded African traditions. The chances of a large social gathering of these small cells of slaves was extremely unlikely; the owners, always wary of insurrection, did not encourage such assemblies. Even those slaves who might have wanted to play their part in a full African musical ensemble had little opportunity to do so. Their music-making seems to have been restricted to singing, chanting, hand-clapping and playing percussion on anything readily available.

The growth of the cotton, tobacco, sugar and rice industries brought the need for huge labour forces housed close to their place of work. This meant that, in many locations, hundreds of slaves were within easy hailing distance of each other. African musical traditions began to revive, stimulated by the constant influx of new slaves arriving direct from Africa. Collective music-making again began to flourish. The art of playing, and of *understanding* the atumpan 'talking drums' had not left those whose agonising journey across the Atlantic had taken place decades before.

Drumming was not tolerated on every plantation, but most owners encouraged their slaves to sing hymns or work-songs. Many owners believed that their slaves should become Christians, but when the Africans sang European hymns of worship they did so in a manner that was immediately heard to be different.

The musical scales that governed the structures of the hymns were unlike anything the African had heard before, compounded as they are by a series of evenly-spaced whole tones and semitones (exemplified by a piano keyboard). The African was used to a more flexible, and more intricate, system of music-making, employing many quarter tones and countless even-smaller variations of pitch as though each note on a keyboard had several subsidiary devices for heightening or lowering its pitch. This gliding up to and away from notes was not part of the European singers' technique. The African concept of singing European religious music became known as 'spiritual singing' (later re-named 'gospel' music). Eventually a name was given to the notes that the American Negroes inflected in their own individual way: they became known as 'blue' notes. This process of transplanting the African system of pitching was also used when the slaves began playing European instruments.

The owners had good reason to encourage work songs. The performance of the African chants was a stimulus to the slaves' work rate, and the music also acted as a safety-valve in dispersing the workers' anger and frustration. The sound of these work songs was completely alien to European ears. Their strangeness was emphasised by the fact that they were sung in rhythms that were also new to the white man. Much European music is syncopated – that is containing notes that do not fall evenly in time with the tap, tap, tap of the music's beat – but the Afro-American music was full of complicated syncopations, some delayed, some anticipated, some lightly emphasised, some heavily accented.

These un-European syncopations, and the use of a 'blue note scale', formed the basis of early jazz. However, it took 200 years of interfusion between African and European music before a recognisable jazz style emerged.

Certain factors appear to have been vital to the development of jazz: the slaves needed to retain some contact with African traditions, they had to have the opportunity to take part in music-making *and* to hear European music, and they needed European instruments.

Three of these factors were probably always available to slaves in New England. However, the slaves there were a tiny minority, and by 1776 only numbered about two per cent of the population. Work songs and drum rituals did not occur there and few Africanisms survived so, in consequence, this area played no role in the emergence of jazz.

In the rural areas of South Carolina (where slaves numbered forty-three per cent of the state's population in 1790), many African rituals were retained, but there the slaves had hardly any contact with either European music or instruments and here again no close links with jazz have ever been discovered.

The locale that supplied all the essentials over a long period was New Orleans, the principal port of Louisiana. Louisiana adopted slavery some while after its Southern neighbour states. The first twenty slaves arrived in 1713 while the territory was still a French colony.

The French attitude towards slaves seems to have been more patriarchal than the approach taken by other European nations, and although a restricting *Code Noir* was formulated during the early days, the percentage of slaves who became freemen was higher in Louisiana than in other Southern States. This process of emancipation continued throughout the eighteenth century, and was not interrupted during the period of Spanish administration (1769–1803). The slave population of the state greatly increased during the 1791–1809 period when thousands of slaves were brought to New Orleans from Santo Domingo by refugees fleeing from slave insurrections in Haiti.

At the beginning of the nineteenth century, four different cultures (French, Spanish, African and Haitian) existed alongside each other in New Orleans. The city also had minority groups of German, Italian and Arcadian settlers, as well as a small number of American Indians. It was justifiably called 'the city of music' and there are many early accounts of the profusion of formal and informal dances held there. Some of the orchestras providing music at these events contained Negro musicians, most often freemen who had received some formal training from Europeans, usually on violin or clarinet. The music played consisted of European quadrilles, cotillions and waltzes. Yet within the same city music that was totally non-European could be heard in Congo Square and on the Mississippi River levee (the raised banks of the river) where hundreds of the city's slaves gathered during their Sunday rest day to dance to music played by fellow slaves.

The juxtaposition of totally dissimilar music was to be a feature of New Orleans life for much of the nineteenth century. The 1803 Louisiana Purchase, by which America obtained the state from France, led to the state becoming part of the Union in 1812. The change of administration had an impact on the main city's ballroom scene. Henry A. Kmen in *Music in New Orleans* cites examples of incoming Americans demanding that their sort of dances (reels and jigs) replace the waltzes and cotillions. The municipal authorities attempted to bring peace to the ballroom by ruling that a set order of dances that pleased all parties was to be adhered to, but this was often ignored. For over twenty years the same dispute was likely to bring violence to the dance floor. In spite of this acrimony, ballroom dancing remained tremendously popular in New Orleans, and even the lowliest hall had a resident orchestra. By 1807, military bands (containing brass instruments and woodwind) were playing for indoor dances held in the city.

Few black people would have been seen at these dances. The only Negroes likely to be admitted would be maid-servants and footmen in attendance. People of colour, whether they were quadroons (one-quarter Negro), or octoroons (one-eighth Negro) were not welcome in the ballrooms. Soon after the 1803 treaty with the United States, which accorded full citizenship to all free people regardless of race or colour, there began a series of quadroon balls. It seems that they featured a mixture of French, Spanish and American dances. Slaves were not welcome at these gatherings, and eventually they were totally banned. The dances presented a positive indication of the complex caste system that played an important part in the early history of New Orleans. The term Creole began to be used as a self-description by Negroes with mixed blood (with French or Spanish ancestry). However the white New Orleanians usually reserved the term for descendants of the elite of early French Colonists.

The slaves continued to hold their outdoor dance ceremonies on Sundays but a decree introduced in 1817 limited these activities to one venue, Congo Square. This was one of a series of restrictions that were introduced as the number of slaves in Louisiana increased. The census of 1810 showed that 40 000 of the 76 556 population were slaves. The recurring slave revolts in the near-by West Indies were one reason for the hardening attitude, another was the rigid discipline needed to control the labour forces employed on the increasing number of sugar and cotton plantations.

Music-making among freemen tended towards formal respectability. The general ambition was to play in a local orchestra or in one of the ever-increasing number of Negro militia bands (slaves who served in the 1812 war were granted freedom on demobilisation). Most of the militia bands were drum and fife units, but occasionally a full military band (with trumpets, french horns, trombones, flutes, piccolos and clarinets) was mustered. The New Orleans newspaper *Times Picayune* published many contemporary reports of musical activities within the city. An 1838 item mentions 'a real mania in this city for horn and trumpet playing'. Several mentions are made of a local Negro musical hero known as Old Corn Meal, a singing street vendor who was celebrated enough to be booked at the St Charles Theatre in 1837. Another local black musician, banjoist Picayune Butler, gained fame all over the Southern States and is credited as being one of the earliest inspirations for Minstrelsy.

By 1830, Louisiana, following the example of other Southern States, had banned the use of drums at slave gatherings, but despite this the Sunday crowds still gathered in Congo Square until the assemblies were banned (temporarily) in 1843. More and more regulations were passed that restricted the social activities of slaves and freemen. Some defied the rules, and an 1841 report details a police raid on an illicit ball 'where the band consists of clarionet, three fiddles, two tembourines and a bass drum'. Regardless of the law the growing number of voodoo ceremonies (witchcraft rituals brought from Haiti) always featured drum music.

The various obstacles that prevented most Negroes from dancing indoors or out gave an impetus to the freemen's marching bands and more and more black ensembles were formed. Many visitors to New Orleans in the mid-nineteenth century wrote, not always flatteringly, about the early morning rehearsals indulged in by the bands. None of the regulations affected the New Orleans Negro custom of having bands to play at funerals – sombre music before the ceremony, joyful marches on the way back from the cemetery. As early as 1819, Benjamin Latrobe wrote about a Negro band playing at a funeral. The tradition of being 'buried with music', as the practice is known locally, continues to this day.

Ordinary people of all races took great interest in the merits of the city's individual musicians and rival bands. The 'cutting contests' whereby two bands would try to outplay each other in the streets were evident by 1850. A *Times Picayune* of the 1860s mentions one such battle: 'Boys, negroes, fruit women and what not followed the procession shouting and bawling apparently delighted.' Those enthusiasts who marched on the sidewalk alongside the bands became known as the 'Second Line' – both the term and the tradition still exist. The Second Line would often be mixed, but the cutting contests were never inter-racial. The four principal ethnic groups of New Orleans, the French-speaking whites, the English-speaking whites, the freed slaves (mostly mulattos of mixed blood), and the Negro slaves, remained separate. The downtown French district of the city, and the uptown American section were two distinct areas, divided by Canal Street. The French and Americans kept their distance socially, and freeman and slave rarely mixed. Occasionally the barriers would be lifted for music, some downtown mixed-blood Creoles studied with European musicians, imported for the Opera House orchestra, and some uptown Negroes had Creole music teachers. No sect lived in a musical vacuum, and musical ideas must have been continually exchanged, albeit unconsciously. However, it was to take a Civil War and a long painful period of Reconstruction before there was any widespread musical fraternisation in New Orleans.

As the nineteenth century passed, so more reports appeared of Negro musicians playing in the country districts of the Deep South. Most were violinists, and the second most common instrument was the banjo – both instruments were similar to cruder African models. Occasionally there was mention of a brass player. The term Negro Jig began to be used on published music. Sometimes a plantation owner would call a field-slave who played the violin up to the big house to provide music for dancing. However, there are no reports of any organised black bands or orchestras in the rural areas. The story was very different in the Southern cities. Richmond (Virginia), Louisville (Kentucky) and Charleston (South Carolina) all had organised black bands (composed of freemen and house-slaves) during the mid-nineteenth century.

Several cities in the North also had regular Negro bands; as early as 1830 an all-black military band was formed in Philadelphia. The early music scene on Manhattan Island gave rise to reports markedly similar to those concerning the Congo Square gatherings. Hundreds of slaves gathered there to take part in exotic dancing on festive days. There are details of slaves playing African-type instruments, and tributes to the skills of the dancers.

A pattern emerges from the mid-nineteenth-century descriptions of Negro music-making in North America. It seems that there were two types of music being played by Afro-Americans. The first, a fairly formal copy of European dance music and dance tunes (music that white people could easily enjoy), the second, a rough and rhythmic music that usually baffled and sometimes displeased white listeners. Occasionally an individual black musician emerged who could blend the two disparates, but usually this man could not write down his own music, so the whole process was not passed on and became a hybrid concept.

The dramatic events that occurred in the USA during and after the Civil War (1861–65) produced a situation that gradually led to the two elements being brought together permanently. The place where this fusion first took place seems to have been New Orleans. It was as though the musical climate of that city forced up a root that had spread underground throughout the United States.

Those slaves who had anticipated that the end of the Civil War (when the North and the South fought each other) would bring total and instant freedom suffered bitter disappointment. The period immediately following the War, known as the Reconstruction era, brought many fresh problems and hardships to the ex-slaves. However, all restrictions on music-making disappeared and from this era many fountains of Negro musical expression began to flow.

Minstrelsy had flourished in America since the 1840s, but all the early troupes featured white entertainers who blackened their faces with burnt cork and gave exaggerated imitations of Negro songs, speech patterns and dances. After the Civil War several professional Negro troupes were formed and some of them became renowned enough to tour Europe. From the ritual finale of the minstrel show, which involved a rhythmic 'walk around', the Cakewalk, one of the most popular dances of the nineteenth century emerged. The Fisk Jubilee Singers, a group of black college students who specialised in spirituals and plantation songs, began widespread touring in 1871, and during the following year made the first of many trips to Europe. Several touring circus bands hired black musicians.

Each succeeding year after the Civil War ended brought new opportunities for musical blacks to display their skills. Seemingly, a craze for music-making took place among the emancipated – anyone who could afford to buy a musical instrument did so. In 1874, a method for playing the guitar, written by a Negro Justin Holland, had been published. It was at last possible for a black musician to work as a professional.

Even New Orleans, with its long tradition of music-making, was affected by the surge of enthusiasm for performing. The number of Negro music teachers grew from seven in 1870 to fifty-three in 1880. The number of black marching bands doubled, yet there was still work for all of them. However, there was still no sign of any mixed bands. If anything, the feeling between those who were freemen before the Civil War and the emancipated slaves worsened when the War ended, one cause being that in 1861 10 000 slaves had poured into the city from country districts to seek refuge. The distinctly separate music-making continued as it had done before the War.

One of the strangest of jazz myths concerns the immediate post-Civil-War period. Some jazz historians have stated that the Confederate Troops departing from New Orleans left behind a profusion of various band instruments; the ex-slaves picked them up, blew them and thus created an embryo jazz. There is not a shred of evidence to support this theory. The acquisition of European instruments by Negroes took place gradually during the fifty years preceding the War.

The most dramatic change in the possession of instruments by ex-slaves during the period following the Civil War concerned pianos and organs. References to Negro keyboard players in pre-Civil War days are few, though one item mentions a Negro pianist whose piano style suggested banjo playing. However, a pianist of natural genius, the twentieth child of a slave, did become famous. This was Blind Tom Bethune. His talents made him well-known before the Civil War and nationally famous thereafter. It is conceivable that this man's example inspired many fellow blacks to concentrate on piano. Whatever the reason, many Negro families underwent hardships in order to purchase their own keyboard instruments. The result was that by the 1890s there were many fine black pianists playing in all the Mississippi River valley states. From these men a style of music emanated that illustrated a blending of two aspects of European and African music. The African system of 'bending' notes cannot be applied to the fixed pitch of notes on a keyboard, but it is possible to transfer African rhythms to piano playing. This is what the emergent black pianists did: their left hands provided the basic pulse of the music, while their right hands played a variety of complex counter rhythms. This style of playing was originally called jig piano. It later became known as ragtime. The music developed most speedily in Missouri. Its principal exponent, and foremost composer, was Scott Joplin, a Negro who arrived in St Louis from his home state of Texas at the age of seventeen.

The new music very quickly became nationally popular. It could be written down accurately, and soon black and white pianists were playing the music in saloons and dance halls all over the USA. Orchestrators began producing ragtime arrangements for military bands, brass bands, string trios, and every sort of musical combination. Here was the music that might have linked all the various musical elements of New Orleans, but in reality it highlighted their differences. White, Creole and Black musicians all played ragtime tunes, each in different ways. The schisms were personified by three of the bandleaders who emerged in New Orleans during the late 1890s: the Creole violinist John Robichaux, the white drummer Jack (Papa) Laine, and the Negro trumpeter Charles (Buddy) Bolden. Each of these men contributed much to the New Orleans music scene around the turn of the century, but it was from the Negro section that the improvisations which were to link ragtime with early jazz were first heard.

Recommended Reading

Bebey, Francis *African Music* (A useful introduction which covers a wide area), G. Harrap, London, 1975

Blassingame, John W. *Black New Orleans 1860–80* (Concentrates on social and economic backgrounds; it includes a wealth of information on population and occupation statistics), University of Chicago, USA, 1973

Blesh, Rudi and Janis, Harriet *They All Played Ragtime* (A fascinating, and well-researched history of ragtime and its principal exponents), Oak Publications, USA, 1971

Gammond, Peter *Scott Joplin and the Ragtime era*, Angus and Robertson, UK, 1975

Haskins, James *Scott Joplin* (The Man Who Made Ragtime), Doubleday, USA, 1978

Jasen, D. and Tichenor, J. *Rags and Ragtime* (A Musical History), Seabury Press, USA, 1978

Jones, A. M. *Studies In African Music* (Two Volumes) (Volume One discusses African instrumentation, drum techniques, work songs, cult music, etc.) (Volume Two is devoted to musical examples), Oxford University Press, 1971

Kmen, Henry A. *Music in New Orleans 1791–1841* (An extensively researched history), Louisiana State University Press, USA, 1966

Mellers, Wilfrid *Music in a New Found Land* (A detailed survey of all aspects of American music), Barrie and Rockcliff, London, 1964

Oliver, Paul *Savannah Syncopators* (African retentions in the blues; a brief, but highly informative and scholarly work), Studio Vista, London, 1970

Roach, Hildred *Black American Music* (A concise survey, with an emphasis on Negro composers), Crescendo, Boston, USA, 1973

Rousseve, C. B. *The Negro in Louisiana* (Aspects of his history and literature; also contains numerous statistics), Johnson Reprint Co., USA, 1970

Southern, Eileen *The Music of Black Americans* (Covers the entire history from 1619 onwards, with chapters on ragtime, blues and jazz), W. W. Norton, USA, 1971

Stearns, Marshall and Jean *Jazz Dance* (subtitled: 'The Story of American Vernacular Dance'). A comprehensive history, covering slave dancing and dancing in Broadway shows – complete with diagrams of dance steps), Macmillan, USA, 1968

Toll, Robert *Blacking Up* (*The Minstrel Show in Nineteenth Century America*) (A detailed history and analysis), Oxford University Press, 1974

2 New Orleans – the cradle of jazz

The improvising black bands of New Orleans experiment by blending dissimilar musical styles, including blues and ragtime; many young white musicians are intrigued by the results and one five-piece band, The Original Dixieland Jazz Band, is offered lucrative work in Chicago and is subsequently the first jazz group to make recordings.

By the end of the nineteenth century, New Orleans's position as America's most active centre of music-making was unchallengeable. Classical works, operas, burlesque ballads, ragtime and marching music were all being expertly performed within the city. Only the merest excuse was needed for an elaborate carnival to be assembled, complete with several parading bands, the city's climate being mild enough to allow outdoor festivities to continue all through the year. The climax of each year's celebrations was the world-famous Mardi Gras.

The one form of music not mentioned in any of the early contemporary accounts of festivities in New Orleans was the blues – the indigenous American music that came into being when the black slaves sang their variations of European folk-songs. Their renderings of religious music, which culminated in gospel music, were discussed in the previous chapter. The slaves' transmutation of the European settlers' folk-songs was a later development, which was to greatly affect all subsequent American popular music.

The blues consist of songs that last for twelve bars, each of those bars containing four beats. The first stanza is repeated, followed by a variant line, usually of explanation:

Feel so lonely, wish that I were dead,
Feel so lonely, wish that I were dead
My gal has left me, with nothing but an empty bed.

Originally, the blues were vocal music, unaccompanied songs of sadness, with no set length. The performer, unrestricted by the European system of measuring music by pre-ordained divisions of the beat, made the songs as long, or as short, as he, or she, thought fit. After years of listening to the songs of the white settlers, the slaves began adjusting their own songs to the harmonic patterns of European music, still retaining their own phrasing, feeling and system of 'bending' notes.

It was perhaps because New Orleans was so full of band and orchestral music that the blues did not play an important part in the city's music until late in the nineteenth century. But even if the city had wanted to, it would not have been able to shut out the blues. Being the principal port on the United States' southern seaboard, and the main terminus for cargo boats going to and from the vast Mississippi delta area, its labour force was continually in contact with itinerant workers from all over the Southern States. In the years immediately following the Civil War, many of the New Orleans workers were themselves recruited from the Southern States. These men brought with them the music they had known in Georgia, Tennessee or Mississippi. In consequence, the songs heard on the levee differed greatly from the ballads heard in the French Quarter of New Orleans.

Fate Marable, one of the most renowned bandleaders in early jazz history, said about this quayside music: 'Jazz was the outgrowth of roustabouts loading cotton boats, singing with perfect rhythm as they lifted the bales.' Although cornetist Dominic La Rocca was to champion white jazz musicians during his later life, he too stressed the importance of the levee music: 'A bunch of us at New Orleans started a band of our own. We got out stuff from the coloured bands that hung around the wharves.'[1]

When the levee workers had finished their labours they rarely moved far from the dockside area for their entertainment and relaxation. To meet their needs, a series of modest saloons opened. Itinerant guitarists, and untutored violinists (playing a robust style known as alley fiddle) realised that they could make a living from the tips that the rough-and-ready customers gave them – providing they played congenial music. After a while, the more ambitious bar-owners bought pianos and sometimes a drummer or a wind instrumentalist was added. A style of music developed within these rowdy taverns that became known as tonk music or barrelhouse music. It was highly rhythmical, and stylistically similar to the songs that the workmen sang during their quayside labours.

Gradually, this compound of syncopated blues and European folk-song permeated into the local Negro brass bands and dance bands. At the beginning of the twentieth century, there were within New Orleans several bands who did not use any written music, simply because their members could not read it. They made up their arrangements by listening to those bands that could read music and copying the sounds by ear, whether it was a dirge played at a funeral, a standard marching tune, or the latest ragtime orchestration.

These 'fake' bands (as the non-readers were called) added some of the tunes that drifted into the city, via waterfront and plantation, to their repertoires.

The short simple themes, attractive though they might be, would not stand the many repetitions necessary to make their performance as long in duration as a standard arrangement. To eliminate identical repetitions of the same tune, musicians played variations on the melodies. From within the ranks of these bands came a number of fine improvisers and blues players, among them trumpeter William (Bunk) Johnson.

One of the earliest bands known to have fused together the elements of tonk music, the blues and ragtime, was a unit led by Bunk Johnson's one-time colleague trumpeter Charles (Buddy) Bolden. Bolden's Band is said to have played in a rugged style that featured current ragtime tunes, local folk-songs, burlesque songs, blues tunes, popular hymns, and some of Bolden's own compositions. The band was never recorded.

During the 1890s, two pieces of Louisiana legislation were passed which had a decisive effect on music-making in New Orleans. One in 1894, greatly reduced the civil rights of many working-class Creoles, and in some cases forced them to move their homes into the uptown section of the city, which had a heavy black population. The other, from 1898, formulated a new voting system which took away the right to vote from many non-white people (black and Creole), and gave direct encouragement to a whole series of racial restrictions. In 1893, 130 344 non-whites were allowed to vote in Louisiana elections, by 1900 the figure was reduced to 5320.

Initially, these restrictions added to a mutual resentment that had been building up between the Creoles and the blacks since the end of the Civil War. In general, people who had been freed from slavery before Emancipation felt socially superior to those who had to wait for a nationally proclaimed freedom. The legislation of the 1890s, in forcing the two groups together, created a spirit of competitiveness within each sect. The competitiveness extended to music-making; it also stimulated each ethnic group to organise its own entertainment. When the resentment mellowed into restrained co-operation it led to a sharing of cultures which was highly beneficial to all the musicians involved.

During the late 1890s, several new dance halls opened in the uptown section of New Orleans. There was also a great increase in the number of elaborate functions organised by the ever-growing number of black fraternal societies.

Buddy Bolden's wide repertoire was readily accepted at all of these events, for he guaranteed to provide a band that could play indoors or outdoors. His usual line-up was an amalgamation of military band instruments (cornet, valve-trombone and clarinets), and the most popular instrumentation used by dance-hall trios in New Orleans (violin, string-bass and guitar or mandolin). Several members of Bolden's Band were able to read music, but mostly they relied on playing by ear. The leader himself was an extremely colourful character, a great favourite with the patrons of the uptown dance halls, and, as his popularity increased, he organised several subsidiary bands. After his death in 1931 he became a legendary figure, whose exploits seem akin to a mythological folk-hero, making it very difficult to sort fact from fiction. It is said that the wild excesses of his wine-women-and-song life-style eventually caused him to suffer a complete mental breakdown. It is a fact that in June 1907 he was committed to the Insane Asylum at Jackson, Louisiana, where he spent the remaining twenty-four years of his life. The cause of his insanity was given by the New Orleans authorities as alcohol.[2]

In a 1938 interview, published in *Tempo* magazine, one of Louisiana's most famous trombonists, Edward (Kid) Ory, gave a vivid description of Bolden at work:

> 'Buddy Bolden had a band in the Skating Rink in Lincoln Park. John Robichaux played for a dance in the same pavilion, separated from the Rink by a partition. Robichaux played the tunes of the day in strictly legitimate style; Bolden improvised on them, also played his own tunes in his own style. Bolden was a sensation. When he would start in at four o'clock, Robichaux would have a large crowd, having begun earlier in the afternoon. Bolden would warm his band up for a couple of numbers, then in the middle of one would say, "Well, let's call the children home". Whereupon he would go over from the platform to stick his cornet out of the window to play his solo. The crowd would come running, leaving the dance floor bare.'

This was one of a whole series of confrontations between black musicians and their Creole counterparts. Clarinettist George Bacquet remembered Bolden disparagingly referring to Robichaux's Band as 'those Frenchmen [*sic*] from down town'.[3]

Robichaux's Band offered no scope for improvisers. Multi-instrumentalist Manuel Manetta recalled: 'Robichaux's Band played strictly from music, including Scott Joplin numbers. The only number they played by ear was "Home Sweet Home".'[4] In contrast Bolden encouraged his musicians to embellish and improvise. This musical freedom allowed each instrumentalist to play a different musical line to that being created by his colleagues. The cornet, trombone, clarinet and violin all took turns at playing the melody, leaving opportunities for the non-melody players to improvise a descant, or counter-melody.

George Bacquet supplied the best description of the difference between Bolden's Band and Robichaux's; he was able to do so because he sometimes played clarinet with both bands during the course of the same evening. Bacquet, a Creole, toured with a Minstrel Band from 1902 until 1905, then returned to his home city and joined Robichaux, whose evening programme he described: 'A typical set opened with a one-step, continued with a schottische, a mazurka, a rag, a waltz, and ended with a quadrille. At evening engagements they ran through eight sets, all with the same sequence, and an intermission between each.'[5]

This was a programme, which apart from the rag and the one-step, could well have been used fifty years earlier. Bolden's Band played material that was decidedly less formal, as Bacquet realised when first he heard them. One evening, after a celebration, he and some friends decided to call in at the Oddfellows' Hall where Bolden's Band was playing. Years later he recalled:

> 'I remembered thinking it was a funny place, nobody took their hats off. It was plenty tough. You paid fifteen cents and walked in. When we came in, we saw the band, six of them, on a low stand. They had hats on too, and were resting – pretty sleepy. We stood behind a column. All of a sudden, Buddy stomps, knocks on the floor with his trumpet to give the beat and they all sat up straight, wide awake. Buddy held up his cornet, paused to make sure of his embouchure (the place on his lips where he positioned his mouthpiece), then they played "Make Me A Pallet On The Floor". Everybody got up quick, the whole place rose and yelled out "Oh, Mr Bolden, play it for us Buddy, play it". I'd never heard anything like that before. I'd played legitimate stuff. But this! It was something that pulled me. They got me on the stand that night, and I was playing with them. After that, I didn't play legitimate so much.'[6]

Initially, Bolden's white musical contemporaries paid little heed to the uptown experiments. The performance standards of some of these white marching bands was world class, but the improvisational capabilities of the musicians was never cited. One of the only pre-1900 white New Orleans groups that attempted to play a fake style was a children's band originally organised by Emile (Stalebread) Lacoume when he was thirteen years old. Lacoume, and some of his pals, formed a street band, playing home-made instruments constructed from cigar-boxes and tea-chests. This novelty group, which later added orthodox instruments, gained considerable publicity; it was later erroneously described as the first-ever jazz group.

George Laine was the leading white bandleader in New Orleans at the turn of the century. He began making music as a fifteen-year-old drummer, and soon became the leader of a drum-and-fife band. Later, he learnt to play brass instruments and organised his own Reliance Band. Laine realised that there was considerable demand for organised bands in New Orleans. When his band became booked up for a year in advance he formed up a second Reliance unit, then a third, until eventually he controlled six Reliance bands. Laine's original band were non-readers; they played by ear, learning arrangements aurally from other bands. After being coached by two light-complexioned Creoles, multi-instrumentalist David Perkins, and clarinettist Achille Baquet, Laine's musicians developed into a fully-fledged reading band. But even during the time that the band played by ear they concentrated on reproducing a standard arrangement, without improvisation.

Laine introduced many youngsters into his Reliance bands, and this gained him the nick-name Papa Jack. Several of his young recruits made their mark in jazz history, among them trombonists Tom Brown and Eddie Edwards, clarinettists Gusby Mueller and Alcide Nunez, multi-instrumentalist Arnold Loyocano and cornettist Dominic La Rocca. Laine did not encourage these youngsters to improvise, but by the early 1900s all of them had heard, and had begun experimenting with, the sounds of the new musical concepts that floated to them on the uptown air.

Many young musicians in Louisiana, black and white, were affected with the same enthusiasm that had overtaken George Bacquet. These young men had grown up listening to marching bands, Creole orchestras, alley fiddle players, tonk pianists, gospel singers, and the songs of the longshoremen. For them the small Negro bands of the early twentieth century, typified by the one led by Bolden, seemed to present a music that fused together elements from all of these varied forms, in a way that was challenging and exciting.

Groups of Negro musicians emerged from parishes in and around New Orleans, who could play their instruments well, but who were not 'legitimate' players, having shunned intensive studies of written music in order to develop their skills as improvisers. They included the cornet players Joe Oliver and Freddie Keppard, trombonist Kid Ory and clarinettist Johnny Dodds. These young men did most of their playing in cabarets and dance halls, but they also participated in the city's marching bands. It was their influx and predilection for improvisation that drastically changed the musical format of several of the long-established brass bands. By the early 1900s, such bands as the Eureka and the Olympia were playing printed arrangements *and* allowing improvisations.

Very few of the improvising musicians of the pre-1910 era were professionals. They played regularly but relied on day-work for the main part of their wages. Many of the Creole players were craftsmen, following trades like cigar-making, engraving, cabinet-making or brick-laying. The Negro players did a wide variety of jobs; Joe Oliver was a butler, Johnny Dodds worked as a labourer in a rice mill. Parade work tended to bring the Creole and Negro musicians together more than any other form of musical engagement. Even violinist Robichaux, the society leader, played drums in the Excelsior marching band. Gradually an *entente cordiale* was established between the two factions. Creole music teachers disregarded past prejudice and took on young pupils without considering their antecedents. The Creoles had long enjoyed a tradition of excellence on clarinet; their teaching skills, and those of a noted family of clarinettists from Mexico, the Tios, were responsible for producing many wonderful players. Sidney Bechet, Jimmie Noone, Albert Nicholas, Lawrence Duhe, Lorenzo Tio Jr and Alphonse Picou were just some of the fine New

Orleans clarinettists who combined the advanced musicianship of their teachers with the soulful sounds of the new music.

Many of the young Creoles encountered family opposition when they went to play in Negro bands. Dr Leonard Bechet was candid about his family's reaction to his brother Sidney's choice of musical colleagues: ' "Big Eye" Louis Nelson and them played that low-down type of music, when us Creole musicians always did hold up a nice prestige, you understand, demanded respect among the people, because we played nice music. So we didn't like Sidney playing with them.'[7]

Ferdinand La Menthe, better known as Jelly Roll Morton, also encountered family disdain over his music-making. Morton was one of the most flamboyant characters in a profession full of extroverts. He became famous as a bandleader, pianist, vocalist and composer, but during his formative years he concentrated on playing the piano, learning much from the ragtime specialists and translating it into his own personal style. He also gleaned a lot from the pianists who worked in the elegant brothels of New Orleans. These musicians were generally known as 'professors' and their place of work was usually referred to as 'the sporting house'. The emphasis in these places was on refined décor and the music was usually a sedate mixture of quietly played ragtime themes and sentimental ballads. The blues were rarely heard there, as they were patronisingly associated with rural areas. Country simplicity was something that few professors were likely to boast about.

Bands were never employed in these high-class bordellos. The pianist usually worked as a soloist, although on special occasions a trio might be employed. None of the pianists employed in the sporting houses was interested in giving up the huge amounts he earned in tips to play subsidiary roles in bands. Details of the renowned brothels were published in the notorious *Blue Book of New Orleans*, but there were countless places fulfilling the same function that went unlisted, particularly after the ordinances of the 1890s, which segregated whites from coloured. Those prostitutes who had mixed blood had, by law, to move to an area designated by Alderman Sidney Story. This man's zeal in enforcing the regulation has given him an everlasting place in jazz history: the area became known as Storyville. The musicians who worked in that area preferred to call it the Red Light District, the Tenderloin District or simply The District. As in the more luxurious establishments, the main instrumentalists were pianists, but they tended to play in a more earthy style, using lyrics that were more risqué than those heard in the downtown hostelries; even the blues were sung.

On a series of recordings made for the Library of Congress, Washington, DC in 1938, Jelly Roll Morton recalled how he became a waiter at one of these brothels simply to learn a particular blues that was played and sung there by Mamie Desdoumes. Morton reminisces in great detail about the music that could be heard in New Orleans at the turn of the century, dwelling not only on the various personalities of the city, but also explaining how he introduced what he called a 'Spanish tinge' into his piano playing. This was a linking of ragtime with rhythms that had been taken from Africa into Spain by the Moors centuries earlier, then brought to America via South America and the Caribbean Islands during the days of slavery.

During the period that Morton was formulating his style, several of his white contemporaries were also experimenting with new musical ideas and new instrumental permutations. Nick La Rocca played in several groups consisting of the popular string trio (violin, guitar/mandolin and string-bass) with his cornet added. Later, some of these groups added a clarinet, and then a valve-trombone, but from listeners' and participants' descriptions, the interplay between cornet, clarinet and trombone, which became the hallmark of the Dixieland style, was still in embryo. Often the instrumentalists all played the same note (in unison), without working out any harmony parts. Any variations were usually slight, and incidental to the main theme. However, the young white musicians were beginning to imitate the timbre and inflections of the coloured players. The next stage was in applying them to ragtime pieces and popular tunes.

A change of instrumentation had a vital effect on the overall sound of all the small bands in New Orleans. This occurred when the slide-trombone replaced the valve-trombone (which looks like a huge trumpet, complete with three valves). Often, as La Rocca said, the valve model ponderously doubled the same note that the trumpet was playing. The slide-trombone, on which the musician produces his notes by pushing the slide in and out, is able to produce glissandi (dramatically slurred notes) and sudden rips which sound like human shouts. A style of playing developed that became known as the 'tailgate style'. It derived from the era when bands advertised forthcoming events by playing on the back of moving lorries. The trombone player needed more room than other musicians by virtue of his extensive slide, and so was always placed at the back of the lorry, looking outwards over the tailgate.

The popularity of the slide-trombone grew rapidly in New Orleans. No one has established why the slide model, which is one of the most ancient of all brass instruments, was rarely used in pre-1900 New Orleans. Alphonse Picou (b. 1878) said that during his formative years he could only remember one man playing a slide-trombone. George (Pops) Foster (b. 1892) said in his autobiography: 'The first slide-trombone I ever saw was brought into New Orleans by a cousin of mine, George Williams.'[8] Manuel Manetta (b. 1889) said that his uncle, Deuce Manetta, was the first to play the instrument in New Orleans.[9] None of these recollections unravels the facts, but they indicate how uncommon the instrument was in New Orleans during the 1890s.

During the last quarter of the nineteenth century several New Orleans Brass Bands left Louisiana to go on extensive tours. The much heralded sixteen-piece

Excelsior did a six-month tour of Northern and Eastern states in 1887. Acknowledgement of the prowess of Louisiana musicians became more widespread. Many circus bands, and minstrel troupes recruited their musicians in New Orleans, but often their offers were declined because the part-time musicians were reluctant to give up the security of a trade that they had assiduously learnt for the hazards of a professional musician's life. But when those who went on tour returned to their home city they did much to convince the local musicians that people far afield were reacting favourably to the New Orleans style of presenting music. The prospects of the travelling life seemed less uncertain.

In 1912, bassist Bill Johnson took a seven-piece band from New Orleans to tour throughout near-by states. It was called The Original Creole Orchestra, the term Creole being thought prestigious billing material, though in fact the group contained Negroes and Creoles. The band's clarinettist George Baquet recalled: 'We went on a hustlin' trip all over Dixie, making money barnstorming, just as the German bands used to do at the time.'[10] The rest of the personnel consisted of Freddie Keppard on cornet, Eddie Vincent on trombone, Jimmy Palao on violin, and a guitarist, bassist and drummer.

The band soon realised that their prospects were not limited to the Southern States. Bill Johnson went out to California to evaluate prospects, and in the summer of 1914 sent for the rest of the band to join him there. The West Coast bookings proved to be the beginnings of three years of continual touring, during which time the band travelled from one coast of America to the other.

Booking-agents began to feel that there might be a novelty value in hiring New Orleans musicians. All over America, thousands of bands were playing ragtime songs, yet none, it seems, could be mistaken for a New Orleans band.

When comedian Joe Frisco worked in New Orleans, late in 1914, he was impressed by the band that played his accompanying music (it was led by trombonist Tom Brown). Other visiting entertainers also found the group's music appealing, and this led to the band being offered six weeks' work in Chicago. In May 1915, Brown's Band from Dixie land, as they were billed, became the first white dixieland band to travel North.[11] The personnel, which contained several Papa Laine alumni, consisted of Raymond Lopez on cornet, Tom Brown on trombone, Gus Mueller on clarinet, Arnold Loyocano on piano, (doubling string-bass) and Bill Lambert on drums.

Administratively, nothing went quite right for Brown's Band. The Chicago booking ended in August 1915; the group then changed their name to the Kings of Ragtime and began touring the vaudeville theatres. After playing dates in New York, they worked briefly under yet another title, The Ragtime Rubes, before gloomily disbanding in February 1916. Their trip to the North got them some publicity but it quickly evaporated. Another white band from New Orleans, a five-piece unit featuring Florian (Curly) Lizana on clarinet played bookings in New York shortly afterwards, but they too failed to attract any substantial interest.[12]

In December 1915, a Chicago café owner, Harry James, visited New Orleans to see a prize fight. Whiling away the time he stood listening to one of Papa Laine's groups performing; Nick La Rocca was in the band. James got into conversation with La Rocca who told him that the 'real music' could be heard later that night at the Haymarket Café. James went along there and heard a five-piece band consisting of La Rocca on cornet, Leone Mello on trombone, Alcide Nunez on clarinet, Henry Ragas on piano, and the leader, Johnny Stein, on drums. He soon realised the commercial potential of importing the group into his Chicago club and offered the group a ten-week contract. With Eddie Edwards on trombone, in place of Mello, the band opened at Schiller's Café in March 1916.

The band was an immediate success in Chicago. Harry James had the shrewd, eye-catching idea of using a dubious slang word on the band's advertising posters. Each night, hundreds of customers filed into the café past a big banner announcing 'Stein's Dixie Jass Band'. At this time, jass and jazz were interchangeable. The first traceable use of the word jazz in print appears in the San Francisco Bulletin dated 3 March 1913, when a sports writer used it to denote pep and enthusiasm.[13] Veteran musicians remember it being used as a colloquialism for sexual drive. The etymology of the word has been argued about for many years but, whatever the word's origin, it provided the new music with a name. Until then, most New Orleans musicians had continued to call their band music ragtime, long after it had developed into something quite different.

Johnny Stein's Band continued to play at Schiller's for two months, gaining considerable publicity but no increase in wages. Stein was deposed, and La Rocca elected leader by the remaining members. The new organisation chose The Original Dixieland Jass Band as its name, and in June 1916, the ODJB (as the quintet were forever after known) opened at another venue in Chicago.

The news of the band's success in Chicago quickly dispelled any remaining reluctance to travel North that lingered within New Orleans musicians. Tony Sbarbaro willingly left Louisiana to replace Stein on the drums, as did clarinettist Larry Shields who took Nunez's place.

In January 1917, the ODJB began a trial residency at the famous Reisenweber's Restaurant in New York. A payment of 750 dollars a week was promised if the experiment succeeded. Succeed it did. The band was described by one New York newspaper as 'a musical riot'. New Yorkers, unused to the 'new' music, staggered away to tell their friends of the sensational happenings.[14]

According to La Rocca's apocryphal story, graffitti-scribes kept obliterating the 'j' from the band's posters. To stop people making an ass of the ODJB the billing was changed to The Original Dixieland Jazz Band.

Soon the ODJB were being hailed as 'the originators of jazz'. This they were not. They were not even the first jazz band to leave Louisiana. They were, however, the first jazz band to gain national (and later, international) publicity. Their widespread and relatively sudden success may have been the reason for La Rocca's later protestations that the ODJB was the first band to play jazz. His campaign reeked of megalomania, yet the ODJB deserved praise. As jazz improvisers, all except the clarinettist Larry Shields were undistinguished. A clipped, stilted rhythm pervaded all of the group's recordings, closer to the stiff formality of ragtime's beat than to jazz. Nevertheless, La Rocca had much to be proud of: his group presented to the world a sound and a style that most had not heard before. The exact combination of trumpet, trombone, clarinet, piano and drums was rarely used by white bands in New Orleans and, as far as can be traced, no band of Creoles or Negroes ever regularly used precisely that line-up, though it is said that Freddie Keppard temporarily used that instrumentation at the Tuxedo Club when forced to cut down the size of his band for economic reasons.

La Rocca lived long enough to hear many of the ODJB's compositions become standard items in the repertoires of dixieland bands. The band's detractors often cite earlier pedigrees for some of the ODJB's tunes, but there is no doubt that La Rocca and his men had a good deal of natural compositional sense and a knack of assembling melodic numbers.

It was inevitable that the rapidly-developing gramophone-record industry should seek out the young men who were creating the sounds that had all Broadway talking. The Columbia company offered the band a trial recording session, but insisted that they record a standard tune of the day as their main side. The company considered the experiment a failure and decided not to sign a contract with the band. Their main competitors, the Victor Talking Machine Company, stepped in and offered the band a free choice within the recording studio. In February 1917, the ODJB recorded two of their own tunes, 'Livery Stable Blues' and 'Dixieland Jazz Band One-Step'. The first pressings were issued two weeks later, and soon the record was selling in vast quantities all over the United States. The Jazz Age was about to begin.

Recommended Reading

Allen, W. C. and Rust, B. *King Joe Oliver* (Biography and Discography), Sidgwick and Jackson, London, 1958

Armstrong, Louis *Swing That Music* (A ghosted autobiography of Louis's early years), Longman Green, London, 1937

Armstrong, Louis *Satchmo – My Life in New Orleans* (Autobiography), Peter Davies, London, 1955

Asbury, Herbert *The French Quarter* (An informal history of the New Orleans underworld), Alfred Knopf, USA, 1936

Bechet, Sidney *Treat It Gentle* (Autobiography), Cassell, London, 1960
Brunn, H. O. *The Story of the Original Dixieland Jazz Band* (A history of the first jazz band to record), Louisiana State University Press, USA, 1960
Charters, Samuel *Jazz New Orleans 1885–1963* (A detailed index of the Negro jazzmen of New Orleans), Oak Publications, USA, 1963
Dodds, Warren *The Baby Dodds Story* – as told to Larry Gara (Autobiography), Contemporary Press, USA, 1959
Foster, George and Stoddard, Tom *Pops Foster, New Orleans Jazzman* (Autobiography), University of California, USA, 1971
Gillis, F. J. and Miner, J. W. *Oh, Didn't He Ramble* (The life story of New Orleans trumpeter Lee Collins), University of Illinois, USA, 1974
Jones, M. and Chilton, J. *Louis* (The Louis Armstrong Story 1900–71), Mayflower Books, London, 1975
Lord, Tom *Clarence Williams* (A bio-discography), Storyville Publications, London, 1976
Lomax, Alan *Mister Jelly Roll* (Biography on Morton), Duell, Sloan and Pearce, USA, 1950
Manone, J. and Vandervoort, P. *Trumpet on the Wing* (Autobiography of Wingy Manone), Doubleday, USA, 1948
Marquis, Donald *In Search of Buddy Bolden* (A detailed investigation into the life of the early jazz trumpeter), Louisiana State University Press, USA, 1978
Meryman, Richard *The Life and Thoughts of Louis Armstrong* (A long, revealing interview with Louis Armstrong), Eakins Press, USA, 1971
Panassié, Hugues *Louis Armstrong* (A portrait of Louis and a summary of his work), Scribner's, USA, 1971
Rose, Al *Storyville, New Orleans* (An illustrated history of the notorious district), University of Alabama, USA, 1974
Rose, Al and Souchon, Ed *New Orleans Family Album* (Illustrated biographies of many New Orleans jazzmen), Louisiana State University Press, USA, 1967
Schafer, William J. *Brass Bands and New Orleans Jazz* (An illustrated summary of marching bands in New Orleans, with a discography), Louisiana State University Press, USA, 1977
Williams, Martin *Jazz Masters of New Orleans* (Detailed summaries of the work of many important jazzmen from Louisiana), Macmillan, USA, 1967

3 Chicago nurtures the new sounds

Many jazz musicians, black and white, leave New Orleans to play residencies in Chicago; small bands are augmented for ballroom work, uncompromising groups take up residencies in clubs on Chicago's South Side; gradually work in Chicago diminishes for both small and large bands and musicians leave the city to seek work elsewhere.

Listeners in many parts of the United States might have been confused by their first hearing of the ODJB's recordings, but that reaction did not occur in New Orleans. For the band's music was a disciplined and distilled form of the music that had been played uptown for many years. The American Press gave sensational coverage to initial reactions to jazz, and this hullabaloo brought forth comment from a conservative element in New Orleans. In a June 1918 editorial the *Times Picayune*, which had regularly brought its readers news of the precursors of jazz, took issue: 'In the matter of jass, New Orleans is particularly interested since it has been widely suggested that this particular form of musical vice had its birth in this city, that it came, in fact, from doubtful surroundings in our slums. We do not recognize the honor of parenthood.'

Others in the Crescent City could not have felt too pleased with La Rocca's startling success. Many of the young musicians in Papa Laine's Bands had been experimenting with similar ideas, but their rancour cannot have been greater than that of the non-white musicians. There seemed no justice. Freddie Keppard had particular cause to be rueful. His Original Creole Orchestra had been offered a chance to record in New York prior to the ODJB's début. He had refused the offer, because, it was rumoured, he felt that it would be easy for other musicians to steal his style by learning exactly what he had played on the recording. This seems doubtful. It has been said that the real reason for Keppard's refusal was that the record company wanted him to play unsuitable material in an alien style – a more probable explanation in the light of the ODJB's initial studio disappointments.

The whole story of the development of jazz, and its acceptance, might well have been totally different had Keppard's recordings preceded the ODJB's. There was considerable opposition to the ODJB's music. 'Unspeakable Jazz

Must Go', blazoned the *Ladies' Journal*; 'The jazz band view of life is wrecking the American home', said another report,[1] and worthy Judge Maberton of Illinois commented that 'three-quarters of the divorces in his court were caused by jazz'. Despite this opposition, the first jazz recordings got distributed from coast to coast in the USA, and sold handsomely. In the social climate of the 1910s, the position would have been very different if the records had been made by black musicians. It is extremely unlikely that the records would have been distributed at all throughout at least a dozen American states. The ODJB personnel represented to America a band of energetic, get-up-and-at-'em, young men. To their advantage, though not by design, the band represented a wide cross-section of second-generation Americans, the members being of Italian, Scottish, German and Irish descent. Despite the howls from the self-appointed guardians of good taste, the American people took to the group, and to their music. There was something exactly right, for the dancers of that era, in the pep and vitality of the ODJB's music.

The ODJB's success stimulated a nation-wide demand for other small bands from New Orleans. Throughout 1917 offers were being continually sent to every organised jazz band in New Orleans. Later that year there was to be a dramatic change in the night life of the city. In November 1917, following a series of vicious fights involving sailors and civilians, the US Secretary of War issued an order that literally closed up the brothel area of Storyville, dispersing the prostitutes to areas further away from the Naval base.

The closure of Storyville did not suddenly make the jazz musicians of New Orleans redundant, as is often suggested. Those most affected were the solo pianists. Other musicians who worked in the dance halls and cabarets in the district suffered too, but there was no question of total unemployment. The timing of the Government's edict, coming simultaneously with the continued offers of well-paid work in other parts of the country, sped up a migration that had already begun.

Booking-agents in cities as far apart as San Francisco and New York were continually offering work to New Orleans musicians, black, white and Creole. As a result, a number of musicians left New Orleans for California during the late 1910s. Several never moved back to Louisiana. Among them was Kid Ory. Ory had exchanged his valve-trombone for a slide-model as the vogue for change reached New Orleans. He became one of the city's leading exponents of the tailgate style of playing, and also one of its most successful bandleaders. Even so, he was determined to achieve wider success. He moved to California, partly for the climate, but also because of the musical possibilities there. He soon sent for several of his former sidemen to join him, and was thus able to form his own Sunshine Band on the West Coast. In 1921, they became the first Negro band to record jazz.

Ory, always a shrewd businessman, as well as a fine jazz musician, based his line-up on the ODJB's five-piece format. They made a fairly convincing attempt to reproduce the commercially successful sounds of the white group but the obscure company that made the records had no nationally organised distribution scheme. The sales figures were low, and it was to be two years before a Negro band from New Orleans again entered a recording studio. Even then, the band had to move to Chicago to be noticed by recording company executives. Chicago was to be the next important site for the establishment and development of jazz.

The Illinois city was then entering a period of great prosperity. Much of the grain and livestock consumed in the East of the United States was channelled through Chicago, the biggest railway centre in the land. Chicago's meat-packing plants and steel-works were among the largest in the world. They needed large workforces, and, to fulfil this need, vast numbers of black manual workers were recruited from all over the Southern States. The Negro population of Chicago rose from 44 000 to 109 000 during the years between 1910 and 1920 – an increase of 148 per cent. During the same period, the white population increased by 21 per cent.[2]

A great proportion of the black newcomers settled in and around the south side of Chicago, in an area that was quickly dubbed The Black Belt. In ghetto-like conditions black families from all over the South began adjusting to urban life. The higher wages of city work meant that, for the first time in their lives, they were able to spend money on entertainment. Within a small area, hundreds of clubs mushroomed (not dissimilar to the tonks of New Orleans). Several theatres and dance halls catering for black customers opened, all of them offering work to musicians.

The beginning of Prohibition in January 1920 also provided jazz with a great stimulus. Within months of the US government's enforcement of the eighteenth amendment, which banned the sale of alcohol, it was estimated that there were 20 000 illicit drinking establishments in Chicago alone. They ranged from high-class night-clubs to sleasy one-room speakeasies. In 1920, there were no juke-boxes, radios or powerful gramophones. It was live music or nothing. Jazz was usually the sound that broke the silence. Many of the professors deposed from Storyville followed the example of the great pianist and singer Tony Jackson and moved to Chicago, as did countless band musicians.

It was not only black musicians who made the twenty-six-hour train journey to Chicago for the ripe pickings. Several of New Orlean's finest young white jazzmen found lasting fame in Illinois, among them trombonist George Brunies, bassist Steve Brown, clarinettist Leon Roppolo and trumpeter Paul Mares. These four provided the nucleus of a band that became known as The New Orleans Rhythm Kings. In Illinois, they subsequently recruited local musicians, including drummer Ben Pollack, pianist Elmer Schoebel and saxophonist Jack Pettis. The seven-piece band produced a music that sounded like a cross between the ODJB and a band led by black cornetist Joe Oliver. The NORK as they became known, developed into one of the most popular jazz groups of the early 1920s and their outstanding clarinet player, Leon Roppolo, was one of the growing number of white musicians who could play convincing blues.

During the early 1920s, the young white teenage jazz musicians of Chicago had two favourite bands, the NORK and King Oliver's Creole Jazz Band – Joe Oliver had by then adopted royal billing. These youngsters spent many hours listening to, and learning from, the imported sounds of the Louisiana musicians. Among those who hung around the band-stands were several players who became world famous jazzmen, including Benny Goodman, Gene Krupa, Bud Freeman, Muggsy Spanier, Jimmy McPartland, Joe Marsala, Dave Tough, George Wettling and Joe Sullivan.

Billed on the record label as 'The Friars' Society Orchestra' the NORK made their recording début in 1922. The issues sold well and, eventually, the same record company (Gennett) realised that there could be a big potential in recording black jazz. Accordingly, in the spring of 1923 they sent to Chicago for King Oliver's Band to come to their ramshackle studios in Gary, Indiana. Despite the appallingly low sound quality on these early recordings, and the poor internal balance between the instruments, one can still hear why the music of Oliver's Band caused such a sensation in Chicago.

Above all, one is aware of the surging rhythms generated by the group. Their beat has a subtle, relaxed feel, which the ODJB's music never had. The jerkiness of La Rocca's Band is replaced by an insistent and exciting pulse. Clarinettist Johnny Dodds plays fine broad-toned phrases that soar over the beautifully linked duel-cornet parts, while trombonist Honore Dutrey fills out the lower register with sonorous counter-melodies. On the recordings, Baby Dodds, was not allowed to use his full drum kit, in case the vibrations disrupted the recording-engineer's equipment. In spite of this restriction he manages to play a carpet of subtle rhythms for the players to improvise on. From an historical point of view the recordings are tremendously important, not least because they were the first ever made by cornetist Louis Armstrong. Armstrong's solos and skilful ensemble playing on his début records show that, even then, he possessed great musical creativity and a superb rhythmic sense. He was destined to become the first colossus of jazz.

Louis arrived in Chicago from New Orleans during the summer of 1922, in answer to a telegrammed offer from his mentor Joe (King) Oliver. He joined Oliver's Band, playing second cornet, the older player taking the lead. All sorts of motives have been put forward to explain Oliver's strategy (himself a cornetist), in bringing in a young man who was already being spoken of by musicians as the greatest jazz prospect ever.

The fact is, the musicians were long-time friends. Oliver, some years older than Louis, was one of the first to give the young Armstrong cornet lessons.

Louis, born in poverty in New Orleans, had no birth certificate and eventually chose 4 July 1900 as his birthday. Neither his father nor his mother were musical, but Louis was gifted with a talent that was tantamount to genius. He became the first great jazz soloist; he was also a superb ensemble leader, and one of the most influential jazz vocalists. In appearance he was purely West African, short of stature, broad-chested, strong-necked and iron-lipped.

Louis's career paralleled the emergence of jazz, and he lived long enough to hear its sounds spread around the entire world. He received his initial musical training in the Colored Waifs' Home in New Orleans, having been sent there for illegally firing a pistol in the street during his early teens. Later, he worked at various menial jobs, such as delivering coal, all the while taking in the wealth of music that filled New Orleans. Louis did his first paid musical work as a teenager and went on to fulfil a classic New Orleans jazz apprenticeship: playing in tonks, dance halls, street parades and at open-air picnics and fish-fry lawn parties. Thomas (Mutt) Carey, a much respected New Orleans trumpeter, whose brother Jack was a distinguished bandleader, described his admiration for Armstrong's talents:

> 'I remember once when Louis came out to Lincoln Park in New Orleans to listen to the Kid Ory Band. I was playing trumpet with the Kid then, and I let Louis sit in my chair. Now at that time I was the "blues king" of New Orleans, and when Louis played that day he played more blues than I ever heard in my life. I give Freddie Keppard and Joe Oliver credit too. They were great boys, but there's no-one who ever came close to Louis.'[3]

Most of King Oliver's repertoire consisted of 'head' arrangements, whereby bands learn their parts, not from written music, but from memorising a carefully rehearsed routine. Fitting in to such an ensemble could have been extremely difficult, but Louis's innate musicianship enabled him to augment the band without any problem. His cornet-playing blended exactly with Oliver's in-phrasing, harmony and timing.

Almost every band in Chicago which featured jazz imported its soloists from Louisiana. It took some while before local musicians grasped the finer points of the new style. The roll-call of New Orleans jazzmen who worked in Chicago during the 1915–25 decade was vast, including Paul Barbarin, Sidney Bechet, Wellman Braud, Natty Dominique, Ed Garland, Tubby Hall, Minor Hall, Tommy Ladnier, Roy Palmer and Manuel Perez. Some of these players were only transitory figures in Chicago jazz history; several found the climate, and the way of life, in the Northern city unattractive. But for a time it seemed that for every one musician who moved back to New Orleans, two set out for Chicago. New Orleans musicians have always had a reputation for being cliquish and information about lucrative residencies was quickly passed from one to another. Kinship played its part, for many of the Creole musicians were related. Bob Shoffner, a trumpeter who moved to Chicago from St Louis in 1921, acknowledged the influence of the New Orleans musicians, and noticed their clannishness: 'The New Orleans jazzmen were influencing everyone, but the musicians here in Chicago pretended to look down on them, because many of them could not read, or did not have technical mastery of their horns. So the New Orleans men hung around together.'[4]

Gradually, the musicians who moved to Chicago from the South and Mid-West became immersed in the ways of jazz by playing alongside the New Orleans men. Shoffner was one of those who learnt his craft that way, as was cornetist George Mitchell from Kentucky, and Paul (Stump) Evans, a highly regarded saxophone player from Kansas. The one instrumental role in Chicago bands that was rarely filled by a New Orleans player was that of the pianist. Few New Orleans band pianists, a rare breed anyway in early times, moved to Chicago; notable exceptions were Richard M. Jones and Gideon Honore. The pianist's place in King Oliver's Band was filled by a woman from Memphis, Lil Hardin, who married Louis Armstrong in 1924.

That same year marked the disbanding of King Oliver's Creole Jazz Band, and the break-up of the New Orleans Rhythm Kings. Internal dissensions and individual ambitions were the main reasons for the disintegration of each group. A newly-formed white jazzband, called The Wolverines – without a single player from New Orleans – made its record début in 1924, and excited a lot of comment among musicians. The main talking point was the playing of the band's cornetist Leon Bix Beiderbecke. Bix, as he was known, was born in Davenport, Iowa of German stock. He had been a child prodigy on piano, but later concentrated on teaching himself the cornet, developing a mellifluous tone that was highly individual.

Bix, who was a keen admirer of Nick La Rocca and Paul Mares, avidly learnt their solos from gramophone records; his translation of their efforts produced vastly superior music. He never possessed an expansive high register, but he was able to impart an attack to his notes that gave them a bell-like quality. The style of his improvisations was unlike anything that had gone before in jazz; the solos, which were the antithesis of ruggedness, were full of lyrical mellowness. Beiderbecke dominated white jazz during the late 1920s, but after his death in 1931 no one seemed able to develop his style any further. To this day, many fine players are content to try to recreate Bix's solos, and imitate his exquisite tone. As a personality, Bix can be likened to a fiction writer's characterisation of a young American drinking his way through Prohibition. Unfortunately for Bix, the continuous intake of alcohol shattered his career and shortened his life.

Bix's place in the Wolverines was taken by Jimmy McPartland, one of the young Chicago musicians who had gained their initial inspirations from the

NORK and King Oliver. The effect jazz had on attentive ears was summarised by Muggsy Spanier, who described his first hearing of King Oliver: 'I knew the minute I heard him, that's the way I wanted to play. I said, that's the man I want to play like or as close as I can',[5] and also by drummer Gene Krupa: 'I know the first time I heard Dave Tough play I said "Wow man". He said, "Hell, this ain't nothing. Let me take you to hear Baby Dodds".'[6] McPartland and his friends, including Tough and Krupa, became known as the Austin High School Gang (though not all of them actually attended the school). At first they found it very difficult to make a living by playing jazz. Most of them had to take commercial jobs, playing in big dance bands. All of the clarinettists had to double on saxophone for this type of work.

The saxophone rapidly gained popularity during the 1920s. It had been introduced into America from Europe by Eustach Strasser in 1868,[7] but was slow to gain favour. During the early twentieth century, two groups who toured the vaudeville theatres, The Brown Brothers and the Musical Spillers did something to increase the appeal of the instrument, as did the Sears Roebuck mail-order company who began advertising the 'C' Melody model in their catalogues. Total sales figures for the entire United States of America were around 20 000 per annum in 1919; by 1929 it was estimated that 500 000 saxophone players in the USA were getting paid for their musical efforts.[8] Before 1920, saxophones had been used in some New Orleans bands, but sales figures there were proportionally no higher, or lower, than elsewhere. Somehow, the instrument's general lack of popularity gave rise to a viewpoint that the saxophone was deliberately shunned by New Orleans ensembles. This was not so. The growing national popularity of the instrument affected New Orleans in a way that was typical of the national pattern. King Oliver showed no reluctance to add saxophonists – his 1924 band had two, Albert Nicholas and Rudy Jackson. Thereafter, all Oliver's bands featured saxophone sections. Later in the 1920s, two New Orleans bands (Sam Morgan's, and the Jones–Collins Astoria Hot Eight) who both recorded exemplary jazz in their home city, featured saxophones.

The recording industry developed rapidly during the early 1920s. One of its successful selling innovations, devised at that time, was the introduction of what were called 'race labels'. This meant issuing records by black performers intended solely for black purchasers. Louis Armstrong was one of the early stars of this series. After leaving King Oliver in 1924, Louis went to New York and played in Fletcher Henderson's Orchestra for a year before returning to Chicago. The recording-manager of the Okeh Company in Chicago, E. A. Fern, sensed that the time was ripe to record the young trumpet star, using a small band format. The billing chosen for the group was 'Louis Armstrong's Hot Five'. It was a studio group, formed solely for recording purposes, and not for making live appearances. All of the musicians involved had previously worked with Louis. Four of the five, Louis, Kid Ory on trombone, Johnny Dodds on clarinet and Johnny St Cyr on banjo, were from Louisiana. Louis's wife, Lil, from Memphis was the one outsider.

The Hot Five assembled for rehearsals, learnt the routines on the tunes to be recorded (which were either written by themselves, or by close associates), and then proceeded swiftly to record one jazz masterpiece after another. All the zest, invention and passion of New Orleans music at its best are embodied in these recordings. On 'Heebie Jeebies', Louis recorded one of the first examples of 'scat singing', a style of improvising wordless vocal sounds. The recordings enjoyed a wide success, not only with black people, but also with whites who were captivated by the astonishing improvisation of the group. In 1927, the group added Baby Dodds on drums, and Pete Briggs on tuba, to become Louis Armstrong's Hot Seven. The results were no less sublime. In May 1927, the group recorded 'Potato Head Blues' which contains a chorus of improvisation by Armstrong that is often cited as a perfect example of jazz improvisation.

During the years 1927–29, Louis's solo playing began to take on new dimensions that were to affect and inspire countless jazz musicians – whether they were pianists, trombonists, saxophonists or whatever. The stream of seemingly endless variations that poured from Louis's trumpet needed agile and gifted accompaniment. In Chicago, Louis found the perfect foil for his inspired improvisations in the shape of pianist Earl Hines, from Pittsburgh, Pennsylvania. Hines, who had developed an impressive local reputation, moved to Chicago. Inevitably, his path crossed Armstrong's. The two men recorded the most intricate jazz duet of the 1920s on a composition by King Oliver called 'Weather Bird', and, as part of a 1928 version of the Hot Five, the breathtaking 'West End Blues'.

Despite the brilliance and artistry that Louis and Earl show on these recordings, neither made their living solely from playing jazz. Both played ballroom and club dates, and did theatre work playing semi-classical overtures during intermissions, or sometimes accompanying the silent films. They were not unique. Often men who played scintillating jazz in the recording-studios went straight on to work in a big band that churned out waltzes and novelty songs of the period. If musicians wanted, they could improvise to their heart's content in the many all-night sessions that flourished in Chicago.

Fortunately, we can gain from recordings a clear picture of all the various jazz styles that flourished in Chicago during the 1920s. We hear Louis Armstrong in a small band featuring a washboard player (who created rhythm by striking the sides of a washboard with metal thimbles), and also working within a big theatre band. We can hear the young white Chicagoans' embryo efforts; Johnny Dodds with the band he led at Kelly's Stables, Jimmie Noone with the sextet he led at the Apex Club, and countless other musical combinations, all of them possessing a degree of individuality.

Jelly Roll Morton made some of the most interesting Chicago recordings during this period. After leaving New Orleans, Morton worked in many cities, east and west, before making Chicago his base. There, in 1926, he arranged a series of recordings that showed that all his boasting about musical prowess could be substantiated. His 'Red Hot Pepper' recordings, which mostly feature tunes that he had composed and arranged, show how skilfully he could blend the tone colours of a small band, yet still retain the inspired feeling of a New Orleans ensemble. All but one of the players were from Louisiana. They too were a 'pick-up' band who recorded with Morton but did not work with him regularly. Clarinettist Omer Simeon, who was given prominence on the recordings, only ever worked with Morton once, for a week, apart from in the recording studio. Morton gave each player a written musical sketch of the effect that he wanted to create, outlining an orderly introduction, and bridge passages that linked together the various sections of the tunes. Beyond that, he left the musicians to their own improvisational devices. The records bear out Morton's dictum that 'Jazz is to be played, sweet, soft, plenty rhythm'.[9]

For Chicago ballroom-dancers, the novelty of listening to small band jazz was short-lived. At first, to rekindle interest, the bands compromised by using wider repertoires. Then, as the bigger ballrooms were built, they augmented their personnel. In the pre-amplification era, a large number of musicians were needed to project sound to the most distant corner of a big, crowded hall. A twelve-piece band might contain some musicians who had never worked together before. As a result more and more bands began using written arrangements; they were the only alternative to hours of intensive rehearsals or musical anarchy. As the bands got larger more effort was spent on presentation and the development of showmanship. Solo space for the jazz improvisers was often cut to a minimum, and even a star soloist might have a long wait before he was featured.

In the South Side clubs, the size of the bands remained small and written arrangements were hardly ever used. Clarinettist Johnny Dodds was typical of a number of jazz players who did not want to work in big bands. Some made the choice because they did not read music fluently, others because their real enjoyment came in soloing. New Orleans guitarist-vocalist, Lonnie Johnson, who specialised in blues playing, found the atmosphere in the small Chicago clubs particularly compatible. Just as the roustabouts changed the tonk music of New Orleans, so did the manual workers from the South have their impact on Chicago club music. Throughout the 1920s, the blues played an increasingly important part in bands working in the South Side clubs. A particular sort of piano blues became popular there. It was highly rhythmical, and featured the left-hand playing repeated bass patterns, while the right hand improvised incisive blues phrases. It became known as boogie woogie. Its origins were in the Southern states, some said in the social-shacks of the wood-cutting and turpentine manufacturing camps. Two of its greatest early exponents lived in Chicago during the 1920s, Jimmy Yancey and Clarence (Pine-Top) Smith.

While blues and boogie-woogie flourished, the general jazz scene in Chicago began to look bleaker as the 1930s approached. Many of the gangsters who had sponsored, or partly owned, the venues that employed jazz musicians closed up and moved into less ostentatious pursuits. The advent of talking pictures meant that dancers drifted away from the ballrooms and dance-halls. This was a national trait throughout America but it possibly hit Chicago harder because of the high proportion of entertainment venues in relation to its population. Some musicians worked on stage in cinemas, playing in between shows, but overall there was considerably less work for jazz players in the late 1920s than five years earlier. Earl Hines took his own big band into the Grand Terrace Ballroom in late 1928, and enjoyed continued success there in Chicago throughout the 1930s, but many of his former colleagues decided to look for work in other cities. Record sales began to fall drastically and they were to be decimated by the Depression in 1929. The place to go seemed to be New York, which had a highly organised entertainment scene. Within months of each other, scores of jazzmen, including Louis Armstrong, left Chicago and made the journey across to the city that was referred to as 'The Big Apple'. Chicago's days of importance as a jazz centre were temporarily over. At the time that it was relinquishing its dominant position in the world of improvised music, other cities were nurturing sensational new jazz talents.

Recommended Reading

Condon, E. and Sugrue, T. *We Called It Music* (Lively reminiscences), Peter Davies, London, 1948

Condon, E. and O'Neal, H. *Eddie Condon's Scrapbook of Jazz*, St Martin's Press, USA, 1973

Freeman, Bud *You Don't Look Like a Musician* (Anecdotes from a famous Chicagoan), Balamp Publishing, USA, 1974

Freeman, Bud *If You Know a Better Life* (Anecdotal humour), Bashall Eaves, Dublin, 1975

Hadlock, Richard *Jazz Masters of the 20's* (Covers the major figures of a lively decade), Macmillan, USA, 1965

Mezzrow, M. and Wolfe, B. *Really the Blues* (A vivid autobiography), Random House, USA, 1946

Miller, P. E. and Venables, R. *Esquire's Jazz Book* (A compendium of the 1944/5/6 Esquire Jazz Books, with an illuminating chapter on Chicago Jazz), Peter Davies, London, 1947

Sudhalter, R. M. and Evans, P. R. *Bix – Man and Legend* (A bio-discography of Bix Beiderbecke), Arlington House, USA, 1974

4 Jazz from coast to coast

Riverboat bands and radio programmes help to spread the sounds of jazz; by the early 1920s hundreds of jazz bands are flourishing throughout the United States; many fascinating regional jazz styles are recorded; big bands begin to gain popularity.

Neither New Orleans, nor Chicago, had a monopoly on live jazz performances during the early 1920s. By then, most American cities had coteries of jazz players. Styles differed from territory to territory, but the message everywhere was very similar – even if it was delivered in a fascinating variety of regional accents. Musicologists have unearthed many widespread turn-of-the-century reports of skilful musical improvisers playing variations that loosened the rigid ragtime format. Once these men grasped the style, and the method of jazz, they easily channelled their talents into it. Their first inklings of the new music came when they listened to musicians who brought the Louisiana style to them via travelling shows, circus bands and riverboat orchestras. Not all of these musical messengers were from Louisiana, but those that were not had listened intently to the New Orleans players and duly passed on their own imitations and reinterpretations.

One of the most important figures in twentieth-century black music had no direct connections with New Orleans. This was W. C. Handy, who became known as The Father of the Blues. Handy, who was born in Alabama, joined Mahara's Minstrels as a cornet player in 1896, and began extensive touring. During his widespread travels in the Southern States he noted down some of the folk-songs and blues that the black workers sang. Many of these melodies became the basis of his compositions (the second section of his most famous composition, 'St Louis Blues' is said to have also been inspired by the Habañera rhythms he heard while touring Cuba).

Handy always took a slightly disapproving attitude towards jazz improvisers. He was one of the old school of well-educated Negroes who felt there was something unbecoming and dishonourable about the music. Even ragtime seemed highly dubious to some members of the black establishment. *The Negro Music Journal* of September 1902 called on its readers to 'help banish this ragtime epidemic'. The bands that Handy led from 1906 contained several much-respected players, including William (King) Phillips, the clarinettist from Florida, and trombonist George Williams, from New Orleans – a cousin of Pops Foster. Handy never claimed to be a jazz-band leader and was usually described as a composer and publisher. His compositional gifts enabled him to distil and re-arrange a whole variety of ethnic ideas into one short opus, providing jazzmen with themes with which they felt at ease – perhaps because they realised, consciously or unconsciously, the Afro-American feel of Handy's tunes.

Several of Handy's most famous compositions were published in Memphis, Tennessee, a city which produced several fine individual musicians, but which did not play a significant part in the birth of jazz. Johnny Dunn, from Memphis, who worked with W. C. Handy, was one of the most famous black trumpeters in the early 1920s. A born natural, he is said to have mastered the high register of the trumpet within a fortnight of starting to play. He made a great impact on Northern listeners with the variety of sounds which he coaxed from his instrument, blowing into rubber plungers, ice-buckets, bottles and various mutes. He was a great performer, rather than a great jazz improviser. His recorded work indicates that he was never able to effectively change from ragtime phrasing to jazz phrasing; his playing had a stilted stiffness never found in the best jazz performances. Clarinettist William (Buster) Bailey was another famous Memphis musician who worked with Handy. Bailey got closer to mastering the transition in-phrasing that eluded Johnny Dunn, but even his work always bore traces of his early musical environment. Later, when Memphis was well acquainted with the sounds of jazz, it produced many fine players, including two superb rhythm-section players, drummer Jimmy Crawford and bassist John Williams.

St Louis, Missouri, gained an important place in the history of American Music by nurturing ragtime during the last part of the nineteenth century. The city continued to produce admirable pianists long afterwards; its brass players, too, became noted for the excellence of their tones and technique. As the hub of a vast network of riverboat organisations, St Louis was a distribution centre for new musical ideas. In the early 1900s, boats sailed from there for huge distances along the Mississippi river, from New Orleans to St Paul, Minnesota, and on the Ohio river from Cairo through to Pittsburgh. Throughout the century, hundreds of cargo and passenger boats regularly sailed the 750-mile river journey between New Orleans and St Louis.

In 1901, the Streckfus Steamer Company of St Louis launched the steamer 'JS', the first in a series of ships built exclusively for passenger excursions; the 'JS' could carry 2000 passengers and had a maple dance floor measuring 2700 square feet. The Streckfus Company booked a regular trio of musicians to work aboard the steamer. It consisted of two white musicians, Emil Flindt (violin) and Tony Catalono (cornet), together with a black pianist, Charlie Mills. The trio's personnel was not a deliberate attempt at integration. Catalono later said that the choice of pianist was obligatory since none of the white pianists of St Louis would go up on the open deck to play the caliope (a steam-powered pipe organ), which was deemed to be part of the band pianist's duties.[1] The experiment was a success. When Mills left, another Negro, Fate Marable, took his place. By then the group had added drummer Earl Wiley.

Captain Joe Streckfus, himself an amateur musician, soon recognised that Fate Marable had a great sense of musical organisation. He appointed him leader of the band which played the Streckfus lines summer cruises, and which then wintered in New Orleans, playing during afternoon and evening excursions. Marable gradually augmented the band, usually by recommending that Streckfus sign on musicians from New Orleans.

Marable's own piano-playing had no discernible influence on jazz developments, but his skill at coaching musicians was so remarkable that other players spoke of Marable's Band as the 'floating conservatory'. Without discouraging natural improvisatory gifts, Marable schooled his musicians in theory, harmony and reading music. Numerous jazz players were to benefit from this tuition; as a result, Louis Armstrong, Baby Dodds, Pops Foster, Johnny St Cyr and many others, were well prepared for their subsequent work in Chicago and New York.

Marable's 1919 band contained several magnificent jazz players. These men, sailing up and down the Mississippi, were heard by thousands of people, at dozens of ports of call, long before any jazz recordings by Negro musicians had ever been issued.

Louis Armstrong recalled the impact that he and two colleagues, Marable and mellophone player David Jones, had when they made guest appearances at a St Louis social gathering: 'We three sat down to one side of the band, and listened to them play. The leader would try to swing them away from the score, but they didn't seem to know how. I thought I could see he knew what we were thinking, because every once in a while he would look over to us and smile, but not as if he was sure we were liking it.' Later, the trio of visitors were invited to play: 'Every one of us three was a natural swing player, and didn't need any scoring at all. We almost split that room open. Well they all liked it fine. They stood up and yelled for more, and the band's boys were all on their feet too, and the leader came over and shook our hands.'[2]

David Jones, realising Armstrong's enormous potential, gave him individual tuition. Jones, who is remembered as a well-schooled musician, also had an effect on the Marable Band's rhythm section. According to Marable's trombonist, William Ridgley, it was Jones who got the band to play four beats in each bar for the dancers, instead of the two-beat style which had previously been in favour.[3] Marable's Band gained great popularity with the excursion dancers. Soon the Streckfus Company were hiring bands who could play jazz for their other passenger boats. This meant employment for scores of musicians, black and white.

During the early 1920s, there were at least six white bands playing regularly on the Streckfus steamers and their success led other companies to employ organised bands. Among their personnel were a number of young men who became famous jazz players, including pianist Jess Stacy, trumpeter Wingy Manone and clarinettist Charles (Pee Wee) Russell.

The number of white jazz musicians in America developed steadily after the first ODJB records were issued and many local bands enthusiastically attempted note-for-note copies of them. Later they used the same approach with the NORK's discs. White musicians emerged whose styles amalgamated white and black influences; the leading example was Jack Teagarden, one of a large musical family raised in Texas. Young Teagarden listened intently to records of the New Orleans Rhythm Kings, and to Louis Armstrong's recorded accompaniments to blues singers. He could equate with both, having heard black people sing the blues throughout his Texan childhood. Jack's trumpet-playing brother, Charlie, also became a well-known jazz musician.

In the early 1920s, there existed tiny pockets of white jazz musicians dotted all over North America. Each had been smitten by an undying love of jazz, usually kindled via recordings. Many of them were united with others of a kindred spirit. Young musicians who learnt their craft from nationally-issued jazz records were able to improvise compatibly with fellow-devotees, even though their respective home towns might be thousands of miles apart. From these caches of jazz appreciation came musicians like Tommy and Jimmy Dorsey from Pennsylvania, Danny Polo from Indiana, Brad Gowans from Massachusetts, Wild Bill Davison from Ohio and Frank Trumbauer from Illinois. Trumbauer and Tommy Dorsey became prime examples of a phenomenon that was often to occur in jazz. Originally they based their style of playing on soloists whose roots lay in black music, but they did this in such an original way that they, in turn, later influenced the styles of some black players.

Jean Goldkette was an early bandleader who specialised in bringing together white jazzmen from diverse backgrounds. Goldkette, a conservatoire-trained pianist from Europe, was not a jazzman himself, and did not play in his own bands. As a business protégé of a former drummer Charles Horvath, Goldkette was given the task of organising a big band to be resident at the Graytone Ballroom in Detroit. The venture was so successful that Horvath and Goldkette took over other venues and formed several other versions of the Jean Goldkette Band. Goldkette's Number One Unit, contained what was virtually the *crème de la crème* of contemporary white jazz soloists, including Tommy and Jimmy Dorsey, Frank Trumbauer, Don Murray, Bix Beiderbecke, and two very talented first-generation immigrants from Italy and Sicily, violinist Joe Venuti and guitarist Eddie Lang (whose real name was Salvatore Massaro).

In 1926, the National Amusement Corporation, as the Horvath–Goldkette organisation was called, created something of a sensation by signing a seven-piece black band from Springfield, Ohio, at that time billed as the 'Synco Septette'. The band reluctantly changed their name to McKinney's Cotton Pickers (their manager was William McKinney) but willingly took agency advice and signed a very talented band arranger, Don Redman. Redman wrote some scintillating arrangements for them, and coached and rehearsed the recently augmented band, which now numbered thirteen, into being one of the best big bands of the 1920s. Most of the band were from Ohio and neighbouring states; none was from Louisiana. Their success indicated that skilfully orchestrated rhythmic music, with occasional jazz solos, could keep a young ballroom crowd as happy as the most inspired collective improvisation.

A white band, signed by the same agency, bore out the same indications. This band was originally called The Orange Blossoms. Later, they took the name of The Casa Loma Orchestra following a successful residency at a hotel ballroom of that name in Toronto, Canada. Within the band were several dedicated jazzmen, but the emphasis in the band's music was in its arrangements; soloists played a secondary role. The band, in this respect, was a precursor of the coming Swing Era.

Both McKinney's Cotton Pickers and the Casa Loma Orchestra gained widespread popularity from their regular broadcasts. The advent of broadcasting in 1920 gave jazz a huge fillip and by 1922 several jazz groups were being featured on radio. As transmissions became more powerful, a band's area of appeal was greatly increased. Radio bands played to the limits of these areas, appearing for one performance in a succession of different towns. These 'one-night stands', as they became known, developed into a source of huge earnings for popular bands, who played in huge ballrooms for a percentage of the admission money taken at the box office.

Often, the first hearing of authentic jazz played by a touring band had a traumatic effect on young musicians. Bassist Walter Page from Missouri, who became a stalwart of the Kansas City jazz scene, described his first hearing of bassist Wellman Braud, then touring with John Wycliffe's Band: 'I was sitting in the front row of the high school auditorium, and all I could hear was the oomp, oomp, oomp, oomp, of the bass, and I said that's for me. I was just getting started with Bennie Moten then.'[4]

Pianist Moten was for many years, until his death in 1935, the leading bandleader in Kansas City. His progress was typical of many regional bandleaders: he started with a trio in 1919, and gradually augmented until he had a twelve-piece band. His early records denote how strongly the band was influenced by King Oliver's band, but subsequently they developed a highly individual approach. The Kansas City black musicians gained a wide reputation for their instrumental skills; much of this prestige was due to the efforts of an outstanding Negro teacher, Major N. Clark-Smith. Many of Clark-Smith's Kansas City pupils became famous musicians. His efforts at Tuskegee in Alabama, and also in Chicago produced remarkable results.

Most travelling bands felt uneasy about playing in Kansas City, because of the competitive attitude of the local musicians, who made a point of inviting, or rather, challenging, visiting players to join them in all-night informal blowing sessions. Due to a flexible political administration many clubs in the city remained open until dawn, and beyond. They were the scene of some of the most fiercely competitive musical gatherings ever assembled, and these get-togethers became known as 'jam sessions'. The competition stimulated invention, and many great soloists first gained recognition by taking part.

Two important saxophonists of the 1920s came from Missouri. One, Coleman Hawkins, became one of the most influential of all jazzmen. He is often cited as being the first saxophonist to play jazz, though he himself said that Paul (Stump) Evans from Kansas was an exact contemporary. Hawkins, a child prodigy, who played the cello before taking up the saxophone, did national tours with famous musicians while still a teenager.

At the time that Hawkins was a young man, music was one of the few professions that was open to the American Negro, and even then the choice did not involve classical music, no matter how brilliant the performer. American symphony orchestras were then bastions of segregation. Other than by working at menial or manual jobs, black people's chances of making a lucrative living rested in sports, the stage, or in playing jazz. Many black parents, only too aware of the restrictions, made great sacrifices to purchase musical instruments for their children. Occasionally, a town had benefactors who supplied poor children with free instruments. Such was the case in Louisville, Kentucky, where an enterprising social worker, Mrs Bessie Allen, persuaded local businessmen to donate instruments for the children at the Booker T. Washington Community Center to learn on. From this source alone came several important jazz players: trumpeter Jonah Jones, trombonist Dicky Wells, drummer Bill Beason, and trumpeter George (Buddy) Lee.

Charleston, South Carolina, was one of the most remarkable centres of black music during the early twentieth century, and most of the interest concerned the activities of the Jenkins Orphanage Band. The Orphanage Institute, which was founded by the Reverend Daniel Jenkins in 1892, specialised in teaching young black waifs various trades and crafts, including music. A boys' band was formed which made local tours to raise funds for the Orphanage. The tours proved so successful that they led to the formation of other bands; eventually six bands from the Orphanage were kept busily touring during the summer months. They would give open-air performances and then collect from bystanders. The bands travelled all over North America, and on three occasions visited Europe. At least a dozen of the young orphans became top-class musicians, and the bands of Fletcher Henderson, Duke Ellington and Jelly Roll Morton all contained, at one time, ex-Jenkins musicians. Perhaps the most gifted of them was the prodigious trumpeter, Cladys (Jabbo) Smith.

The rigorous schedule of tuition that the boys underwent ensured that they would develop instrumental technique; their jazz styles were gleaned from bands that they heard during their travels. Often, runaway boys worked with distant bands. When they were forced to return to the Orphanage they taught the other boys the new tunes, phrases and harmonies that they had picked up. Thus a musical idea that might have originated in Florida could soon be carried to Boston, via Charleston.

Some theorists believe that the charleston – probably the most popular novelty dance of the 1920s – emanated from a step that the Jenkins Band did as a prelude to their musical performances. The Charleston Dance Committee goes as far as citing the place of the origination on King Street, Charleston.[5] What is certain is that the movements were similar to a dance step that was popular with the Geechie people who lived in the near-by Georgia Sea Islands – these people are said to be the black Americans who retained the closest links, in speech and custom, with African traditions. Pianist James P. Johnson composed the Charleston melody while playing at a dance casino in New York City. Most of the male patrons there were merchant seamen from Charleston, and the coast of Georgia, who sailed between South Carolina and the port of New York. These sailors and longshoremen wanted to impress the New York girls with their style of dancing. James P. Johnson, in searching for a suitable accompaniment to their steps, wrote a tune that became an international success. He said: 'It was while playing for these southern dancers that I composed a number of "Charlestons" – eight in all – all with the same rhythm. One of these later became my famous "Charleston" when it hit Broadway.'[6] New York was to become the clearing-house for many other regional ideas.

During the 1920s, most of the jazz action was taking place in the eastern half of the United States, roughly east of a line drawn from San Antonio, Texas up to the Canadian border. Across to the West, in California, jazz records were being made regularly. They showed that the musicians there were keeping in touch with developments elsewhere without adding anything new. The large number of New Orleans musicians who moved there in the period 1917–27 either drifted into commercial bands, or left full-time music. In Denver, Colorado, violinist George Morrison led a Negro Band that was famous throughout the area in the 1920s, and was still flourishing thirty years later. Two of his band members went on to become well-known leaders, Andy Kirk, whose 'Clouds of Joy' became famous in the 1930s, and Jimmie Lunceford. Lunceford, who studied music at Wilberforce College, then went to Fisk University where he gained his degree, later becoming a music teacher in Memphis. That occupation ended when he formed a touring band – comprised of his former pupils, including the brilliant saxophonist Willie Smith.

At Wilberforce, one of Lunceford's white music teachers was W. J. Whiteman, whose son, violinist Paul, was then leading his own little orchestra in California, having previously played with various symphony orchestras on the West Coast. The young Whiteman was shrewd enough to realise that white American ballroom dancers preferred refined, rather than vigorous, stimulation. He perceived that he might transplant certain jazz effects into his own orchestra without alienating the very people who were decrying jazz. From the time he instigated this idea, through to the end of his career, he always had some jazz musicians in his ensembles. He did not interfere with what these men played in their solos, but usually their improvisations filled only a tiny part of the arrangement, and often they were accorded musical backgrounds that were totally unsuitable. Their task was to provide a jazzy spice to some very stodgy cuisine. Whiteman's formula made him one of the most famous musicians of the 1920s.

Whiteman has been described as an ogre, who made musical slaves of jazzmen. This is a totally false picture of a skilful musical entrepreneur, who was extremely popular with employees, and who often retained more jazz soloists than he had space to feature simply so that they would not be out of work. The ludicrous aspect of Whiteman was the title of 'King of Jazz', bestowed on him by his New York publicists.

The 'Empress of the Blues' was another title born in the 1920s, but this time, the accolade was fully justified. Its recipient was Bessie Smith, a black singer born in Chattanooga, Tennessee. Bessie had no need to go to New York to receive her title. It could have been bestowed at any one of the hundreds of tent-shows, cabarets and theatres that she worked in after becoming a professional singer in 1912, for she was unquestionably the greatest woman blues singer who has ever lived. She did ten hard years of touring before making her recording début in 1923. After that she rapidly became rich and famous, working regularly until her unfortunate death in an automobile accident. Bessie Smith was not the first blues singer to record; that distinction went to another black singer, Mamie Smith (no relation). The situation could be likened to the ODJB preceding superior jazz groups into the recording world: Mamie Smith's 'diluted' blues singing prepared the public for the expansive emotions of Bessie's magnificent voice.

Gertrude (Ma) Rainey from Atlanta, Georgia was the first woman to sing the blues professionally. In 1902, when she was already a touring artiste, she decided to introduce a blues as an encore to her act. The song elicited such response that she eventually specialised in singing the blues. Her success surprised her and she herself said that she had frequently heard similar songs in the course of her travels.[7] All of the travelling blues singers who trekked through the Southern

States in the forty-year period following the Civil War were males. The pure novelty of hearing a woman singing the blues on stage may well have accounted for Ma Rainey's initial success.

The early blues singers, usually accompanying themselves on guitars or banjos, sang about the woes of life in the Deep South. Their blues told of flood disasters, drought, crop failures, cruelty, disease and unrequited love. Occasionally, a wry blues told of good fortune, or the manifold successes of imaginary heroes. These bluesmen eked out a living by taking a collection after each performance, which might have taken place outdoors on a side-walk, or indoors at a tavern, or in a plantation's social hut. Later, some blues singers found work with 'medicine shows', literally acting as singing salesmen for the dubious concoctions which the travelling quack doctors dispensed. The full story of blues singers, and of specialist blues players, is the subject of another book. Superb blues players like Little Brother Montgomery, Cow Cow Davenport, Lonnie Johnson, Art Hodes and Sam Price are mentioned because most of their work was performed in a jazz environment. Regularly, for the past fifty years, one or another forms of the blues have found their way into the lists of best-selling records.

The role of recordings in a singer's professional life, or in a band's career, became progressively more important during the 1920s. Rival companies, vying with each other for greater profits, sent out roving talent-scouts to scour America for new stars. In order to strike while the iron was hot, some companies had mobile recording units travelling with their scouts. Often, they brought back fascinating examples of regional jazz: from St Louis, Fate Marable's Band, and Charlie Creath's Orchestra; from Kansas City, George E. Lee's Orchestra and Walter Page's Blue Devils. Other examples were The Blue Ribbon Syncopators from Buffalo, J. Neal Montgomery's Orchestra from Atlanta, Georgia and Troy Floyd's Band from San Antonio, Texas.

Occasionally, Southern Bands were coaxed to the North for a recording session, and, if the results sold well, the bands were called back to record more titles. During the 1920s, many Territory Bands were formed, the name describing bands that worked primarily in their home state, and in other states directly adjoining their own. Some of the bands who restricted the area of their tours (and thus reduced their overheads) earned more than their big-city counterparts, but by the late 1920s all the musicians concerned realised that national reputations only came to those who played regularly in New York City. By then, jazz recordings were being sold all over the world and while success in New York usually meant fame throughout the United States, it could also quickly lead to international acclaim. More and more bands like The Missourians and The Alabamians gambled a steady future for the big prizes and moved to New York.

Recommended Reading

Albertson, Chris *Bessie* (A biography of Bessie Smith), Stein and Day, USA, 1972

Dance, Stanley *The World of Earl Hines* (A biography, plus many anecdotes from Hines's musicians), Scribner's, USA, 1977

Dexter, Dave *Playback* (A renowned jazz journalist and record producer surveys his career), Billboard Publications, USA, 1976

Dixon, R. and Godrich, J. *Recording the Blues* (The Story of recording companies' activities in the blues field – much interesting data), Studio Vista, London, 1970

Handy, W. C. *Father of the Blues* (Autobiography), Macmillan, USA, 1955

Hentoff, N. and McCarthy, A. *Jazz* (A series of excellent essays – the one by F. S. Driggs on Kansas City Jazz being a landmark in that area of research), Cassell, London, 1960

Lee, George W. *Beale Street – Where the Blues Began* (Background to Memphis music-making), Robert O. Ballou, USA, 1934

McCarthy, Albert *Big Band Jazz* (Much useful information on Territory Bands, and famous big bands), Barrie and Jenkins, London, 1974

Murray, Albert *Stomping the Blues* (An illustrated summary of the great blues instrumentalists), McGraw Hill, USA, 1976

Oliver, Paul *The Story of the Blues* (A detailed survey), Barrie and Jenkins, London, 1969

Russell, Ross *Jazz Style in Kansas City and the South-West* (Coverage of an important jazz area), University of California, USA, 1971

Schiedt, Duncan *The Jazz State of Indiana* (A lovingly assembled, well illustrated history of one state's jazz activities), Published by the author. Pittsborough, Indiana, USA, 1977

Waters, Ethel *His Eye on the Sparrow* (Autobiography), Doubleday, USA, 1951

Waters, Howard J. *Jack Teagarden's Music* (A bio-discography), Jazz Monographs, New Jersey, USA, 1960

5 New York - the metropolis of jazz

Work prospects entice almost all of America's leading jazz exponents to New York City; Louis Armstrong is recognised as the first great jazz soloist; big bands gradually gain favour; first mixed (black and white) recording sessions take place.

By 1930, New York City was established as the jazz centre of the world, simply because of the enormous number of top-class musicians who had moved there. The practical reason for the mass-migration was that all of America's most important band-bookers and agents had their principal offices there. It was also the site for the nation's main radio and recording studios. Success in New York brought handsome rewards, and this made competition particularly fierce. The players themselves had a saying: 'If you're not big in New York, you're not big anywhere.' Collisions between the musically ambitious took place regularly. The intensity of the challenge caused many young musicians to pack their instruments away and return to the less demanding atmosphere of their home town.

None of this early competitiveness was inter-racial. White musicians did not clash with blacks for vacant jobs, nor blacks with whites. Black people danced and listened to white bands, and vice versa, but during the 1920s there were no regular mixed bands working in New York City. The two musical communities, black and white, moved along parallel, but unconnected, paths throughout the decade.

As mentioned in chapter two, Freddie Keppard's Band had appeared in New York before the ODJB's first visit. Their engagement at the American Theatre in December 1915 was described by a contemporary reviewer as 'one of the hits of the afternoon'.[1] Other press reactions were less favourable. Most of the band's work in New York consisted of theatre bookings, where they appeared as an act on a variety bill. They did not play for dancing and had they done so their impact would surely have been greater, for the whole East Coast was then in the grip of the new 'fox-trot' craze, which provided work for several Negro orchestras, the most popular of which was led by James Reese Europe.

After receiving a musical education in Washington, DC, Jim Europe moved to New York in 1904, hoping to take advantage of the growing opportunities for black musicians in stage shows. Eventually, he formed his own dance orchestra, and in 1910 became the central figure in a New York organisation for Negro musicians, called The Clef Club.

Europe's Society Orchestra regularly accompanied the English ballroom dancers, Irene and Vernon Castle, then touring America. Europe passed on to them a variation of the schottische dance that had been taught to him by W. C. Handy; these steps became the basis of the fox-trot. Europe's syncopated music was ideal for the new dance; his Orchestra played ragtime, quasi-ragtime novelties, and popular songs of the day, such as Irving Berlin's 'Alexander's Ragtime Band'. In 1917, when America entered the First World War, Europe enlisted in the Army and sailed to France as the Commander of the 369th Infantry Band. The band became renowned during their stay in Europe, and Jim Europe returned to the United States as a hero. His end was tragic: in May 1919, while on a nationwide tour, he was fatally stabbed by a drummer in his band. Europe was a distinguished pioneer in the organisation and presentation of black musical talent. His place in jazz history was transient, but he did provide, by example, inspiration for many Northern Negro musicians, some of whom became important figures in jazz. Many of these men were pianists.

Both Lucky Roberts and Dr James (Eubie) Blake have given ear-witness accounts of many fine pianists who were prominent in the Northern States during the early years of this century. They were musicians who had absorbed the far-reaching effects of the Afro-American keyboard styles that preceded ragtime. They were able to blend easily with jazz bands when the piano eventually gained a permanent place in them.

These pianists fared better in the transition to jazz than many of the Northern wind instrumentalists, most of whom had great difficulty in adapting their playing styles to the revolutionary jazz. Expert trumpet players like Jack Hatten and Addington Major found it impossible to change their styles to meet new demands. It was like the great stars of silent movies being unable to cope with changes required by the new techniques of talking films. Reed-player Garvin Bushell summarised the players' problems: 'New York "jazz" then, was nearer the ragtime style, and had less blues. There wasn't an Eastern performer who could really play the blues. We later absorbed that from the Southern musicians we heard, but it wasn't original with us.'[2]

Pianist James P. Johnson was probably the most brilliant performer in the North during the early 1910s. He became the dean of all the stride pianists in New York (they were so called because of the power and accuracy of their left-hand playing). His early mentors were Lucky Roberts and a shadowy hero called Abba Labba. James P. (as he was affectionately known) said of fellow pianists he heard during his adolescent years: 'If they had anything I didn't have, I listened and stole it.'[3] Thus he became a brilliant performer, and an eclectic of earlier piano styles. One striking facet of his technique was that he was able to span ten white notes on the piano keyboard, with his left hand, not just spanning them but also able to play accurate phrases at that stretch with great speed. It was a device that his favourite pupil, Thomas (Fats) Waller, later incorporated into his style.

Besides being a brilliant performer, James P. Johnson was also a skilful composer. During the early 1920s he wrote the score for one of the first of the all-black stage revues, 'Shuffle Along'. New York theatres were among the first to stage these spectacular extravaganzas, which blended the panache of minstrelsy with the rhythms of jazz, and added an uninhibited chorus-line of dancers. The mode of these new presentations were to have a lasting effect on the American Musical. The lure of possible employment in these shows brought large numbers of black musicians into New York but an even bigger incentive for moving to the Metropolis were the growing opportunities in the field of recording.

The big breakthrough for black recording artistes came in November 1920, when the Okeh Record Company released 'Crazy Blues', composed by a black composer, Perry Bradford and sung by Mamie Smith, a black singer, accompanied by black musicians. Not far from the New York recording studios, where the session took place, lay Harlem, then the most densely populated black district in the USA. The record created a sensation there, selling 75 000 in the first month of issue. This success led the New York a-and-r men (short for a record company's selectors of artistes-and-repertoire) to record several other black blues singers, most of whom were accompanied by black bands. The sounds of black instrumental jazz reached the Northern record-buying public, albeit in small doses.

For the undiluted mixture, New Yorkers needed only to visit one of the countless cabarets and speakeasies that were dotted all over Harlem. Most of them employed small groups, usually consisting of five or six musicians. White businessmen, observing the success of black artistes in Broadway shows, also saw the commercial possibilities of presenting Negro musicians in palatial surrounds.

As part of this strategy, the Club Alabam, a basement supper-club on West 44th Street, Manhattan, signed a band led by Fletcher Henderson who was originally from Georgia. Henderson moved to New York in 1920 to make use of his degree in chemistry, but soon found that his erstwhile hobby of playing the piano could earn him more money. His introverted manner did not make him an ideal bandleader, but he was a conscientious organiser, and an accomplished musician. Don Redman, who was originally his chief arranger, was also a consummate musician, who played every instrument in the band, but specialised on saxophone and clarinet. The members of Henderson's original band came from various States, but not one of them was from Louisiana. However, the music of New Orleans was to have a revolutionary effect on the band, as in October 1924 they were joined by Louis Armstrong.

A rigidity of rhythm mars every recording that Fletcher Henderson's Band made before Louis arrived. As soon as Louis had settled in, the phrasing of the whole band became buoyant. Henderson first heard Louis in 1922, while on a theatre tour which included New Orleans. He had tried to get Louis to join the band then, but was met with a refusal because he could not offer a place to Louis's close friend, drummer Zutty Singleton. Louis's exceptional gifts were unforgettable and when Henderson heard that he had left King Oliver's Band in Chicago, he offered Louis a job in New York, which the cornetist accepted. Henderson's sophisticated musicians looked on in amazement as the tubby young man, wearing outrageously unfashionable clothes, strolled into his first rehearsal. Henderson's drummer, Kaiser Marshall, described the scene: 'He had on big, thick-soled shoes, the kind that policemen wear, and he came walking across the floor, clump-clump, grinned and said hello to all the boys.' Don Redman also remembered the traumatic meeting: 'He was big and fat, and wore high top shoes with hooks in them, and long underwear down to his socks. When I got a load of that, I said to myself, who in the hell is this guy? But when he got on the bandstand it was a different story.'[4] Any laughter quickly died away when the Band heard Louis play.

During Louis's thirteen-month stay, his concept of rhythmic improvisation transformed Henderson's Band from a sedate, often boring, dance orchestra, into the first exciting big band. Henderson sidemen like cornetist Joe Smith and trombonist Charlie Green were talented improvisers with sonorous tones, but neither had Louis's rhythmic genius. The band's star soloist before Louis's arrival was saxophonist Coleman Hawkins and recordings show how dramatically the sax player's solos improved after he began working alongside Armstrong. Arranger Don Redman openly admitted that Louis's phrasing and harmonic ideas were his inspiration in pioneering new concepts of orchestration.

By coincidence, a twenty-seven-year-old musician from Louis's home town was also in New York at the same time. This was Sidney Bechet, who had already been acknowledged as one of New Orleans's leading clarinettists before he left the city as a teenager. By 1924, he was specialising on a soprano saxophone, playing it with considerable skill, and great intensity. A third Louisianian, songwriter–publisher–pianist Clarence Williams, who had moved to New York, coaxed the two musicians into recording together. This was no easy task, since both Armstrong and Bechet had already developed a wariness of each other that was to prove life-long. The result of their early partnership is a series of magnificent recordings which exhibit both musicians' superb solos, and their inspired accompaniment to Williams's wife, singer Eva Taylor.

Bechet had done a great deal of travelling before he reached New York. In 1925, he resumed globe-trotting, but not before he had played a part in shaping a band led by Duke Ellington. Ellington became the foremost composer in jazz and also the most important big-band leader.

At the time of the first Armstrong–Bechet recordings, Duke Ellington was playing piano in a small New York club called The Kentucky with a five-piece ensemble called The Washingtonians, none of whom were from the South. When Duke was later elected leader of the band, he began adding musicians to the line-up. Their first recordings sound highly reminiscent of those made by Fletcher Henderson's band *before* Louis Armstrong joined. Early signs of Duke's superb arranging talents soon became apparent, stimulated by regular encounters with Bechet (who worked briefly with Duke), and by inspiration provided by a remarkable New Jersey pianist, Willie (The Lion) Smith.

Edward Kennedy Ellington did his first engagements while still in his teens, when he played piano at an ice-cream parlour in his home town of Washington, DC. He then lived with his parents in a comfortable, middle-class home, studying commercial art at a near-by school. Piano-playing was meant to take second place to art, but Duke (as he was nicknamed during childhood) was regularly asked to accept musical work. He joined up with other musically ambitious youngsters and formed a band, one of whose members, drummer William (Sonny) Greer, was the envy of all, for he had actually played in New York City. Inevitably, the commercial art projects were abandoned and Duke and his colleagues set out for New York.

In late 1927, after a long stay at the Kentucky Club, the band, now under Duke Ellington's name, successfully auditioned for New York's Cotton Club, one of several Harlem entertainment venues that catered for a 'white only' audience.

The provision of music for the Cotton Club's floor-shows inspired many of Ellington's most brilliant ideas. The mood of the Club (designed for tourists) was a jungled exotica. Duke responded by orchestrating parts for growling trumpets, moaning trombones and wailing reeds. All of these effects were presented with a stunning artistry, and juxtaposed round the improvised solos of his sidemen. By 1927, he had an all-star cast of players, including two eloquent plunger-mute players, trumpeter Bubber Miley, and trombonist Tricky Sam Nanton, the inimitable baritone-saxophonist Harry Carney, and two great individualists from New Orleans, clarinettist Barney Bigard and string bassist Wellman Braud. In assembling these musicians, Duke showed a trait that marked the rest of band-leading life. He was able, by his arrangements, to present highly individual musicians to the public, in a way that enhanced and developed their originality. After his Cotton Club début, Duke continued to add unique stylists to his band. They included the talented and versatile trumpet player, Cootie Williams, the exhilarating cornetist Rex Stewart, the trombonists Juan Tizol and Lawrence Brown, and, on alto-saxophone, Johnny Hodges, who had been personally coached by Sidney Bechet. Hodges developed into the most consistent of all jazz soloists. Duke's Orchestra became a veritable galaxy of all-American jazz stars, and had only one close rival in the late 1920s, which was Fletcher Henderson's Band. Henderson too had also signed many fine jazz musicians, including one of the finest trombone players of the era, Jimmy Harrison, two superb jazz trumpeters, Tommy Ladnier and Bobby Stark, and multi-instrumentalist Benny Carter, whose arranging skills were as remarkable as his playing.

Occasionally, fully formed bands, as well as individual players, made their way to New York seeking employment. One early arrival was the Scott Brothers' Band (which featured reed-player Cecil Scott). They arrived from Ohio and achieved a fair degree of success in New York ballrooms, which encouraged them to stay in New York permanently. Such was not the case when a band comprised entirely of New Orleans musicians, led by Creole violinist Armand Piron, played briefly at the Roseland Ballroom, New York, in 1924. Piron's music was well received, but socially their presence alongside the all-white personnel of Sam Lanin's Band led to some ill-feeling. The *New York Clipper* commented: 'The dual performance of a white and coloured orchestra under one roof, in itself unusual, is reported to have had its bad results. The Lanin personnel does not fancy the idea much.'[5]

Lanin's Band was a straightforward dance band of its era. In contrast, by 1924, there were a growing number of organised jazz bands comprised of young white New York musicians. Following the ODJB's initial success, a number of five-piece bands formed up in the North to imitate the group's music. Most of them emulated only the superficial effects that the ODJB featured – the cornetist imitated a horse neighing, the clarinet was made to cluck like a hen, and the trombone to bray like a donkey. However, the more serious young musicians did not only resort to hokum. Among these was a quintet who, while playing at a Coney Island Dance Hall in the summer of 1917, named themselves The Memphis Five (inspired by a W. C. Handy composition 'The Memphis Blues'). From this group came one of the first white musicians to show jazz originality, trombonist Milford (Miff) Mole. Another white original came from within the ranks of The Californian Ramblers (actually a group from New Jersey). This was Adrian Rollini, who joined the band on vibraphone and piano, but who, within weeks of buying a bass-saxophone, astounded his colleagues and the audience with the dexterity and inventiveness he showed on the usually ponderous instrument. Both Miff Mole and Adrian Rollini met in New York the stars who had worked for Jean Goldkette, until that leader had disbanded in 1927. Bix Beiderbecke, Frank Trumbauer, Joe Venuti, Eddie Lang, Bill Rank, and other ex-Goldkette sidemen moved to the East Coast together, and were signed *en bloc* by Paul Whiteman.

Loring (Red) Nichols, who worked briefly with Paul Whiteman, became one of the best known instrumentalists of the 1920s. Besides the recordings he made with his own Five Pennies he was also featured on countless other sessions as a freelance. Nichols, who made no secret of his great admiration for Bix Beiderbecke's playing, became noted for the smoothness of his small band arrangements, which included novel ideas like single-string guitar solos, and the use of tympani (the large, tuned drums which are part of an orchestral percussionist's equipment). Nichols's recordings were widely distributed and achieved big sales.

By 1925, the ODJB's popularity was considerably diminished. They had made big-selling records after their return from London in 1920, but a growing internal dissension and a realisation that the group's great days were in the past caused them to disband. Even though La Rocca had never been more than a pretender to the jazz throne, he saw his retirement as a willing abdication. Nevertheless, he must have been astounded to hear Paul Whiteman soon hailed as the 'King of Jazz'.

The fake crown was given to the white violinist who had brought his small orchestra to New York from California in 1920. Whiteman himself made no pretence that he could improvise jazz. He arrived in the East at exactly the right time. By then, many people wanted to be connected with jazz without getting too emotionally involved, or without making any amendment to their outlook on racial issues. Whiteman's portly, solid appearance and confident stage presence always commanded an audience's attention. He told people they were listening to jazz when he presented the tunes of the day arranged in a way that would not displease, or confuse, their ears, and they wanted to believe him.

Whiteman himself had no doubts about the origins of the music he was caricaturing. In 1926, he wrote *Jazz*, one of the very first books on the subject. Its opening paragraph reads, 'Jazz came to America three hundred years ago in chains'.

His dream was to popularise a rhapsodic style he called 'symphonic jazz', and he hoped to do this via concert-hall performances. The first big realisation of his ambition came in February 1924 when he organised a concert at New York's Aeolian Hall. Whiteman's twenty-three-piece orchestra played a very varied programme, which began with a version of the ODJB's tune 'Livery Stable Blues' and ran through twenty popular melodies before reaching the moment when George Gershwin premiered his composition 'Rhapsody In Blue'. The evening then concluded with Elgar's 'Pomp and Circumstance'. 'Rhapsody In Blue' was regarded by the critics as the most significant number in the programme. In a way, this composition epitomised Whiteman's ambitions – it was a tuneful example of modern American music, with frissons of jazz rhythms and blue notes. Elegantly composed, certainly, but in no way jazz.

Today, the only reason jazz-lovers listen to Whiteman's recorded curios is to hear the short improvised solos on them, played by Bix Beiderbecke, Andy

Secrest, Frank Trumbauer, Jack Teagarden, and other fine jazz musicians. It seems that Whiteman himself saw the limitations for his orchestral attitude to improvisation, for he was candid enough to report the departing comments of one of his early stars, clarinet-player, Gus Mueller: 'I just can't play that pretty music that you all play. And you fellers can't never play blues worth a damn.'[6]

Not all the white jazz in New York was stifled by over-orchestration. In the late 1920s a ten-piece band led by the ex-drummer of the NORK, Ben Pollack, featured the improvisations of an array of jazzmen. Pollack, who led in Chicago and California before moving to New York, employed several of the Austin High School Gang, those young jazz musicians who had learnt their skills first hand from the great Chicago jazz groups, and included Benny Goodman, Bud Freeman, Jimmy McPartland and his guitar-playing brother Richard. Several other young Chicagoans moved to New York in the late 1920s, among them drummer Gene Krupa, clarinettist Frank Teschemacher, pianist Joe Sullivan, and an adopted Chicagoan, guitarist Eddie Condon. These young men often found it hard to make a living from playing their brand of jazz. Paul Whiteman had temporarily convinced the masses that jazz was a polite form of music and when the rough-toned, lively Chicagoans performed they often met with stern disapproval. Rather than move back to their home city, they did brief, well paid penances in commercial bands.

But, if a jazz group, black or white, were fortunate enough to get a booking in a sympathetic New York venue, they could play unrestrained jazz to enthusiastic audiences. One such place was the Roseland Ballroom on Broadway, which opened in 1924, and featured most of the top bands of the era, including, on occasion, a double-bill consisting of Fletcher Henderson's Band and Jean Goldkette's. The Savoy Ballroom, a rival to the Roseland, opened in 1926, and the dancers there soon produced a style of unrestrained movements that became known as 'jitterbug dancing'.

These big ballrooms needed big bands to fill them with sound, but all over Harlem there were late-night clubs that only employed small bands, usually of five or six pieces. The usual front-line there consisted of a trumpet and a saxophone, backed by piano, string-bass and drums, and sometimes with the addition of a guitar. None used the dixieland line-up of trumpet, trombone and clarinet.

King Oliver and Jelly Roll Morton, two ultra-important figures in the development of jazz in New Orleans and Chicago, both tried their luck in New York during the late 1920s. Oliver brought his band from Chicago to New York, via St Louis where he signed on two up-and-coming New Orleans players, trumpeter Henry (Red) Allen and bassist Pops Foster. The band played a short season at the Savoy Ballroom in 1927; the audience liked the music, but the impact was insufficient to gain a long booking. Oliver was given the opportunity to audition for the Cotton Club (where Duke Ellington became established) but lost the chance by submitting too high a quotation. King Oliver developed severe trouble with his teeth, and this often made it impossible for him to play satisfactorily. The band were forced to quit New York, and began working on an arduous, and poorly paid, touring circuit that proved to be a slow descent to poverty. Oliver, who died in 1938, spent the last part of his life as a janitor in a pool-room at Savannah, Georgia.

Morton's decline was not as swift as Oliver's, but it was almost as decisive. He too had aspirations of leading a big band in New York. In 1928 he secured a residency at the Roseland, but this proved to be his only lengthy engagement in the city. Like Oliver he was forced to go on tour. Morton continued to record, but the skills which had delicately manipulated the tone colours of the early Red Hot Peppers seemed to have evaporated. Occasionally he got his musicians to blend their talents in a good arrangement, as they did on the beautifully poignant 'Deep Creek Blues', made in 1929. But little that Morton did in the late 1920s suggested that, a few years earlier, he had justly been considered a great jazz innovator.

Even if Morton and Oliver had been able to maintain their incredibly high musical standards there would have been no assurance that they would have retained big followings. The listening and dancing public of the 1920s were no different from their counterparts in subsequent decades. They wanted a continually changing array of new personalities to bring them music. By the late 1920s, both Morton and Oliver were middle-aged; the time was ripe for younger bandleaders to catch the New York public's attention.

Duke Ellington and Fletcher Henderson were two of the new names in big band jazz. Others who gained their initial popularity as leaders in the late 1920s were Luis Russell, Claude Hopkins, Benny Carter and the diminutive drummer Chick Webb, who became the idol of the Savoy Ballroom crowds. Vocalist Cab Calloway, a showman extraordinaire, who became one of the highest paid bandleaders of the 1930s, came to New York from Chicago in 1929 to appear in a show called 'Hot Chocolates'. Also in the same show was Louis Armstrong, who had recently made the same journey as Calloway.

It was in 1929 that Louis took part in one of the first mixed recording sessions with black and white participants. No enormous planning went into this historic breakthrough. The musicians involved had shared an all night spree, which preceded the morning on which Louis was to record with Luis Russell's Band. Louis invited his drinking pals to make a record as a preliminary to the main session and the result was a superb example of impromptu blues improvisations, appropriately called 'Knocking a Jug'. If the personnel had been selected with the utmost care it could not have presented a wider cross-section of the men who were making jazz in New York during the late 1920s. Three of the musicians were black, Louis on trumpet (from New Orleans), Kaiser Marshal on drums (born in Georgia) and Happy Caldwell on tenor-saxophone (from Chicago). The other three were white: Jack Teagarden on trombone (German stock from Texas), Joe Sullivan on piano (an Irish-American from Chicago) and Eddie Lang on guitar (first-generation immigrant from Sicily).

The session was a precursor of many jazz collaborations between various races, not only on record, but in thousands of jam sessions – spontaneous gatherings where musicians improvised by the hour for their own pleasure. Ten years after the 1929 recording many black musicians were working alongside whites in mixed bands. All of these changes came into being during the period known as the Swing Era, but before they occurred the United States was to undergo its greatest economic crisis. The Wall Street Crash of October 1929 eventually brought unemployment to 1 500 000 people in New York City alone. The music industry was drastically affected, but this did not seem to deter young musicians from making their way to its centre in New York. Many of these youngsters, black and white, were to suffer hard times in keeping the jazz flame bright during the Depression.

Recommended Reading

Allen, Walter *Hendersonia* (The music of Fletcher Henderson and his musicians), Jazz Monographs, New Jersey, USA, 1973

Bradford, Perry *Born With the Blues* (A black composer's own story), Oak Publications, USA, 1965

Calloway, Cab and Rollins, B. *Of Minnie the Moocher and Me* (Autobiography), Crowell, USA, 1976

Charters, S. and Kunstadt, L. *Jazz – A History of the New York Scene* (A well-documented survey), Doubleday, USA, 1962

Chilton, John *McKinney's Music* (A bio-discography of McKinney's Cotton Pickers), Bloomsbury Book Shop, London, 1978

Haskins, Jim *The Cotton Club* (A pictorial and social history), Random House, USA, 1977

Kaminsky, Max *My Life in Jazz* (Autobiography), Harper and Row, USA, 1963

Kimball, R. and Bolcom, W. *Reminiscing With Sissle and Blake* (The life stories of two famous black musicians), Viking Press, USA, 1973

Kirkeby, Ed *Ain't Misbehavin'* (Biography of Fats Waller), Peter Davies, London, 1966

Smith, Willie 'The Lion' *Music on My Mind* (Autobiography), Doubleday, USA, 1964

Waller, M. and Calabrese, A. *Fats Waller* (A biography by the pianist's son), Macmillan, USA, 1977

6 Theory (I) the basis of jazz improvisation

Great jazz musicians all share the gift of being able to improvise solos that are full of melodic and rhythmic variations. Many other forms of music have given scope to improvisers, but the uniqueness of the rhythmic phrasing which marks all good jazz performances, coupled with the way that a jazz player interprets his melodic ideas against the accompanying harmonies, ensures that no one could ever mistake an improvised passage from a classical work for a jazz solo.

The rhythmical differences would best be demonstrated by listening to a classical musician play a phrase that could be easily copied. If a jazzman immediately repeated the passage note-for-note at exactly the same tempo there would be a difference, and that difference would be in the phrasing. The jazzman, by accenting certain beats more than others, would give the piece a different rhythmic impetus. The placement of his notes would emphasise the pulse of the music in a unique way.

If we experimented further and asked a folk musician to play the melody of the centuries-old song 'Careless Love', then compared the results with a master jazz musician's rendering of the same theme, we would hear that the jazz performance would be full of nuances of rhythm not present in the folk version. In comparison, some notes would be held fractionally longer, others made shorter, some would be heavily stressed, others lightly accented. The jazz piece would be phrased in a way that encouraged the listener to tap his feet, or drum his fingers, in time with the music. The jazz musician would hopefully expect his performance to 'swing'.

A description of the verb 'to swing' is said to be the most difficult jazz activity ever devised. A group of musicians will play a tune one night and it will swing, yet the same players might not swing on the same tune on the very next performance. Swing is a placement of notes so exquisitely rhythmical that each beat seems to be flexibly linked to the preceding and succeeding beat in a way that eliminates any degree of stiffness or rigidity; the change from one beat to another is markedly smooth. The difference in position of the beats played by a swinging band and a non-swinging one might be minuscule, but within that difference is the secret of swing. It is not simply a matter of precision – the process of non-swinging can be likened to a squad of soldiers who are marching badly. No one is out of step, all the arms move together, yet the tread seems heavy and listless. On another day, the same men marching at the same pace develop a simultaneous feel for correlated movement. The unification becomes immediately apparent, and it seems too that every moving sinew within the unit is perfectly co-ordinated; in effect, they are swinging.

The great jazz musicians have an in-built ability to swing at any tempo, ranging from the slowest blues to the fastest show-stopper. It is this rhythmic gift, even more than the skilful way that they can improvise melodic phrases, which makes them great jazz musicians. Often a top-class jazz improviser will repeat the same note several times, but each repetition is subtly held for a different length of time. Some of the notes are syncopated (syncopation is the accenting of a note on a normally weak beat); in contrast, some notes are emphatically on the beat. Every great jazz soloist also knows exactly where to leave periods of silence in his improvising, knowing that these gaps surprise and interest listeners.

Besides the rhythmic differences between the two versions of 'Careless Love' there would also be melodic differences. The jazz musician might deliberately alter the pitch of some melody notes by hitting them slightly flat, before swiftly taking them up to the correct pitch. Conversely the player might hit the note true and then immediately lower the pitch for effect. This would represent a jazz musician's embellishments of the melody of 'Careless Love' (figure one), and if the player then proceeded to improvise variations on that tune (figure two) the uniqueness of jazz would become instantly apparent.

The jazz solo would be presented in segments that lasted exactly the same length of time as a chorus of the melody. In technical terms the chorus of 'Careless Love' lasts for sixteen bars, each bar containing four beats. If you tapped your feet on the beat for a full chorus you would total sixty-four beats (sixteen bars of four beats). The jazz musician would construct his improvisations on the same harmonies that accompanied the folk-singer, but his interpretation of the melodic potential of those harmonies would differ from those of a non-jazz musician.

The jazz player would regard blue notes as perfectly suitable ingredients for his solo (the ethnological background to the Afro-American habit of altering pitch was discussed in chapter one). Technically, it is easiest to explain blue notes in relation to a piano keyboard. If we play the scale of C major, the ascending notes will be C, D, E, F, G, A, B, C. If, instead of playing the E note, we substitute the black note immediately below it we will have established a blue note (in technical language that E flat – the E note flattened by a semitone – will be described as a minor third). If we play a phrase containing this altered note, such as C, D, E flat, F, G, we will immediately hear the sombre nuance that this altered note has introduced. If we move further up the scale of C major and alter the B to the black note just below it we will have B flat (a minor seventh), another blue note. Next we play the whole 'altered' scale: C, D, E flat, F, G, A, B flat, C.

At first this sounds odd, as if the musical phrase had not been concluded, but if we play permutations of the notes of the altered scale in small clusters we will hear how elementary jazz phrases are shaped. Play a B flat for two beats (two taps of the foot), follow it with a G (held for two beats), next move down to the E flat (held for two beats), then conclude the phrase by playing a C for two beats. A variant pattern would be G (two beats), F (two beats), E flat (one beat), D (one beat) and finishing on C (two beats). You will have played two phrases in the key of C major, lasting for two bars (eight beats) and containing blue notes.

Next, experiment with four-bar phrases (sixteen beats). Play C (three beats), D (one beat), E flat (three beats), D (one beat), C (two beats), B flat (two beats), G (four beats).

A jazz musician need not include blue notes in every phrase that he plays. He can revert to straightforward scalic patterns, using the third and seventh notes unaltered. This can provide a lively, happy-sounding contrast to the passages tinged with blue notes.

Figure 1 Melody of 'Careless Love'

Figure 2 Improvised variations on 'Careless Love'

The majority of phrases in the very early days of jazz lasted for either two bars or four bars, but the length was arbitrary, depending entirely on the performer's imagination. Great jazz musicians use their sense of rhythm to create phrases of consistently varying length, improvising patterns that last for five beats, seven beats or seventeen, etc. The jazz soloist is indulging in instant composition, continually varying his selection of notes, and altering the rhythm value that he gives to those notes. The permutations of possible phrases are countless.

There are no rules governing the length of the phrases that go to make up an improvised chorus, but the chorus itself is of a fixed, pre-determined length. The soloist must adhere to that length (which is exactly the same as the chorus of the tune that he is improvising on), and his note selection must be appropriate to the harmonies of the tune. The option is given to the soloist to take more than one chorus. Having played completely through the harmonic progression that forms the basis of the tune he can return to the beginning and follow the same chordal landmarks for another chorus. The guidelines that tell him exactly where he should be in the chorus (during his improvisations) are provided by chords played by the accompanying instruments (usually the rhythm section: piano, string-bass, guitar/or banjo).

If we strike (on the piano) the first note in the scale of C major, together with the third note in the scale (E) and the fifth (G), we will have produced a three-part chord known as a triad. This particular chord is the C major triad; C, the first note in that scale, being the most important. The first note of any scale is referred to as the tonic (it can also be called the root note, or the key note). The distance between two musical notes is described as an interval. If we play notes from another scale, the scale of F major, using the same intervals that formed the C major triad, we will produce the chord of F major: F (tonic), A (third note of scale) and C (fifth). All major triads are built on identical intervals: for B flat major we combine B flat (tonic) with D (third) and F (fifth); for G major, G, B and D. In jazz jargon, chords are often referred to as 'changes'.

The blue notes appropriate to the scale of C have been described. The full piquancy and effectiveness of blue notes is attained when the soloist plays them 'against' the orthodox chords provided by his accompanists. If the soloist plays a phrase that contains the note E flat, this will clash with the unaltered E (the third of the scale of C) that the accompanists are playing. The sound of such a musical conflict is one of the hallmarks of jazz improvisation. The effect produces momentary tension in the listener which is resolved as soon as the soloist plays a note that is part of the accompanying chord. It was this effect which caused some people vehemently to denounce early jazz – their ears were slow to accept the dissonance that resulted from a musical transplantation of one style of music (African) on to another (European).

Top jazz musicians are able to play intricate improvisations solely by using their sense of hearing. Their ears identify chords, and some are able to do this without studying the theoretical side of music. If a pianist, guitarist or banjoist strikes a chord, they can instantly improvise a phrase on the notes of that chord, in much the same way as some untrained singers can instantly harmonise in a vocal choir. The 'ear' musician knows instinctively when and where to play blue notes. Great jazz musicians can create a telling effect by playing a note that is a little below, or a little above, the accepted pitch of a blue note.

In early jazz there was a great deal of collective improvisation, which meant that all the members of the front-line (the wind instrumentalists) were improvising simultaneously. A musical anarchy would have resulted had not the front-line players disciplined their individual lines by basing them on the chords played by the rhythm section and thus achieving harmony with their colleagues. Each man improvised a different musical line. In technical terms they achieved polyphony, and as each player also chose different rhythms in which to couch his phrases, several rhythmic patterns were being created simultaneously. The players thus achieved polyrhythmic effects.

The simultaneous use of different notes of a chord by a small band is best illustrated by a Dixieland band, using a three-piece front-line consisting of trumpet, trombone and clarinet. The trumpet usually plays the melody; in jazz jargon he takes the 'lead'. If the melody started on the note C, the clarinet, which usually plays above the trumpet, would start his improvisations on the note E. The low-voiced trombone would commence with a G. The three musicians have formed a triad on the chord of C major (C, E, G). Throughout the piece the three instruments will try to weave individual phrases that are in harmony with each other.

The three notes of a triad chord can be presented in any order: C, E, G or E, G, C or G, C, E. The components are the same, but their rearranged patterns are called inversions. In this example in C major; C, E, G is a chord in the root position; E, G, C is the first inversion; and G, C, E the second inversion.

Early jazz improvising was not limited to major triads. Each major triad has seven related chords, and by the mid-1920s most bands used all of them in their harmonic vocabulary. For those 'non-ear' players, who required a visual indication of a tune's harmonies, a musical shorthand system was devised which indicated chords by symbols:

C meant simply C, E, G.

C 6th meant C, E, G, plus the sixth note of the scale A.

C 7th meant C, E, G, plus the flattened seventh of the scale B flat.

C major 7th meant C, E, G, plus the ordinary seventh B.

C minor meant C, E flat, G.

C minor 7th meant C, E flat, G, plus the flattened seventh B flat.

C° or C diminished meant C, E flat, G flat, and A.

C+ or C augmented meant C, E, G sharp.

A professional jazz player would be expected to be conversant with every major chord in each key of the twelve notes that exist between one C and another C. They are: C, C sharp, D, D sharp, E, F, F sharp, G, G sharp, A, A sharp, B, C. It must be remembered that all the black notes on a piano have two different names. The black note between C and D can be referred to as C sharp, or as D flat, between D and E as D sharp or as E flat, between F and G as F sharp or G flat, between G and A as G sharp or A flat, and between A and B as A sharp or B flat. Each of the major chords also has seven related chords; an F major chord would have F 6th, F 7th, F major 7th, F minor, F minor 7th, F and F+. Once all of these chords had been learnt, the improviser would approach any popular tune and be able to solo on its harmonies; for instance,

'When You and I Were Young Maggie', a thirty-two-bar song, whose chords are given in figure three (each stroke, or virgule, represents one beat).

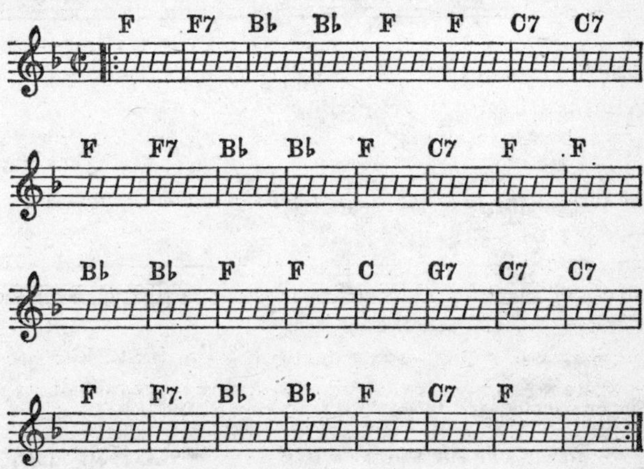

Figure 3 'When You and I Were Young Maggie'

Or the basic twelve-bar blues in figure four.

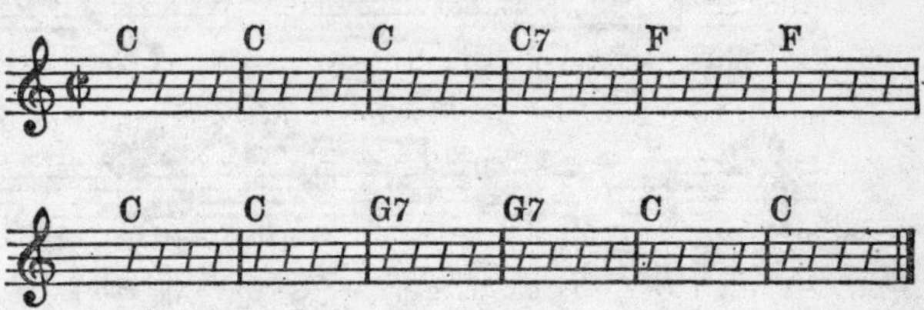

Figure 4 The basic twelve-bar blues

The structure of the blues is the same in every key: three bars of the tonic chord, one bar of a seventh of the tonic, two bars of the fourth note of the major scale, back to the tonic chord, then to a seventh chord built on the fifth note of the scale, concluding on the tonic chord. Thus, the blues in G will be:

G G G G^7 C C G G D^7 D^7 G G

The chords of the blues have provided the raw material for some of the greatest jazz solos, and for some of the most inspired accompaniments – particularly where a call-and-answer pattern is used between singer and accompanist. The singer's stanza covers two bars:

GET THE BLUES EVERY MORNING, GET THE BLUES EVERY NIGHT

The instrumentalist's answer fills the next two bars (figure five).

Figure 5

The singer then repeats:

GET THE BLUES EVERY MORNING, GET THE BLUES EVERY NIGHT

The instrumentalist responds (figure six):

Figure 6

The singer concludes:

NEVER GET THE BLUES WHEN MY BABY TREATS ME RIGHT

Which is answered by (figure seven):

Figure 7

The methods used by jazz musicians to create their improvisations have been outlined. The elements that make up an outstanding jazz solo are: firstly, the rhythmic content of the phrasing; secondly, the ingenuity of the melodic patterns; thirdly, the timbre with which the soloist projects his ideas. Most great jazz players aim at producing a vocal-like tone on their instrument and in order to do this they add vibrato. Vibrato is the wavering pulsation that can be imparted to a note, usually by moving the instrument rapidly while the note is being created. The shaking of the instrument takes the sound alternately over and under its original pitch. Many trombonists and saxophonists/clarinettists, prefer to vibrate their jaws while blowing to produce vibrato. Guitarists, banjoists and string-bassists add vibrato by trembling their fingers on the string of the note that they have just played. Pianists cannot alter the pitch of the notes they play: instead, by alternating their fingers rapidly on the keyboard they produce a tremolo effect which imitates vibrato. The use of dynamics is also a feature of a memorable jazz solo. The volume of sound is constantly changed, ranging from soft (pianissimo) to loud (fortissimo). The subtle shadings are particularly effective when the accompanists adjust their dynamics in sympathy with the soloist.

In early jazz, most players used pronounced vibratos: Johnny Dodds, Louis Armstrong, Coleman Hawkins, Sidney Bechet and trombonist J. C. Higginbotham being notable examples.

Some players carry the vocal effect a stage further and actually growl into their instrument while soloing. Trumpeters in particular use this device and the sound of the manoeuvre becomes even more effective when the musician holds a rubber plunger (such as used by plumbers) over the bell of his instrument. King Oliver and Johnny Dunn were adept plunger-players, both able to imitate roosters crowing, horses neighing and babies crying. But the plunger was used to best advantage by Duke Ellington's brass-players, notably Bubber Miley, Cootie Williams and Tricky Sam Nanton. Ellington's immense talent enabled him to orchestrate these effects into his arrangements and the vigorous tone colours produced were called jungle sounds. The plunger is one of several mutes available to the trumpeter and the trombonist. Others are: the harmon mute, through whose funnel-like stem a column of air can be interrupted by the palm of a brass player's hand producing a 'quacking' effect (when the cup is removed the mute produces a soft, husky tone); the cup mute, which mellows the sound; the straight mute which decreases the volume but still retains an incisive sound; and the metal bowler-hat (or derby) which when placed over the bell of a brass instrument produces a horn-like sound. Occasionally, the bowler-hat is waved over the end of the bell to produce punctuated phrases.

Duke Ellington also made effective use of cornetist Rex Stewart's ability to coax unusual-sounding notes from his instrument by pushing his valves only half-way down and blowing normally. The cornet is the trumpet's closest relation. It is a shorter, more compact instrument whose main difference is that its piping is conical, while the trumpet's is cylindrical. Both have three valves, both have similar mouthpieces, and both fulfil the same role in a jazz group. Preferring the cornet's mellower qualities to the brilliant sound of a trumpet is simply the personal choice of an individual instrumentalist.

There are two types of trombone, and they are quite different. The most common model now in use is the slide-trombone, on which the player produces his notes by moving a slide into seven basic positions. Less common is the valve-trombone, which looks like a very large trumpet, complete with three valves. Its disadvantages are that it cannot produce the glissandi (gliding between notes), or ripping sounds that are easily created by rapidly moving a slide in and out.

The usual type of clarinet found in jazz is known as the B flat model. In the very early days of jazz some bands occasionally used the slightly smaller C clarinet, which then sometimes played the melody in place of a trumpet. An even smaller E flat model was used in parade work, where its shrill sounds enabled it to be heard clearly above the ensemble. Originally, two models of clarinet with different mechanisms were used in jazz: the Albert system, and the more recently designed Boehm. Many New Orleans pioneers swore by the Albert system, but gradually the flexibility of the Boehm system won them over. As far as the listener is concerned, there is little to choose between the two systems.

Clarinets and saxophones are known as reed instruments because sound is produced on them by blowing into a mouthpiece which vibrates a reed fixed within. The saxophone was slow to gain universal popularity. Originally the C melody model sold best, but it was superseded in popularity by the E flat alto, the deeper B flat tenor, the even lower E flat baritone, and the lowest, the B flat bass saxophone. Novelty models, like the high E flat sopranino, and the monstrous E flat contra-bass, found little favour. The B flat soprano did however become popular mainly through the playing of Sidney Bechet.

Pianos, trombones, oboes, violins and string-basses are non-transposing instruments (as is the C melody saxophone), which means that they sound a note at exactly the pitch that it is written, whereas a B flat trumpet or a B flat tenor-saxophone has to play each note on a pianist's music a tone up. When the pianist plays the note C, the trumpet or tenor-saxophone have to play a D in order to create a note of the same pitch as the pianist. An E flat alto-saxophone (which is pitched four notes higher than a B flat tenor) needs to play a note four scale-steps higher than the tenor-saxophone's D – the note A – in order to produce the sound of the pianist's C.

In jazz groups, the pianist is usually classified as a member of the rhythm section. He actually plays a double role, playing chords that accompany the front-line musicians, then soloing in his own right. The solo pianist obviously has no one to provide a guide-line for his improvisations. He keeps the pattern of the tune (and its harmonies) in his head, and supplies his own bass part by playing a strong line with his left hand. The improvising bonus for a pianist is that he can effectively place a blue note against his own 'normal' chords. Boogie-woogie, the piano style which first became popular in the 1920s, highlighted both the strong bass line and the blue note effect. Boogie-woogie, which was improvised on the twelve-bar blues, featured an ostinato bass, which means the use of a figure that keeps repeating itself. The rhythmic insistence of these left-hand figures created an eight-beats-to-the-bar effect, which contrasted with the four, or two, beats to the bar that were then prevalent in jazz. Simultaneously, the pianist's right hand improvised totally independent patterns. The leading boogie pianists were able to play many widely differing bass-hand patterns.

The Harlem pianists, typified by James P. Johnson, were all proud to demonstrate the power and accuracy of their left-hand work by playing stride piano which entailed using a 'walking bass' effect, which was the playing, by the left hand, of a strong counter-melody to the tune. Unlike boogie-woogie there was no continuous pattern; the stride player might easily change his musical line at any point during the chorus. Earl Hines, an outstandingly individual jazzman, proved that it was possible for the improvising pianist to make use of complete independence in both hands. Hines used each hand to improvise 'against' the other, and, in doing so, produced a fascinating mixture of complex counter rhythms.

During the 1930s, the amplified guitar played a double role in jazz, being used both as a rhythm and a solo instrument. In the 1920s, its solo potential was rarely used, being then unamplified and so having little volume. Guitarists then were restricted to playing four beats to each bar, as part of the rhythm section. Many guitarists also doubled on banjo, and gradually the louder-sounding banjo became used more often than the soft guitar. The volume advantage meant that the banjo could be more easily heard in large dance-halls. The increase in sound also made it more suitable for early recording techniques. As soon as recording techniques advanced, most of the banjo players reverted to guitar (but years later, in the 1940s, there was a revival of interest in the banjo). Several great jazz guitar soloists like Eddie Lang, Lonnie Johnson and Django Reinhardt had sufficient talent to ignore changing fads.

A large number of bands used brass-basses instead of string-basses during the 1920s. There are two sorts of brass-bass: the tuba, which sends sound straight up into the air, and the sousaphone, which is wound around the player's body and projects its sound forward. Brass-basses could easily send sound to every corner of a big ballroom, but they are not as dexterous as the string-bass and, when amplification ceased to be a problem, most bands preferred the string model. Talented brass-bassists can play admirable solos, but in early jazz their main role was in emphasising the rhythm, usually by playing on the first and third beat of each bar. Their selection of notes usually gravitated between the tonic and the fifth of each chord. Players of the calibre of Cyrus St Clair were able to make the instrument sing out a highly rhythmical part, but often brass-bassists were responsible for ponderous, grunting, highly monotonous sounds.

The string-bass can either be played pizzicato (meaning its string can be plucked by the finger-tips), or the strings can be bowed. It is impossible to ascertain which jazz bassist first played pizzicato; so many have claimed that they originated the effect in jazz. Whoever did made a most important contribution to the sound of a jazz rhythm section. During the 1920s the majority of top-class string-bassists came from New Orleans. They included Wellman Braud, Bill Johnson, Pops Foster, Johnny Lindsey, Steve Brown and Al Morgan.

Attempts to record a full drum kit brought many problems to sound-engineers during the 1920s. It was not until the end of that decade that drummers were finally allowed to use their bass-drums on recordings. When King Oliver's Band first recorded in 1923, drummer Baby Dodds was restricted to using only part of his kit. His excessive striking of a wood-block was not from choice but from the necessity of trying to replace sounds that he was used to creating on his full array of percussion equipment. A typical drum kit of the 1920s would consist of a bass-drum (which was struck by a beater manipulated by a foot pedal), a snare drum, a tom-tom, woodblocks, a gong, and various cymbals. In effect the drummers were attempting to fulfil the combined roles of an African percussion group. Their tasks in a jazz ensemble were to ensure that the tempo of the piece remained steady, to punctuate each segment of the tune with neat rolls, and to play polyrhythmic patterns that enhanced what the front-line were playing, without distracting them. Most drummers of that era stressed all four beats in each bar, but some, particularly those in Dixieland bands, emphasised only two of the four beats, the first and third. These are usually referred to as the 'on beats', whereas the second and fourth in each bar are called the 'off beats'. It is general custom, when clapping out rhythm in time with a jazz performance, to clap on the second and fourth beats.

During the 1920s, most drummers added a new piece of equipment to their kits. This was the high-hat (or 'sock') cymbal, consisting of two linked-cymbals which clashed together when a foot-pedal was lowered. Drummers can use sticks to produce sound, or wire-brushes which produce quiet effects when stroked across the drumskins. Few early jazz drummers played long solos; there were exceptions, but generally the habit did not become popular until the 1930s. Most early drummers' solos were restricted to playing breaks. A break, which is usually two bars long, occurs when the band stops completely to allow one musician to play an improvised phrase. Another device is the stop-time chorus where the band only play on the first beat of each bar so as to give the soloist added prominence.

By 1930, many drummers were experimenting with vibraphones, or vibra-harps (rival trade names for similar instruments). The vibes, as they are known, consist of layers of strip-metal of graduating lengths, which, when struck by felt-tipped mallets, produce sounds that are amplified in long, hanging, resonant metal tubes. The revolving discs attached to the tubes are powered by electricity and the player is able to control vibrato effects by pedal manipulation. The vibes are usually included in listings under 'miscellaneous instruments', as is the flute (which during the 1920s and 1930s had few jazz practitioners) and the violin. During the 1920s and 1930s, several excellent jazz violinists made recordings, including Joe Venuti, Stuff Smith, Juice Wilson, Eddie South and Stephane Grappelli, but they were soloists and not section players. Occasionally, throughout the history of jazz, violins have formed part of string-sections working with jazz groups, but none of these ensembles have played a significant part in the development of jazz.

Recommended Reading

Bryce, Owen *Let's Play Jazz* (Books One and Two) (An introduction to chords and chord sequences), EMI Music Publishing, London, 1978

Coker, Jerry *Improvising Jazz* (A treatise with musical illustrations), Prentice-Hall, USA, 1964

Coker, Jerry *The Jazz Idiom* (A concise but valuable aid to understanding the theoretical side of jazz), Prentice-Hall, USA, 1975

Dankworth, Avril *Jazz* (An introduction to the musical basis), Oxford University Press, London, 1968

Schuller, Gunther *Early Jazz* (A most detailed musical survey of pre-Swing Era jazz), Oxford University Press, USA, 1968

7 The swing era begins

Many American bands undertake overseas tours; the first influential jazz books and magazines are published in Europe; the 'one-night stand' system of band touring begins; the Depression affects attendances – and musical tastes – but its aftermath gives a stimulus to big bands that feature jazz soloists; the sounds of the Swing Era develop in the ballrooms.

Despite the economic rigours brought about by the Wall Street Stock Market Crash there was no mass exodus of jazz musicians from New York City. The total number of American jazzmen embarking on overseas' tours in 1930 was little different from the figures in any pre-Depression year.

Groups of black singers and musical entertainers regularly toured Europe in the late nineteenth century, and by the early 1900s, American Negro musical acts were known throughout the world. An unsubstantiated rumour has it that Scott Joplin, the ragtime 'king', went to Britain about 1902. The Jenkins Orphanage Band certainly did three tours of Europe before the outbreak of the First World War.

Louis Mitchell, a black drummer from Philadelphia, made a big impact with musicians in Britain during his visit in 1914. He went back to the USA and worked with Jim Europe, then returned in 1915 for a long sojourn in Europe, later leading his Jazz Kings in Britain and France.

The first American group to get national front-page publicity in England was the ODJB, who, after their successes in New York, became the talking-point of the dancing world. They arrived in England in April 1919, and after receiving mixed reactions for their theatre appearances (which included the London Palladium), they moved into the vast Hammersmith Palais, a West London dancing arena, where they often played to more than 2000 people nightly. Their fifteen-month visit to Britain had a deep effect on the styles of hundreds of youngsters who were attempting to play the new music – simply because there was no other point of reference, this being before the transatlantic issue of other jazz bands' recordings.

In 1919, Will Marion Cook took the huge Southern Syncopated Orchestra to Britain, including the redoubtable Sidney Bechet as one of their number.

Light classical music was the basis of the Orchestra's repertoire. After playing prestigious theatre dates in Britain, the unit disbanded, leaving behind enough musicians to form several small bands; some of these ex-SSO players remained in Europe for the rest of their lives. Bechet greatly enlivened night-club music in London and Paris for a while, and then returned to New York, but the liking for European life acted like a magnet on him. Before the 1920s had ended, his travels took him as far afield as Russia, where he worked alongside trumpeter Tommy Ladnier.

The all-black shows that had captivated New York audiences in the early 1920s also went on overseas tours. One American hit, 'Plantation Days', went to London in 1923 with an orchestra that included James P. Johnson on piano, Darnell Howard on clarinet, Wellman Braud on string-bass and Johnny Dunn on trumpet.

A whole host of white dance bands and orchestras played in Europe during the 1920s (including Paul Whiteman's). Some of them had jazz soloists in their personnel, but they were rarely featured. One of the most fascinating improvising groups to go to Europe in that era was the Mound City Blue Blowers, a white novelty group consisting of Red Mackenzie, blowing into a haircomb wrapped in paper, Dick Slavin humming into a kazoo, Jack Bland on banjo and the great Eddie Lang on guitar.

Some of the black bands that visited Europe in the 1920s by-passed Britain, including Sam Wooding's Orchestra which played in Germany, Scandinavia, Spain, Turkey and France. Pianist Claude Hopkins' Band also toured several European countries in 1925 and 1926. But Europe was not the only destination for American jazzmen who travelled internationally in the 1920s. Several musicians went to Asia, including pianist Teddy Weatherford, who settled there for life, and New Orleans clarinettist Albert Nicholas, whose engagements took him from Shanghai to Egypt in 1926 and 1927. J. Paul Wyer, a pianist and clarinettist from Florida, who had worked with many jazz pioneers, including Bunk Johnson and Clarence Williams, played in areas as far apart as Britain and Japan.

In 1928, drummer Sonny Clay took his Plantation Orchestra (which featured singer Ivie Anderson) from California to Australia. Three years earlier, Buddy Rich, then an eight-year-old drumming prodigy, toured the Australian variety-hall circuit. During the 1920s, many bands from the USA played in South America.

Throughout the world, the public's initial reaction to their first live hearing of jazz varied, but it was usually apprehensive. Gradually, ears became accustomed to the new sounds, and a sturdy minority actually came to love the music. Departing American jazzmen left behind small cliques of admiring musicians all intent on forming their own jazz groups. It was to be some time before any non-American musicians showed real originality in their attempts to play jazz;

these players were praised not for the merits of their improvising, but for producing a close copy of the work of American stylists.

Some fortunate European bandleaders were able to persuade Americans to work with them full-time: Adrian Rollini, and his brother Arthur, trumpeter Chelsea Quealey, and other jazzmen worked at London's Savoy Hotel. When clarinettist Ted Lewis brought Jimmy Dorsey, George Brunies and Muggsy Spanier to Europe in his 1930 band, all three were inundated with offers to work permanently with local bands. By then, each of these men were celebrities with British jazz fans, who learnt a great deal about visiting musicians from the London-published *Melody Maker* (first issued in 1926), one of the first periodicals in the world to devote space to jazz record reviews, and news columns devoted to American jazz events.

From the turn of the century America had at least two regular magazines published solely for musicians, *Metronome* and *The Orchestra World*. In issues before 1930 there is scarcely even a cursory mention of jazz in either. The situation improved in 1934, when *Down Beat* was launched (it is still published). *Metronome* soon changed its policy and began including jazz news and reviews but both these magazines were pre-dated as jazz magazines by several European publications.

Only a few books on jazz had been published by 1930 and most of them were singularly ill-informed tending to suggest that Paul Whiteman's music was authentic jazz, and that George Gershwin was *the* jazz composer. The first knowledgeable and influential books on jazz were published in Europe: in Belgium by Robert Goffin, *Aux Frontières de Jazz* (1932), and in France by Hugues Panassié, *Le Jazz Hot* (1934). Both were serious attempts to treat improvised jazz as an art form. Guitarist Eddie Condon's retort, on being told of the serious interest being shown in jazz, was that playing the music was no more an art form than shelling peas. Nevertheless, many conservative musicians were beginning to notice the breadth and freshness of Duke Ellington's composing and arranging, and brass players of every school could plainly hear that Louis Armstrong was a virtuoso.

By 1930, many European jazz fans had become record collectors, diligently assembling the few jazz records that were issued each month, and trying hard to find the personnel of the bands that were featured. This was not always an easy task, particularly as pseudonymous recordings were often issued (Duke Ellington's Orchestra being labelled as 'The Ten Black Berries' was one confusing example). Duke Ellington and Louis Armstrong, both of whom toured Europe in the 1930s, were at first surprised and confused when asked complicated questions by European collectors about recordings that they had forgotten making.

During the 1930s, European jazz fans organised their own jazz appreciation clubs, called Rhythm Clubs in Britain and Hot Clubs in France. More often than not, the weekly meetings began with a record recital, generally devoted to the work of one particular jazz musician, and concluded with a jam session comprised of enthusiastic local jazz musicians. A few years later, in 1935, the United Hot Club of America was formed, with Marshall W. Stearns and John Hammond as its presidents.

The Depression had caused record sales in America to fall drastically. None of the companies there saw jazz as the saviour of the industry, but they did realise that there were enough dedicated buyers of jazz discs in Europe to make regular issues an economic proposition. Accordingly, John Hammond was commissioned to organise recordings by American jazz groups solely for distribution in Europe (thus were Bessie Smith's last recordings, and several other jazz masterpieces recorded).

The best-paid jobs for American musicians during the early 1930s were in the radio-studio bands. The prospect of a hefty, regular wage-packet caused a number of white jazzmen, who read music well, to ignore their improvising gifts in favour of security. The big black bands felt the economic recession particularly hard, even those with a high standard like Luis Russell's Band, which included Henry (Red) Allen, Pops Foster, Albert Nicholas, J. C. Higginbotham, Paul Barbarin and Charlie Holmes. Often Russell could not guarantee his musicians a weekly salary, and they were forced to work as and where they could. Fletcher Henderson, one of the most famous leaders of the 1920s, was forced temporarily to disband.

During the early years of the Depression, the American public's musical tastes changed. It appeared that the majority of ballroom-dancers had tired of the vigour and intensity of jazz and were reflecting what seems to be a twentieth-century trait, favouring sentimental and uncomplicated music during times of stress. Both black and white audiences reacted alike. Average attendances at a Harlem ballroom in 1932 were given in a Negro newspaper report as:

> Islam Jones, 3500; Rudy Vallee, 2800; Guy Lombardo, 2200; Ben Bernie, 2000; Vincent Lopez, 1700; Duke Ellington, 700; Cab Calloway, 500; Louis Armstrong, 350.[1]

Amazingly, the five bands that topped the list were all white, commercial dance-bands. Doubtless the tastes of the masses were swayed by the most predominant sounds that came from their radio sets. The smoother-sounding bands, all of which featured the new style of popular singing known as 'crooning' (whose most delightful exponent was Bing Crosby), got the greatest allocation of air time. People reacted by preferring the sounds they heard most often.

By the early 1930s, jazz was generally regarded as a minority interest. There had to be a sensational occurrence before the word appeared in the news pages. Even the death of Bix Beiderbecke in 1931 (the most celebrated white jazz musician of his day), was given only passing mention. Bix, who struggled with alcoholism for most of his brief adult life, was only twenty-eight when he died, his debilitated body being unable to withstand a summer bout of pneumonia. Today, the memory of Bix is revered. During the 1970s, the annual Bix Festivals held in his home town of Davenport, Iowa, regularly attracted thousands of people.

Just as Bix was ending his playing career, Bunny Berigan, a young trumpeter from Wisconsin, was making an impact on New York listeners. The pattern of Berigan's career was markedly similar to Beiderbecke's, even to completing a stint with Paul Whiteman, and having a lifelong drinking problem, but stylistically, the two players were very different. Berigan's power, range, and 'hot' tone contrasted greatly with Bix's mellow sound and lyricism. Berigan was a disciple of Louis Armstrong, and was one of the first white trumpeters to base a style on Louis's playing. Berigan acted as something of a musical translator for Louis's intricacies, and thenceforth scores of white trumpet players began copying Berigan.

After visiting Europe with Hal Kemp in 1930, Berigan settled into a lucrative studio job, playing with dozens of different bands within the course of a single month. In these ensembles he sat alongside a number of white jazzmen who were to become household names in the approaching Swing Era, players such as Artie Shaw, Tommy and Jimmy Dorsey and Benny Goodman. No black musicians were employed in salaried studio bands then, no matter how brilliant their musicianship. During the 1930s, two superb Negro musicians, Coleman Hawkins and Benny Carter, both went to Europe to work with radio orchestras, something they could not have done then in the USA.

Hawkins' departure in 1934 presented Fletcher Henderson with the gigantic task of finding a suitable replacement on tenor-saxophone. He sent for Lester Young, who had made a name for himself in the Kansas City jam sessions. In New York, Lester was soon made to feel ill at ease by his new colleagues, who continually urged him to abandon his light, vibrato-less way of playing in favour of the broad-toned, wide vibratoed style that they were used to hearing Hawkins play. Young left the band and returned to Kansas City rather than make the stylistic adjustment. Two years later, playing in the same manner, he returned to New York in triumph as a member of Count Basie's Band. By then, he was recognised as a true original, who had developed a way of playing jazz on the tenor-saxophone that owed nothing to Coleman Hawkins' work – Lester himself said that one of his only influences was the playing of the white saxophonist, Frank Trumbauer. Hawkins and Young were the twin colossi of the tenor-saxophone during the 1930s who both attracted countless copyists, and their influences were so overwhelming that it was common then for jazz tenor players to be described as being of the Lester Young School, or the Coleman Hawkins school. Two gifted white players, Bud Freeman and Eddie Miller, were notably rare exceptions. Also, several black players including Leon (Chu) Berry, Ben Webster, Dick Wilson and Don Byas, set out as devoted copyists, but found originality and became important jazz tenor-saxophonists in their own right.

Coleman Hawkins had an oblique influence on one of the most important of all jazz trumpeters, Roy Eldridge. The fiery nature of Eldridge's playing, and his tone and range, were a corollary to Louis Armstrong's style, but the shapes of his improvisations were often markedly different from anything that Louis had done. Much of Roy's style was, as he admitted, based on Hawkins' saxophone work. For his first important audition he chose to play a note-for-note copy of a recorded Hawkins solo. Another black trumpeter a few years older than Roy, Henry (Red) Allen, also developed a style that moved away from Armstrong's influence. Red, whose father was a famous bandleader in Louisiana, had a childhood full of jazz, and this led him to work in the marching bands. He progressed into the riverboat orchestras, and then joined King Oliver and Fletcher Henderson. Along the way, he developed a new approach to jazz improvisation whereby he inserted daring notes into solos that seemed to ignore the rigid beat of the rhythm section. For simple explanation several jazz critics have mapped out a stylistic lineage for early jazz trumpeters which reads: Louis Armstrong – Henry Allen – Roy Eldridge. But Eldridge and Allen, although both inspired by Armstrong, chose entirely different approaches to improvisation.

During the early 1930s, a musician burst forth whose technique was so formidable, even on his début recordings, that it took years before anyone could imitate his work convincingly, even for one chorus. Pianist Art Tatum had a style of playing that belonged to no particular school of jazz and he remains the supreme jazz individualist, impossible to categorise. His legacy to the jazz listener is a whole series of recordings, spanning twenty-five years, which feature a combination of faultless technique and vast imagination. During his lifetime he was revered by his fellow musicians, particularly by pianists. Fats Waller, himself no mean technician, always got up from the piano and said 'God is in the house' whenever Tatum entered the room.

Waller, who became one of the jazz world's biggest earners, found fame through a series of small-band recordings, begun in 1934, and entitled 'Fats Waller and his Rhythm'. On them, Fats projected his effervescent personality through a series of jokey vocals. Fats, a prolific composer, who had successfully done solo playing, band work, and accompaniments throughout the 1920s, was amazed, and some said, slightly perturbed to find that his jovial singing had tripled his income, and made his name a household word on both sides of the Atlantic. There was a serious side to Waller, which was reflected in the records he made playing the organ, but to the world at large he was a plump entertainer, whose powerful left-hand playing rocked the gin bottle that was always on the piano, while his jolly voice humorously ridiculed serious lyrics. Fats's Rhythm, with its trumpet and saxophone front-line, was typical of many bands who played in Harlem clubs during the 1930s. Fats himself was a musical antidote to the Depression. The first issue of his Rhythm recordings coincided with a change of mood which was affecting the American people who, after five years of economic hardship, were making themselves ready for unrestrained enjoyment on the dance floor. A boom period for musicians was just around the corner.

The Swing Era was the general name for the five-year boom period, which lasted from 1935 to 1940. Many bandleaders enjoyed great success during that time and none more than clarinettist Benny Goodman. Goodman was something of a musical prodigy. He joined the musicians' union in his home city of Chicago at the age of thirteen, and at sixteen was with Ben Pollack's Band, where he stayed for four years before becoming a free-lance musician in New York, working in the lucrative studio bands, and in the theatre orchestras that played for Broadway shows. The scuffling, uncertain life that many of his jazz friends endured (so that they could continue to play jazz), had no appeal for Goodman. He was quite content to hide his formidable technique in a studio band section, occasionally playing a dazzling clarinet solo that proved he was one of the most gifted of all white improvisers.

In 1934, he was persuaded to form his own big band. On the face of it he appeared to be an unlikely bandleader – his personality was never radiant, and he often had problems in communicating with his sidemen. However, he could quickly analyse a jazzman's potential, and was self-evidently a master musician. Goodman soon realised that his band needed arrangements that were exciting and stimulating enough to keep his musicians interested. Fletcher Henderson, who had again disbanded, was the ideal man to provide such arrangements. He not only wrote new orchestrations for the band, but also he re-vamped tunes that his own band had recorded, and passed the written scores on to Goodman. It was not the first time that a black arranger had written for a white band (Don Redman wrote for Jean Goldkette and Paul Whiteman in the 1920s) but it was the first time that a Negro was hired as a staff arranger by a white bandleader. Later, Sy Oliver fulfilled a similar role and completely revitalised Tommy Dorsey's Band. The success of Henderson's arrangements encouraged Goodman, and pleased the critics, but the band's first national tour in 1935 began disastrously with respect to audience response. This all changed when the band reached California, where they were given an ecstatic welcome by an audience in a packed ballroom. The reaction took Goodman by surprise. He later found out that the West Coast dancers (because of their different time zone) had been receiving the band's East Coast broadcasts at peak listening time.

The audience at the Palomar Ballroom in Los Angeles went wild every time that Goodman's Band appeared, and the resultant publicity had a snowballing effect. The national media featured stories of the frenzied reactions, with the result that when Goodman returned to the East Coast vast crowds turned out to listen and dance to his band. The Swing Era had begun.

Almost immediately, radio sponsors, record companies and ballroom owners all wanted to sign up 'swing' bands. In 1936, even the ODJB's leader, Nick La Rocca, came out of musical retirement to form a fourteen-piece band. In effect, the appellation 'swing' was simply a new brand name for an old product. People had been listening to big band riffs (the repetitious playing of a short set phrase to generate excitement – see chapter ten) and call-and-answer patterns for years before 1935, and they were regularly featured by Fletcher Henderson's Band, Don Redman's Band, and by the Casa Loma Orchestra, whose arranger Gene Gifford made a speciality of having one instrumental section answering another. The main difference between big bands before 1935 and after was that the swing era groups paid much more attention to presentation; soloists were encouraged to stand in front of the band while they were being featured and each musician was introduced by name to the audience who were encouraged to crowd around the bandstand at the ballroom.

The ballroom was the birthplace of swing and it continued to be the music's vital outlet. Jitterbugging, which developed in the Harlem ballrooms, became popular with white dancers. The original movements were modified and made less energetic, but the basis of improvising steps and dance patterns to the music remained. An even more restrained approach to improvised dancing developed which eventually became known as jiving. Publicists had a field-day in March 1937 when Benny Goodman played at the Paramount Theatre in New York, for many of the young audience got out of their seats and jitter-bugged in the aisles. On the first day of their engagement, Goodman's Band (doing five shows a day) had played to 21 000 people.[2]

Swing bands were very big business. Goodman was acclaimed as the 'King of Swing', but there were many contenders for the crown. Several of them were musicians who had moved to New York in the 1920s, such as Tommy and Jimmy Dorsey, and clarinettist Artie Shaw, who was for a time a close rival to Benny Goodman. Moreover, mass popularity was not only accorded to white big bands. Jimmie Lunceford's Orchestra, with its immaculate presentation and inspired soloists, was a big favourite with ballroom crowds. As the interest in swing developed, so an increasing number of sidemen were coerced into forming their own big bands. Bunny Berigan, a star soloist in Benny Goodman's 1935 Band, was persuaded to become a leader but the venture ended in a disastrous bankruptcy, as did Jack Teagarden's similar attempt. Sidemen who became leaders found that the change in status was an expensive one, for it was the leader's task to pay for arrangements, the band-bus, uniforms, agency fees and publicity charges.

The popularity of the swing band's sidemen was akin to the adulation that pop stars were later to receive. The duration of the acclaim was only temporary, as with the heroes of any fad. For some jazz musicians, the gimmickry and phoney jargon of the Swing Era was hard to take. It was irksome too for good musicians to hear the worst, but loudest solo of the set, get the most applause. But some Swing Era sidemen enjoyed lasting success with their own big bands, among them several ex-Goodman players such as trumpeter Harry James, drummer Gene Krupa and multi-instrumentalist Lionel Hampton. An ex-Isham Jones musician, reed-player Woody Herman, began his own band in 1936; over forty years later he was still at the top of the big-band profession.

In 1935, Benny Goodman created one of the sensations of the Swing Era by signing black pianist Teddy Wilson. Although Wilson was employed purely on musical merit, his joining Goodman was seen as a direct attempt to eliminate the widespread racial discrimination that existed in the music business. Wilson was specially featured with Goodman and Gene Krupa in a trio within the big band, Goodman next augmented this unit by adding another black musician, Lionel Hampton, on vibraphone. The move may have appalled racists, but for the jazz listener the results were extremely satisfying. Saxophone player Charlie Barnet was also notable for employing black soloists for his big band at a time when most musicians' union branches throughout the USA had two distinct organisations – one for whites and one for blacks.

The most important black big band to emerge during the Swing Era, was led by pianist William (Count) Basie. Basie, who had been the pianist in Bennie Moten's Band, was something of a rarity, a New York stride-pianist who left that city to find fame in Kansas City. Moten's premature death in 1935 eventually led to Bill Basie becoming the leader of Moten's alumni. A radio announcer observing the self-accorded titles in jazz – Duke, King, Earl – called Basie 'Count' and the accolade stuck. Basie's Band played for minuscule wages in a Kansas City club, but one benefit of the residency was that the music from there was regularly broadcast over a wide area. Record-producer and writer John Hammond happened to hear the Basie Band broadcast in 1936, and knowing instantly that he was listening to a highly original jazz unit, he saw to it that Basie was offered work in New York.

Originally, Basie had specialised in the forceful, two-handed stride-piano style, but by the mid-1930s his playing featured exquisitely placed single-note phrases that often seemed like interjections to someone else's solo, producing an immensely rhythmical effect. Basie had several wonderful jazzmen in his band including bassist Walter Page, drummer Jo Jones and tenor-saxophonist Lester Young, who was also a sensitive clarinettist. Basie's other tenor-sax player, Herschel Evans, played with a broad-toned orthodoxy – the contrast between his work and Lester's was to remain a jazz talking-point for decades.

One of Basie's early stars, Oran (Hot Lips) Page, an exciting jazz trumpeter and a splendid blues vocalist, preceded the band to New York to follow a solo career. He was replaced by Wilbur (Buck) Clayton, a trumpeter who presented elegant jazz ideas with a burnished tone that could cut through the sounds of any packed ballroom. Buck was soon joined in the brass section by two other fine jazzmen, trumpeter Harry (Sweets) Edison and trombonist Dicky Wells, whose habit of ending phrases with a sudden burst of fast vibrato made his playing easily recognisable. In early 1937, Basie signed guitarist Freddie Green, whose way of playing four beats in each bar with great rhythmic surety, on unamplified guitar, gave the Basie rhythm section a unique sound. Forty years later, Green was still fulfilling his vital role as Count Basie's guitarist.

Basie's magnificent rhythm section, the rugged power of the brass players – who seemed to have developed an almost telepathic regard for synchronised phrasing – and the exciting inventiveness of the saxophone soloists, all combined to make a dramatic impact on New York audiences. Many of the band's arrangements were not written down. A basic musical 'plot' was memorised, but often riffs would be created spontaneously on the bandstand, and one section would answer the other with a musical aptness that made other bandleaders feel rueful. Jimmy Rushing, the band's male singer, soon became a great favourite. Rushing, a short, fat man, became known as Mister Five by Five (five feet tall and five feet wide), and his rich baritone voice was capable of singing blues, and ballads, with great power and feeling. During 1937 and 1938 Basie also featured vocaliste Billie Holiday, who was already being spoken of as one of jazz's finest singers. Billie, who suffered a hard childhood in Baltimore and Philadelphia, began her singing career in New York clubs in the early 1930s. She made her record début in 1933, but did not begin recording regularly until 1935. On record, Billie was backed by small bands, playing a jam-session-styled accompaniment to her vocals, which were usually on popular tunes of the day. The skill with which she made timeless music out of songs that were often trite, both in lyric and melody, remains one of the outstanding endeavours in any form of jazz.

Billie, who had grown up as an admirer of Louis Armstrong and Bessie Smith, improvised vocal variations on songs in just the way that a jazz saxophone would improvise. The perfect partner for her was tenor-sax player Lester Young – whom Billie named Pres (short for The President). Lester, in turn, gave Billie a nick-name, Lady Day, which was to stay with her forever. Lester Young, and several other Basie musicians, were regularly featured on Billie Holiday's recordings. Basie himself could not take part for contractual reasons and the pianist who was most often on the sessions was the impeccable Teddy Wilson. Billie toured with Basie's Band for almost a year, but then the agency that booked the band dispensed with her services, saying she was too inconsistent.

The jazz world's surprise at this comment was nothing compared to the astonishment that followed Billie's next move. Almost immediately after leaving Basie she began touring with another big band, this time led by a white man, clarinettist Artie Shaw. Billie was not the first black girl singer to work with a white band – both Ivie Anderson and June Richmond had preceded her in that respect – but she was the first to go on full-scale tours that covered Northern and Southern states. Billie's stay with Shaw had many stormy moments. The accompanying musicians were delighted with her artistry and her company, but ballroom managers and band agencies were less happy at being part of the experiment. Billie stayed with Artie Shaw for nine months and then they both went on to greater things apart. Billie never again did long tours with big bands.

During the Swing Era, Ella Fitzgerald who worked regularly with the big band led by Chick Webb was one of Billie's close professional rivals. Chick, who overcame in spectacular style the disability of being a tiny hunchback, became one of the most impressive big-band drummers of all time. His following at New York's Savoy Ballroom was almost messianic, which made playing opposite his band a daunting task for visiting musicians. Ella, too, was a great favourite at the Savoy; she never became as great a jazz artiste as Billie Holiday, but her superlative vocal technique made her more consistently popular with mass audiences.

One of Ella Fitzgerald's early inspirations was the white singer, Connee Boswell. Connee could sing the blues authoritatively, but she virtually ignored that side of her talents, and during the 1930s worked mostly with her two sisters, Martha and Helvetia, in a vocal trio which specialised in ingenious vocal arrangements.

The most publicised jazz vocaliste of the 1930s was Mildred Bailey, who was part Cherokee Indian. She first came to fame with Paul Whiteman's Orchestra, but later made a long series of small-band recordings, many with her husband, vibraharpist Kenneth (Red) Norvo. Lee Wiley, another singer who was also part-Indian, had a dedicated following among jazz musicians. Like Mildred Bailey, she too worked with a big commercial orchestra before realising her true potential was in singing with small bands. One of the best all-round jazz singers of the 1930s, Ivie Anderson, worked exclusively with Duke Ellington's Orchestra throughout the decade. Ethel Waters, who had been a very influential vocaliste during the 1920s, led her own band during the 1930s, prior to becoming a successful actress.

Most of the big swing bands featured both female and male singers, but few had any pretensions to being jazz vocalists. Their task was to present to the public an accurate vocal representation of the composer's and lyricist's intentions, without improvising. A young man who sang with swing bands led by Harry James and Tommy Dorsey became one of the great popular singers of the century: Frank Sinatra.

Male jazz singers are a rare breed. In the 1930s, dozens of jazz instrumentalists often sang with satisfying, and sometimes sublime, results. Louis Armstrong continued to exert an enormous influence on jazz vocalising, and other players like Jack Teagarden, Hot Lips Page, Henry Allen, Woody Herman and Jonah Jones sang on recordings, but the two vocalists who dominated jazz at that time were Jimmy Rushing, and Big Joe Turner, a vast man who occasionally sang ballads, but who sounded much more at home when he sang blues. Counter to the Swing Era, there was a rapidly developing interest among the black populations of some big American cities (notably Chicago and Kansas City) in a style of music that became known as urban blues. It consisted of songs that were concerned with the traumas of city life, as opposed to the content of rural, or country blues. As with all earlier examples of city blues singing, the piano played a big part in the accompaniments. The boogie-woogie style that had flourished during the post-ragtime period became standard backing for several urban blues singers. Big Joe Turner's first trip to New York in 1938 was in the company of Pete Johnson, one of Kansas City's finest boogie players. Through Johnson's prowess, and the skills of Chicago pianists Albert Ammons and Meade (Lux) Lewis, boogie-woogie became increasingly popular with white audiences until it escalated into an international fad. Tommy Dorsey's swing band made a best-selling record of a cleverly arranged version of pioneer stylist Pine Top Smith's 'Boogie Woogie'. The rendering was a far cry from the boogie that became popular in the Chicago South Side clubs during the 1920s but, by the time Dorsey's records were a hit, the musical tastes in those clubs was changing. Guitar groups, or vocalists accompanying themselves on guitar, were gaining popularity. These musicians were utilising a technical development that had been the basis of many experiments during the 1920s – the electrically amplified guitar. A whole new array of tone colours came from these instruments – sounds that became the basis of the world's pop music of the 1960s.

Mass support for boogie-woogie proved to be temporary, though it was later to enjoy several smaller recurrences of popularity. In 1938, it played an important part in one of the first jazz concerts held at New York's Carnegie Hall. The concert, which was attended by 4000 people, presented a potpourri of jazz styles of the 1930s. Benny Goodman's Orchestra was the main feature, with guest appearances by several of Count Basie's sidemen, young Dixieland players like Bobby Hackett, and musicians from Duke Ellington's Orchestra.

Duke Ellington himself did not take part in the concert, but there was nothing sinister in his absence. He might well have smiled wryly at some of the ecstatic praise that was being heaped upon swing bandleaders, but his only pronouncements were full of graciousness. Years before, in 1932, he had written and recorded a song called 'It Don't Mean A Thing, If It Ain't Got That Swing'. To Duke, the Swing Era was no more important than the Charleston Era, or any other era. Throughout the 1930s, he continued to create the finest jazz compositions being written, orchestrating them in his own inimitable way. His orchestra remained, man for man, the strongest jazz group of all.

Bands with less solo strength often had to indulge in novelty numbers to keep the public interested. One craze that affected many leaders was called 'Jazzing The Classics', which meant creating a big-band swing arrangement of a work that was usually part of a symphony orchestra's repertoire. Tommy Dorsey's big-selling version of Rimsky-Korsakoff's 'Song of India' was one of the first of the genre. Examples became more frequent, which produced angry reactions from lovers of classical music; eventually, radio stations threatened a ban on similar parodies. But the main anger engendered by the success of the swing band was felt by those jazz fans who firmly believed in the merits of small-band jazz. The Swing Era, with all its ballyhoo, gimmickry and restricted solo space, seemed too far removed from the early jazz recordings that they treasured.

Only one of the bands that broadcast regularly had a repertoire based on material from the period that jazz fans called the Golden Era and this was the band led by Bob Crosby, a brother of Bing, who had formerly sung with the Dorsey Brothers' Band. In 1935, Bob Crosby was elected leader of a co-operative unit comprised of excellent young musicians, who were, almost to a man, dedicated jazz fans themselves. Several came from New Orleans, including tenor-saxophonist Eddie Miller, drummer Ray Bauduc and guitarist Nappy Lamare (later joined by another Louisianian, clarinettist Irving Fazola). These men, together with trumpeter John (Yank) Lawson from Missouri, and clarinettist Julian (Matty) Matlock from Kentucky, featured their own brand of collective improvisation, embracing many tunes that had been jazz favourites in the 1920s. There was an even more direct link with the earlier jazz heritage, for all the Crosby sidemen mentioned had played in the band led by ex-NORK drummer, Ben Pollack, the leader who had also employed Benny Goodman for four years. Goodman will always be remembered as 'The King of Swing', but by 1940 his band was second in acclaim to a unit led by yet another ex-Pollack sideman, trombonist Glenn Miller. Miller was not a notable jazz improviser but he was a fine trombonist and a brilliant arranger. Improvised solos were featured, but it was Miller's arrangements (and those of Jerry Gray, Bill Finegan and others), and the precision with which the band played them that won widespread popularity. Miller's success was indicative of a process that is omnipresent in American music: the big prizes go to those who adapt, and smooth out, the roughness and vigour of a previous style. Miller, with talent and ingenuity, did just that. The result was totally uninteresting for jazz fans. For them, the smoothness that many swing bands attained was the antithesis of what they wanted. By the end of the 1930s, there existed several magazines produced by devotees of what was then known as 'hot jazz', and their editorial and correspondence columns were full of phrases that expressed discontent with the existing state of jazz. These enthusiasts wanted a full-scale return to what they thought of as a more honest, and sincere, form of music-making. They called for a revival of collective improvisation.

Recommended Reading

Chilton, John *Billie's Blues* (A survey of Billie Holiday's career), Quartet Books, London 1975

Connor, D. R. and Hicks, W. H. *B.G. On the Record* (A bio-discography of Benny Goodman), Arlington House, USA, 1969

Dance, Stanley *The World of Swing* (Revealing interviews with veterans of the Swing Era), Scribner's, USA, 1974

Gammond, Peter (ed.) *Duke Ellington – His Life and Music* (Impressions by various writers), Phoenix House, London, 1958

Goodman, B. and Kolodin, I. *The Kingdom of Swing* (Benny Goodman's Autobiography), Stackpole Sons, USA, 1939

Hammond, John with Townsend, I. *John Hammond on Record* (Autobiography), Summit Books, USA, 1977

Holiday, B. and Dufty, W. *Lady Sings the Blues* (A ghosted autobiography), Doubleday, USA, 1956

Horricks, Raymond *Count Basie and His Orchestra* (Biographies of Basie and his musicians), Gollancz, London, 1957

Sanford, Herb *Tommy and Jimmy – The Dorsey Years* (Biography of two big-band leaders), Ian Allan, London, 1972

Shaw, Arnold *The Street That Never Slept* (The story of jazz on New York's 52nd Street), Coward, McCann and Geoghegan, USA, 1971

Shaw, Artie *The Trouble With Cinderella* (Autobiography), Jarrolds, London, 1955

Simon, George T. *Simon Says* (A survey of the leading figures in the Swing Era 1935–55), Arlington House, USA, 1971

Simon, George T. *The Big Bands* (Background stories of the famous swing bands of the 1930s and 1940s), Macmillan, USA, 1971

Stewart, Rex *Jazz Masters of the Thirties* (In-depth essays on great jazzmen by one of their number), Macmillan, USA, 1972

Ulanov, Barry *Duke Ellington* (An early biography), Musicians Press, London, 1947

Walker, Leo *The Big Band Almanac* (An alphabetical listing of famous bands), Ward Ritchie Press, USA, 1978

Wells, Dicky (as told to Dance, Stanley) *The Night People* (Reminiscences of the ex-Basie star), Robert Hale, London, 1971

8 The renaissance of early jazz

Interest in collective improvisation revives – record companies begin re-issuing 'jazz classics'; veteran New Orleans musicians record in their home city, several important jazzmen cease working in big bands and form their own small groups.

Until the late 1930s, the pattern of jazz's evolvement consisted of adding new dimensions to the concepts of the previous era. Instruments were added to make small bands into big ones, the arrangements that these bands played became more involved, and the harmonies, on which the jazz soloists improvised, became more complicated. Not everyone was ready to change their style of playing to meet new demands, but only the hardiest of musical reactionaries refused to incorporate some facet of the new ideas into their performances. There was a hardening of attitudes during the late stages of the Swing Era when there occurred what might be called the first big schism in jazz. The result was that some musicians deliberately adopted playing-styles that were appropriate to an earlier decade.

Throughout the 1930s, a minority of jazz fans had called for what they saw as the most worthwhile feature of jazz – collective improvisation. The ballyhoo of the Swing Era, and the monotony of playing the same arrangements over and over again, year in, year out, eventually persuaded a small number of jazz musicians to begin thinking along similar lines. No single dramatic event caused them to reconsider their attitude, but gradually a revival of old values gained momentum. Other musicians, who believed that the Swing Era was to be a musical springboard for further technical developments, were appalled at what they considered to be blatant retrogression. A contretemps developed between the factions and, as a result, two distinct schools of jazz came into being during the early 1940s – the modern, and the traditional. It was to be some years before either school could acknowledge each other's music with anything other than open derision.

Even at the height of the Swing Era, a popular spot in many bands' programmes occurred when six or seven of the personnel moved out in front of their music-stands to play an impromptu set. Several name bands had what was called 'a band within a band'; Bob Crosby had The Bobcats, Tommy Dorsey The Clambake Seven, Chick Webb The Little Chicks and Woody Herman The Woodchips, but these small units were only a part of the overall presentation. If big-band musicians wanted to take part in extended collective improvisation they did so, unpaid, at jam-sessions. In the 1930s, a large number of small bands were formed solely for recording sessions. Many jazz musicians were booked to record on a free-lance basis, often as accompanists for singers. Their skills at following musical routines, without needing to have written music, saved the record company money on time (paid for on a musicians' union scale), and arrangers' fees.

The onset of Prohibition in 1920 created a lot of work for musicians but, as the years rolled by and tastes changed, many clubs dispensed with bands and used solo pianists and vocalists. The repeal of Prohibition in 1933, lifting the restrictions on purchasing alcoholic liquor, caused the American public to become fussy about where they drank. They now needed coaxing into the very clubs into which they had previously thronged. Club owners soon realised that a good, entertaining band could be a big factor in attracting customers. As a result, several novelty groups flourished in New York, whose 52nd Street area had several clubs close to each other. One of the most popular groups was called The Spirits of Rhythm, which consisted solely of rhythm instruments. Its two featured members were guitarist Teddy Bunn and a zany vocalist named Leo Watson. This group was the precursor of the highly popular Slim and Slam duo, which featured Slam Stewart, whose gimmick was to sing in unison with his own bowed string-bass solos, and Slim Gaillard, an able guitarist, whose humorous readjustment of song lyrics often gave them a surreal quality.

Early in 1936, another group with an unusual line-up began attracting a large following to New York's Onyx Club. It was led by an exciting jazz violinist, Stuff Smith, whose only other front-line colleague was trumpeter Jonah Jones. The two men's playing and singing was presented with inspired showmanship which soon made them very popular. When Stuff's Sextet left New York temporarily, a sextet led by bassist John Kirby and featuring Leo Watson's vocals was formed to fill the vacancy. The band's alto-saxophone Pete Brown epitomised the type of musician who then worked in the small Harlem clubs. Throughout his life, Brown rarely worked in anything larger than a sextet. He could, if called upon, play trumpet and guitar proficiently, but he specialised on the alto-sax, which he played in a highly individual way. Brown's improvisations always had an urgent, 'jumpy' feeling, so marked that it was called the 'jump style'. Brown's closest colleague in John Kirby's Band was trumpeter Frankie Newton, who, like Brown, was one of the most important small-band players of the 1930s. Neither stayed long with Kirby. Their replacements were two young musicians, who until then had worked mainly in big bands: trumpeter Charlie Shavers, and alto-saxophonist Russell Procope. They joined Buster

Bailey on clarinet, Kirby on string-bass, O'Neill Spencer on drums and vocals, and Billy Kyle on piano. This band soon became even more popular than the ebullient sextet led by Stuff Smith. They achieved their success in an entirely different way: by performing very intricate arrangements, most of which were written by Shavers and Kyle, who were also the band's most brilliant soloists. The band memorised and performed these arrangements immaculately, with a panache that impressed laymen and musicians. Their selection of material was immensely varied, ranging from Tschaikovsky to the 'Royal Garden Blues'; its well-rehearsed dynamics enabled the band to go from a fortissimo roar to a pianissimo whisper with perfect control. They were soon being billed as the 'Biggest Little Band in the Land'. Kirby's Band were extremely versatile and could also play well without using complex arrangements. As sidemen they recorded with Willie (The Lion) Smith, and also accompanied the New Orleans veteran clarinettists Jimmie Noone and Johnny Dodds when they visited New York for recording sessions.

Earlier, in 1935, a group of young white New Orleans players began making their mark on the New York club scene. They were led by the trumpeter and vocalist Louis Prima who brought a six-piece band up from Louisiana which opened at a club called The Famous Door, featuring a blend of dixieland and novelty numbers. Another white trumpeter-vocalist from New Orleans, Wingy Manone (so called because he only had one arm), came to New York to present a similar musical mixture; in 1935, his light-hearted vocal on 'The Isle of Capri' became a best-selling record.

Despite the high quality of small-band jazz that was being played in New York during the late 1930s, the die-hard traditionalists were far from satisfied. They felt the musicians involved were playing jazz only for monetary gain, ignoring the fact that many of them could have earned more money as star sidemen in big swing bands. The dedicated fans wanted the jazz of yesteryear to return, completely unchanged.

It is impossible to pinpoint an exact date on which the traditional jazz revival started, because several events played their part. By 1936, swing bands were reviving tunes that had been originally recorded a decade or so earlier, such as King Oliver's 'Dippermouth Blues' and Jelly Roll Morton's 'King Porter Stomp'. The popular music magazines began featuring articles on jazz pioneers. Big record companies took to re-issuing early jazz recordings and calling them 'jazz classics'. In 1936, Hugues Panassié's book *Le Jazz Hot* was translated for English and American readers into *Hot Jazz*.

Panassié was soon to visit New York where he assembled a recording band that based its style on the collective improvisation of a New Orleans group. It featured two famous musicians from that city, Sidney Bechet and Tommy Ladnier. Earlier (in 1932), these two men had tried, unsuccessfully, to get regular bookings in New York ballrooms for their own exciting band The

Feetwarmers. On the recordings their colleague was clarinettist and tenor-saxophonist Milton (Mezz) Mezzrow. During the 1920s, Mezzrow's hell-fire-preacher-like ravings on the merits of jazz had stirred several young Chicagoans to become interested in playing the music. Mezzrow himself never became a fluent jazz technician, but sometimes, when the musical company was compatible, he could enhance a session. His real contribution to jazz, besides organising interesting bands, was in writing the music's most colourful autobiography, *Really The Blues*. Mezzrow was one of the few American jazz musicians to be imprisoned for drug offences prior to 1941. The use of marijuana was quite widespread among jazz musicians during the 1920s and 1930s, but hard drugs were rarely taken. As we shall see, a more sombre pattern became apparent during the 1940s.

In 1938 Frenchman Charles Delaunay compiled the first edition of his *Hot Discography*, an early attempt to inform the interested jazz fan about who played what, on various recordings. The book also gave the date and location of the recordings, and the record companies' issue numbers. The compilers of such listings became known as 'discographers' and a new word entered the language. They constantly spoke of 'second takes' (meaning the second attempt at recording the same tune) and occasionally more than one take of a tune would be issued. There was much searching by record collectors for the rarer example. It became clear that many groups had recorded under pseudonymns – usually because of contractual reasons – and this added to the fanatical collectors' problems. Rarity often became more important to them than musical quality.

A streak of deep romanticism developed among the dedicated fans, who were delighted to hear any mention of eccentricities that their jazz heroes might have. Often men whose musical abilities were dubious were acclaimed simply because of remarkable personal habits.

Jelly Roll Morton did not fall into this category. He possessed both an extraordinary musical talent and blatant eccentricity. In 1938, he was given the opportunity to demonstrate both of these facets in a series of recordings organised by the folk-music archivist, Alan Lomax. On them, Morton plays piano, sings and in answer to Lomax's questions, reminisces about his early career. They were among the first positive attempts to trace the origins of jazz, and its definitions and remain vital to a close study of the music.

During the 1930s, Morton had, what was for him, a quiet decade, quiet that is until the moment in March 1938 when he heard W. C. Handy described in a 'Believe It Or Not' radio programme as 'the originator of jazz, stomps and blues'. Morton reached for his pen and fired an angry missive at the programme's creator Robert Ripley. Mercifully, the diatribe was preserved, and later published in the *Down Beat* magazine.[1] Never modest, Morton composed a letter that was proud and emphatic. It begins: 'It is evidently known, beyond contradiction, that New Orleans is the cradle of jazz, and I, myself, happened to be the creator in the year 1902, many years before the Dixieland Band organised . . .' The letter, which went on for over 3000 words, was Morton's attempt to put the record straight, as he saw it. He concluded by signing himself: 'World's Great Hot Tune Writer.'

A few weeks later, Morton was contacted by Lomax at the seedy club in Washington where he was reduced to earning a living as a pianist-barman and doorman combined. Morton agreed to start the Library of Congress recordings in May 1938. Soon after the recordings were completed, Morton, fortified by a good deal of publicity, returned to New York in something like his old style. Before he left Washington he attended a dance at the local Lincoln Colonnade Ballroom and listened to Chick Webb's band playing. A local jazz fan saw him there and said: 'The band played your King Porter Stomp, and it sounded fine.' 'How could they miss,' replied Morton. 'The music's right there, all they've got to do is play it.'[2]

The widespread interest in the multi-talented braggadocio's work came too late in Morton's life. His health was failing rapidly but, nevertheless, he organised a few recording-sessions which featured several of his 'home town boys', as he called Sidney Bechet, Albert Nicholas, Wellman Braud and Henry Allen. In late 1940 he moved out to California and died there within a year.

The counter-movements of players disillusioned by the excesses of the Swing Era continued. Broadly, two types of small band were being formed during the late 1930s. The first style featured bands who were positively interested in recreating music, and tunes, of the past. The other type of unit consisted of musicians who wanted to experiment with harmonies and instrumentation. Clarinettist Artie Shaw was one of the latter. He formed up a small group called The Gramercy Five which featured the harpsichord playing of Johnny Guarnieri.

Typical of the former groups was the eight-piece band formed by Muggsy Spanier in Chicago in 1939. In an effort to state that his interest lay in the past, Muggsy, a devotee of King Oliver and a close friend of Louis Armstrong, called his band The Ragtimers (although, in fact, the band did not play ragtime). Muggsy had spent most of the 1930s working in Ted Lewis's Big Band and was persuaded by the growing enthusiasm for Dixieland to form his own band for a hotel residency in Chicago. He was then enticed to make the classic jazz pilgrimage to New York, for further fame and fortune. The regular bookings that were needed to keep the band intact did not materialise, and despite making sixteen excellent recordings, they were forced to disband before a year had ended. Although the band played classic jazz tunes with cohesion and expression, the music did not placate the purists. The music was collectively improvised, but it was thought suspect because it was presented so smoothly. The purists craved for more rugged jazz fare, and they were soon to hear it.

At the time of the Library of Congress recordings, a team of devout jazz enthusiasts were working on a book that was to throw light on Jelly Roll Morton's contemporaries – the men who had played jazz in the early years of the century. The book, called *Jazzmen* (compiled by C. E. Smith, Frederic Ramsey and Bill Russell), was published in 1939. The researchers contacted Louis Armstrong and Clarence Williams for background information, and both men mentioned the name of trumpeter Bunk Johnson as someone whose memory should be consulted. Neither had Bunk's address, but eventually a letter sent to him care of the Postmaster of New Iberia, Louisiana, reached him.

Bunk had not played trumpet for several years; he was working as a driver of a delivery truck. He not only volunteered information to the researchers, but said that given false teeth and a trumpet he could once again play as he used to. Here was talk to thrill all those who yearned for a return to the past – a living legend who claimed to be an ex-colleague of Buddy Bolden, and who was ready and willing to try and recapture lost glories. False teeth were made for Bunk, and he was given a new trumpet. Amazingly the resolute old man began to play himself back into form.

In 1940, Heywood Hale Broun, a jazz magazine editor, decided it was time that he visited New Orleans to record other musicians, like Bunk, who had played a part in early jazz history. Bunk Johnson was offered the chance to play on the session, but he was busy rehabilitating himself by working as a music-teacher for the Works Progress Administration. Instead, a younger man, Henry (Kid) Rena, who had been in the Waif's Home Band with Louis Armstrong, played trumpet on the recordings. His front-line colleagues were clarinettists Alphonse Picou and Big Eye Louis Nelson, together with Jim Robinson on trombone. They were joined by a three-piece rhythm section consisting of guitar, string-bass and drums.

Bill Russell, one of the few writers who could then justifiably be called an expert on New Orleans jazz, wrote in his initial review of the records: 'New Orleans music is played by groups of any size specified by an employer, and ranges from the single piano player in the tonks and whorehouses to the bands of twenty or more used for funerals and Mardi Gras parades.' He went on to say: 'although the records featured a line-up similar to that used by Buddy Bolden's Band, they were not a deliberate attempt to recreate the traditional jazz style of the '20s or even the '90s. They contained a variety of New Orleans music: marches, folk-tunes, composed pieces and improvised blues played by a group of outstanding musicians.'[3] All this made sense, as there never had been a *de rigueur* instrumentation for New Orleans jazz.

All of the participants on the records which Russell was discussing had spent their lives playing within various instrumental combinations. Their outlook typified the relaxed attitude that New Orleans musicians had always shown towards hidebound conventions. For them, the playing of jazz music was a social function in which the listeners, dancers and musicians shared their enjoyment. Many of the purists had not only misunderstood the question of instrumentation, they also had the misconception that the music of New Orleans resembled Rip Van Winkle. They imagined it had remained unchanged since Buddy Bolden's days of glory and all that it needed was an awakening. In truth, much varied music was played in New Orleans during the 1930s, some of it created by young, local-born blues artistes like Fats Domino, who was later to gain widespread fame.

Eventually, Bunk Johnson felt satisfied that his lips were sufficiently strong for him to begin playing regularly in public. In June 1942, he made his long-awaited recording début leading a seven-piece band, consisting of himself on trumpet, George Lewis on clarinet, Jim Robinson on trombone, and a pianist, banjoist, string-bassist and drummer. Despite Bill Russell's thoughtful words, a certain section of jazz followers still insisted that this instrumentation was the only true line-up for a New Orleans jazz band. They argued that it presented the authentic jazz sounds of the early 1900s. This was a tenuous theory because none of the jazz bands from that era had ever recorded, and none of the New Orleans bands of those years ever regularly used that exact line-up. Added to this was the fact that in Bunk's Band there was a wide divergence of age. The leader, born in 1879, could remember the musical style of those days, but clarinettist George Lewis, born in 1900, would have no constructive memory of them. In fact, the members of Bunk's Band did just what Russell would have wished; they played improvised music, each in his own individual way, and the results were a series of jazz sounds, some rugged, some delicate. There were no star soloists; every player's improvisations were intended to contribute towards the overall ensemble. Many listeners found the band's style appealing, and the three men who formed its front-line became among the most important figures in the 'revival'. Many young men listened in awe to the recordings by Bunk's band, and many of them took up musical instruments in order to attempt to recreate what they had heard. It was a repetition of earlier times when young Chicagoans learnt their parts by rote by continually re-playing a gramophone record. Bunk did not live long enough to take advantage of his international fame, but for many years George Lewis and Jim Robinson were able to undertake highly successful foreign tours.

The initial impact of Bunk Johnson's recordings literally split the hot jazz fans into two camps – the call for a return to collective improvisation became secondary to the dispute over what was authentic jazz and what was not. One faction had nothing but praise for Bunk's front-line, and his rhythm section which featured vigorous banjo playing. Their opposites maintained that the band was out-of-tune, monotonous and un-swinging, and that it often played wrong harmonies. It seemed in those days that anyone who liked jazz *had* to develop a prejudice against one style or another. For many, there was no

Sidney Bechet 1897-1959

Jelly Roll Morton 1885-1941

Louis Armstrong c.1900-1971

Edward (Duke) Ellington 1899-1974

William (Count) Basie b.1904

Benny Goodman b.1909

Leon Bix Beiderbecke 1904-1931

Earl Hines b.1905

Billie Holiday 1915-1959

Thomas (Fats) Waller 1904-1943

Bessie Smith 1895-1937

Coleman Hawkins 1904-1969

Django Reinhardt, 1910-1953

Lionel Hampton b.1909

Weldon (Jack) Teagarden 1905-1964

George Lewis 1900-1968

Charlie (Yardbird) Parker 1920-1955

William (Bunk) Johnson 1879-1949

Roy Eldridge b.1911

Theodore (Sonny) Rollins, b.1929

Lee Konitz b.1927

Thelonious Monk b.1917

John (Dizzy) Gillespie b.1917

Stan Getz b.1927

Lester Young 1909-1959

Miles Davis b.1926

Dave Brubeck b.1920

Sun Ra (né Herman Blount) b.1912

John Coltrane 1922-1967

Ornette Coleman b.1930

question of unbiased listening, and often an excellent jazz musician would suffer because his individuality was not part of a particular style.

Out in California, Kid Ory, one of the wiliest and most skilful of all jazz bandleaders, observed all the excitement. He had chosen to retire from music in the early 1930s to settle on the West Coast. During the early 1940s, he felt the urge to resume playing. In 1942, he began taking engagements (or 'gigs' as they had become known), on alto-saxophone and string-bass, but he soon resumed playing his main instrument, the slide-trombone. Years later, he recalled his re-entry into the music profession: 'I thought about forming a swing band when I came out of retirement in the early 1940s, but they went out about then, so I decided on the small group.'[4]

Ory soon secured important bookings for his band, including a widely-heard radio series hosted by actor-director Orson Welles. Ory used several musicians who had played important parts in early New Orleans jazz, including clarinettist Jimmie Noone, guitarist Bud Scott, bassist Ed (Montudie) Garland, drummer Zutty Singleton and trumpeter Mutt Carey. Carey was one of several veterans who were able to return to full-time music through the revival of interest in old-style jazz. He had worked for years as a railway-porter, and by a remarkable coincidence was serving the very train that took Bunk Johnson to California in April 1943.

Bunk journeyed to the West Coast to guest with a group of young white musicians who were forming a repertoire of tunes by King Oliver, Louis Armstrong and Jelly Roll Morton. They called themselves Lu Watter's Yerba Buena Jazz Band. Watters, who played cornet, had grown disillusioned playing in dance bands. He found that some other musicians felt the same way, and allied himself with them to form a jazz band in Oakland, California, that consisted of two cornets, clarinet, trombone, two banjos, tuba, piano and drums. The band were dedicated believers in reviving the style of collective improvisation featured by King Oliver's Band in the early 1920s. They went to their task with great enthusiasm, and in late 1941 began recording.

Bunk's initial session with the band went fairly smoothly, although there was a divergence of thought concerning repertoire between the veteran and the young musicians. Bunk, who followed an age-old New Orleans tradition in selecting tunes to be improvised upon from many sources, wanted the band to broaden their repertoire and play the popular tunes of the day, including one called 'Mairzy Doats, and Dozy Doats'. The young purists were apparently shocked and surprised by this attitude, which had never been mentioned by jazz historians. They, like many other revivalist bands, believed that everything, including instrumentation, repertoire and style, should come from an earlier era. Mercifully, they later became more broad-minded and adopted the attitudes of the men whose music they worshipped.

In July 1944, Bunk Johnson returned to New Orleans and assembled a band to record for Bill Russell. The front-line of Johnson, Lewis and Robinson remained, and after a few experiments the permanent rhythm section consisted of Alton Purnell on piano, Alcide (Slow Drag) Pavageau on string-bass, Laurence Marrero on banjo and Warren (Baby) Dodds (the ex-King Oliver sideman) on drums.

There was talk of the band being booked in the North but some of the band members hesitated about accepting the engagements because they did not want to jeopardize their day-jobs. In the interim, Bunk's old friend Sidney Bechet invited the trumpeter to join his band for a residency in Boston. The reunion, which provoked a clash of personalities between Bunk and Bechet, proved to be short-lived, though they did share one fine recording session in March 1945 which also featured the renowned trombonist Sandy Williams. Sandy, who had one of the most poignant tones of any jazzman, told Swiss jazz-writer Johnny Simmen an anecdote that illustrated how the public's changing tastes could affect a musician's playing style. In the 1930s, Nat Story, a trombonist who worked with Sandy Williams in Chick Webb's band, asked Sandy to help him eliminate some of the mannerisms he had acquired during the years he spent playing in riverboat bands – he felt they were outmoded, and inappropriate in a swing band. Sandy Williams obliged, and gave Story stylistic guidance. Years later, when the demand for traditional jazz began to grow, Sandy realised he needed advice on playing in that style. He promptly went to Nat Story and asked to be shown the nuances and mannerisms of the riverboat style.

In September 1945, Bunk's entire band were persuaded to travel North, and they began a residency at the Stuyvesant Casino on New York's Lower East Side. They were a great success there, and remained for a four-month residency. There was, however, more harmony on stage than off. Bunk said that he wanted to use New York musicians in his band, instead of men from his home state, whom he scornfully referred to as his 'emergency musicians'. The acrimony created by this attitude, and Bunk's fondness for argumentative drinking bouts, eventually caused the band to break up in May 1946. Bunk did some touring, guesting with various bands, then returned to play engagements in New York using musicians based there. He made his last recordings in late 1947, then returned to spend the last year and a half of his life, in poor health, at his home in New Iberia. The old man's brief re-emergence was one of the big factors in the re-popularisation of traditional jazz.

Unaffected by disputes that called for definitions of 'authentic jazz', 'classic jazz' and 'revival jazz', a group of the young musicians who had stood around the bandstands in Chicago were steadily making their own brand of small band jazz more popular. Their unofficial spokesman was guitarist Eddie Condon, who was also a notably fluent wise-cracker. Most of Condon's circle worked in big bands during the 1930s, but they assembled on a semi-regular basis to make small-band recordings, most of which were for a specialist jazz company called

Commodore whose headquarters were in a New York record store. The original clique had been augmented by two fine players from the North, Max Kaminsky on trumpet and Brad Gowans on valve-trombone. Another regular was the extraordinarily individual clarinettist Pee Wee Russell, whose croaking tone in the middle register and spikey sound when playing high notes are unmistakable. In 1939, Eddie Condon and these men joined a band led by a stalwart Chicagoan, tenor-saxophonist Bud Freeman. The Summa Cum Laude Orchestra, as it was called, followed a pattern set by many jazz groups, and only stayed intact for a year. The happy sounds that the band produced encouraged two New Yorkers to open clubs that consistently featured music that was akin to the Freeman's music (and to Muggsy Spanier's lamented Ragtimers). One club, Jimmy Ryan's, opened in September 1940 (it still flourishes today, but at a different venue); the other, sited in New York's Greenwich Village, was sponsored by a jazz enthusiast, Nick Rongetti. Soon after that club opened in 1940, the name Nicksieland was applied to the sounds that were heard there. It was an apt attempt to indicate that the jazz was a blend of Dixieland and jam-session music. There was collective improvisation at the beginning and end of each number but in between there was a succession of solos. Usually, everyone in the band was featured on each tune.

Eddie Condon was a ubiquitous figure at Nick's during its early days, Bobby Hackett, the cornettist, was also a regular. Condon's 'gang' of compatible musicians grew swiftly during the early 1940s, and included trombonist Lou McGarity, baritone-saxist Ernie Caceres, trumpeter Billy Butterfield and pianist Gene Schroeder. Drummer George Wettling was so delighted by the music he heard at Nick's that he quit Paul Whiteman's Orchestra in 1941 to become part of the resident band. During the same year, cornettist Wild Bill Davison moved to New York from Milwaukee and began working at the club.

When the mood took him, Condon could play rhythm guitar in a highly adept way. However, he usually preferred to exercise his vocal chords at Nick's, amusing patrons and musicians with a fund of anecdotes, and improvised humour. He was the ideal host for the first televised jam session in 1942. His widespread fame began in 1943 when he compèred a series of jazz concerts held at the New York Town Hall. His role on stage was that of jam-session organiser (a previously unheard-of function). He pointed out who the next soloist was to be, controlled the volume of the band, and signalled when the last chorus was due. The Town Hall concerts were a notable success. A basic pool of musicians made up the resident band, but guest stars, black and white, were also featured. As a result of these ventures Condon was offered a position as master of ceremonies, and bandleader, at a New York night spot. The Eddie Condon Club came into being in 1947, and continued operating for twenty years. The nucleus of musicians who worked there originally were all old friends of Condon, but over the years they were joined by younger players including

Peanuts Hucko on clarinet, pianist Ralph Sutton, multi-instrumentalist Dick Cary and trombonist Cutty Cutshall.

Sidney Bechet, who was featured on several of Condon's Town Hall concerts, never worked regularly with a big band after he left Noble Sissle in 1938. He too played many dates at Nick's and Ryan's, working with musicians who might be twenty-five years his junior. His artistry transcended any stylistic barriers; he was as creative alongside Muggsy Spanier as he was with Bunk Johnson, and he triumphed at jam sessions whether they were in a Dixieland Bar or in uptown Harlem. His work made a mockery of the views of those who thought that jazz was not homogenous.

Jazz musicians were often amused by the theorising that went on during that era, definition seeming more important to some fans than the music itself. It could be annoying, as Pee Wee Russell discovered. He was continually being classified as a Chicagoan, no matter how often he pointed out that he had only ever worked in that city for a matter of weeks. It took some time before the purists gave a fair hearing to skilful improvisers like trumpeters Sidney de Paris, Joe Thomas, pianist Joe Bushkin, trombonists Jimmy Archey, Vic Dickenson, and clarinettist Edmond Hall, simply because they had worked in big bands for most of the 1930s.

Even Louis Armstrong, the most gifted jazzman of them all, did not escape criticism for touring with a big band. By the late 1930s Louis was internationally known but by then he had appeared in several Hollywood films, and had also made big-selling records, mostly with studio groups, which might range from an Hawaiian band, to a large vocal choir. Louis's own big band was never high in the popularity ratings. It was ironical that the man whose talents had inspired all of the big-band arrangers, and most of the swing soloists, never won acclaim for his own band. Almost every interview with the famous figures of the Swing Era contained ardent praise of Louis's influence; when Harry James was voted as the leading jazz trumpeter in a popularity poll he pointed out in his acceptance speech that the award should surely have gone to Louis Armstrong.

During the mid-1940s, work for Louis's big band became scarcer and he began guesting with small bands at concerts. The climax of these events took place at a much-heralded concert at New York's Town Hall, which featured Louis with a specially assembled all-star band. The evening, which was recorded, was a dramatic success, and led to Louis's agent, Joe Glaser, suggesting that Louis should work only with small bands. As a result, The Louis Armstrong All Stars made their début in August 1947. Originally they featured Jack Teagarden on trombone, Barney Bigard on clarinet, Sid Catlett on drums – soon to be joined by Earl Hines on piano and Arvell Shaw on string-bass. Thus began twenty years of world-wide touring for Louis's sextet. Louis, like Sidney Bechet, never again worked regularly with a big band. Most jazz critics were delighted to see two great jazz improvisers being featured in more congenial musical surroundings. Few young black musicians took any interest, simply because they were not interested in listening to, or in playing, traditional jazz. For them, the style seemed a reminder of eras fraught with pain and humiliation. Their attention was fixed firmly on the new modern concepts of jazz-playing that had developed alongside, but entirely separate from, the revival.

Recommended Reading

Barker, Danny and Buerkle, J. V. *Bourbon Street Black* (A famous musician and a sociologist study Negro musicians working in New Orleans), Oxford University, USA, 1973

Bethell, Tom *George Lewis – A Jazzman From New Orleans* (A detailed biography and discography), University of California, USA, 1977

Colyer, Ken *New Orleans and Back*, Brooks and Pratt Delph, Yorks, n.d.

Fairbairn, Ann (psy.) *Call Him George* (A biography of George Lewis), Crown Publishers, USA, 1969

Fountain, Pete and Neely, B. *A Closer Walk* (The Pete Fountain Story – New Orleans clarinettist), Henry Regnery, USA, 1972

Hodes, Art and Hansen, C. (eds.) *Selections From the Gutter* (Articles reprinted from *The Jazz Record*, a leading American jazz magazine of the 1940s), University of California, USA, 1977

Ramsey, F. and Smith, C. E. (eds.) *Jazzmen* (Dedicated and enthusiastic pioneer work in jazz history), Harcourt Brace, USA, 1939

Shacter, J. *Piano Man* (The story of pianist Ralph Sutton), Jaynar Press, USA, 1975

Sonnier, Austin M. *Willie Geary (Bunk) Johnson* (A career monograph and discography), Crescendo, USA, 1977

9 The birth of bop

Young jazz musicians experiment by using 'new' harmonies and rhythms in their improvisations; club owners begin employing small bands that specialise in these innovations; the jazz world takes sides – old jazz versus new jazz (bop); dancers ignore the dispute and concentrate on enjoying 'rhythm-and-blues'.

The magazine issue (*Down Beat*, August 1938) in which Jelly Roll Morton's diatribe on the origins of jazz appeared, also contained the first national mention of Charlie Parker, a young black saxophonist who was the most important figure in what became known as modern jazz (it was subsequently re-named bop). The magazine news item simply said that Parker was working in pianist Jay McShann's Band at the Antler's Club in Kansas City. Parker began playing saxophone as a teenager and was soon taking part in the highly competitive Kansas City jam sessions where no quarter was asked, or given. His playing was so precocious and unusual that many of his partners in the informal get-togethers were totally mystified by his musical intentions. It seemed to them that Parker's improvisations were full of wrong notes, and that his phrasing was accented in a way that suggested his sense of rhythm was faulty.

If the trained ears of musicians were critical and confused, one can imagine the reactions of the general public when they first heard Parker play. Eventually, when laymen and musicians became attuned to the apparent wrongness of his style they realised that a highly skilful method formulated the passionate sounds that flowed from Parker's saxophone. The first inkling of general acceptance came when Parker arrived in New York with Jay McShann's Band, early in 1942. As with all previous jazz innovations, New York was to be the proving ground for new jazz ideas.

Several other young black musicians, scattered throughout the United States, had musical ideas similar to Parker. All of them were tired of the clichés that had become associated with the Swing Era and wanted to introduce new harmonic and rhythmic ideas into jazz improvisation.

One of these restless young musicians was trumpeter John (Dizzy) Gillespie, who moved to New York from South Carolina in the mid-1930s. Gillespie's first jazz inspiration was Roy Eldridge. While with Teddy Hill's Band in 1937, Gillespie copied Eldridge's solos note-for-note – this was no mean feat of trumpet playing, but it was the antithesis of improvisation. Later, while with Cab Calloway's big band, Dizzy began experimenting with a new style of phrasing, linking it with the use of intricate harmonies. Calloway accused Gillespie of playing 'Chinese music', but some of the band encouraged the youngster to continue with his experiments, and bassist Milt Hinton often rehearsed new chord progressions with Dizzy during the band's intermissions.

Guitarist Charlie Christian was another young experimentalist. During the 1930s he spent several years playing in Territory Bands in and around Oklahoma. He was one of the pioneers in the use of an electrically amplified guitar for jazz improvising. The added volume allowed guitarists to project sounds as loud as a trumpet and they were now able to fulfil a dual role, playing rhythm (usually on each beat of the bar), then, by switching up the volume, they could play melody, joining in with the front-line. Unlike the other innovators of modern jazz, who had a slow climb to fame, Christian became a jazz celebrity overnight after being discovered by John Hammond and Benny Goodman in 1939. Christian immediately became a feature of Goodman's Sextet and moved to New York City.

Off-duty from Goodman, Christian often sat in at the jam sessions held regularly at Minton's Club on 188th Street in Harlem. The club was then managed by Dizzy Gillespie's former bandleader, Teddy Hill. Gillespie himself often participated in the sessions. Another regular was pianist Thelonious Monk. Monk was experimenting with a style of jazz piano-playing that deliberately shunned the use of a rapid technique. Instead he chose to play short phrases full of intricate harmonies and ingenious rhythms. The pyrotechnics associated with modern jazz piano-playing developed a little later when another originator, Earl (Bud) Powell, began performing at the sessions. Another highly individualistic pianist who emerged at about the same time as Powell was Errol Garner, who, like Art Tatum, was an unclassifiable jazzman. The contrast between the adroit, lagging rhythms of Garner's right-hand playing, and his incisive left-hand work, produced an instantly recognisable musical trade-mark. Any attempts to copy Garner's style automatically sounded like pastiche. He was one of the first to record in small bands with Charlie Parker, but he never became closely involved with bop, or with any other jazz style. The two most important keyboard pioneers of bop were Thelonious Monk and Bud Powell. Some of the pianists of the Swing Era, such as Mary Lou Williams, Clyde Hart and Nat Jaffe could provide sympathetic accompaniment for the modernists, as could young up-and-coming players like Billy Taylor and Duke Jordan, but the two key figures of bop piano-playing were Monk and Powell.

Drummers too were beginning to re-think their instrumental roles as many of the drum patterns popular in the Swing Era did not blend with the bop soloists' phrasing. Drummers like Kenny Clarke (and a little later, Max Roach and Art Blakey) pioneered styles that gave the soloist more rhythmic freedom. They did so by accenting basic rhythms on their cymbals, while playing complementary phrases on the snare-drums that emphasised the phrasing of the soloist. They also used the bass-drum for playing irregular accents which became known in bop jargon as 'dropping bombs'.

During the late 1930s and early 1940s, the function of every instrument used in jazz was being reconsidered. Most of the significant changes that occurred on string-bass were the work of one man – Jimmy Blanton. In 1939, Blanton, who was working with Fate Marable's Band in St Louis, was heard by Duke Ellington, and was immediately offered a place in Duke's Orchestra. During the following two years, until ill health forced him to retire, Blanton made a series of recordings that showed new horizons to the jazz bassists. By playing harmonically interesting musical lines with a precision and rhythm that had never previously been heard, he made the string-bass the pivot of the rhythm section. With a bass providing such a pulse, the pianist was able to give full attention to embellishing chord changes, rather than having to stress rhythm forcefully. The bass's new role also allowed the drummer to devote more thought to producing sympathetic tone colours and involved rhythmic fill-in phrases, as opposed to acting as a metronomic time-keeper.

In the early 1940s, a number of eminent jazzmen showed genuine interest in the new musical ideas that were developing. The most sympathetic were the drummer Sid Catlett, and the tenor-saxophonists Coleman Hawkins and Lester Young. They were musically at ease in the young company, perhaps because each of them realised that their styles had played a part in the transition of bop. Hawkins returned to New York in 1939 after a five-year sojourn in Europe. He soon proved that he had been developing his musical ability by recording a version of 'Body and Soul' which was full of daring ideas. While in Europe, Hawkins realised that a jazz revolution was inevitable. As early as 1934, in the London-published *Melody Maker*, he noted that one musical exercise he recommended was 'rather modern, in that it goes counter to the accompanying chords'. Ten years after writing that article[1] Hawkins became one of the first established bandleaders to employ modernists for his recording sessions.

Many acknowledged bandleaders frowned on the young boppers' jazz style, and on the attire that many of them chose to wear. Dark glasses, draped suits and fancy hats became a craze uniform at bop jam sessions, both for the players and their devout fans. However, no one could live solely from playing in jam sessions and several bop pioneers left New York on occasion to tour in bands whose music had nothing of interest for them. They did this simply so that they could return to New York with enough money to enable them to devote time to individual practice, or to playing regularly in jam sessions. When the money ran out, they got back on the musical treadmill again. Charlie Parker's stint in Noble Sissle's Band was typical.

During their travels, the modernists sometimes heard young musicians whose improvisations would not have sounded out of place at a Minton's session. Trombonist Fred Beckett was one of these kindred spirits; another was J. J. Johnson, a trombonist, who at the age of nineteen was heard by Benny Carter, and brought to New York. Johnson's advanced technique made him one of the first jazz trombonists capable of playing the complicated, fast-moving bop tunes while Benny Carter was one of several older players who were admired by the boppers, both for his technique and harmonic knowledge as was Art Tatum. A first meeting between Art Tatum and Jimmy Blanton resulted in the two men interchanging ideas in a series of duets that went on all through the night, and concluded at nine o'clock the following morning.

A band that proved to be an important gathering centre for modernists was led by a veteran of the Chicago era, Earl (Fatha) Hines. Hines gave his musicians free rein during their solos, perhaps mindful that he had sometimes been decried for originality and daring. Hines led a fine big band throughout the 1930s, which gained a reputation for reliability and proficiency rather than experimentation. During the early 1940s, partly due to the Second World War service enlistments, changes occurred which led to Charlie Parker being offered the job of tenor-saxophonist. He temporarily abandoned the smaller alto-sax to get the job. Dizzy Gillespie was also in the band, as were several other modernists. The band's straw-boss (the musician who directs the band in the leader's absence), was a sympathetic alto-saxophonist called Scoops Carry, who let the young men try out new musical ideas during rehearsals. Gillespie and Parker respected each other's creativity – it was, according to Gillespie 'a mutual non-aggression pact'. After leaving Hines the two men worked independently, but soon teamed up again in a new big band which was being formed by Billy Eckstine, formerly a vocalist with Earl Hines's Band. The difference in musical attitudes between Eckstine's Band, and that of his former employer, was that the older man's group contained elements of many jazz styles, old and new, whereas all of Eckstine's young musicians were passionate about modern jazz.

Neither Parker nor Gillespie stayed with the band long, but their places were taken by other musicians who were just as devoted to the new music. Eckstine's band, during its three-year existence from 1944 to 1947 employed many young modernists who were to gain lasting fame, including trumpeters Miles Davis, Howard McGhee, Fats Navarro and Kenny Dorham. Two brilliant young improvisers, tenor-saxophonist Wardell Gray and trombonist Bennie Green remained with Earl Hines.

From the hurly-burly of the jam session came forth a style of small-band bop arrangements which featured front-line instruments all playing in unison (each musician playing exactly the same notes, without harmony). The players then took improvised solos, concluding the piece by replaying the opening theme, still in unison. A big band adopting the same plan would have sounded unwieldy and monotonous. Arrangers like Tadd Dameron, Gil Fuller, Budd Johnson and George Russell not only introduced bop effects and phrasings into their orchestrations, they also used the wide, sumptuous, bop harmonies to create new voicings for each section within a big band.

By 1944, the economic prospects for small bop bands began to look more hopeful. Club owners on New York's 52nd Street were taking notice of the young improvisers who were adding new sound 'flavours' to their resident bands. Early in 1944, the old-established Onyx Club booked a small combo (short for combination of players), whose entire repertoire was devoted to bop. It was co-led by Dizzy Gillespie, and string-bassist Oscar Pettiford (who later became a brilliant jazz 'cellist). Soon afterwards, adventurous record companies began offering recording dates to Gillespie, Parker, Bud Powell, and others in the bop hierarchy.

Recordings were to be a big factor in the wider acceptance of bop. Unfortunately its musicians became involved in a general ban on recordings imposed by the American Federation of Musicians in August 1942, which lasted for almost two years. It meant that no recordings were being made of a new jazz style which needed support to survive. Discerning jazz fans knew, when they first heard bop, that it was a revolutionary new jazz style, but even the most enthusiastic of them often had difficulties in grasping the pattern of the innovator's improvisation. The situation soon changed when fans were able to re-play a 78 r.p.m. recording, lasting three minutes, often enough to become well acquainted with the intricacies of the new music.

Jazz listeners and musicians released from the Armed Services at the end of the Second World War, were in the mood for change. For many, modern jazz seemed exactly right for a new era. The emergence of bop during the Second World War, and its spread of popularity, might be likened to the way Dixieland became popular during the First World War.

All of the new music's innovators were black. Consciously or unconsciously, bop was their protest music. The protest concerned the racial segregation that was still prevalent throughout the music business during the early 1940s. Despite the black man's role in formulating jazz, and the continual stream of black jazz innovators, few Negro musicians received widespread public acclaim in the white media, and fewer still were able to earn wages comparable to white musicians – even if both worked at the same venue. Discrimination against black jazzmen diminished during the bop era, but many of those who pioneered the style did not have the smooth way of life that might come automatically with big earnings. Along the way, many picked up a habit that was no respecter of talent, black or white. They became addicted to a drug jokingly called 'horse' but whose real name was heroin, a derivative of opium. It is not irrelevant to raise the subject of narcotics at this point. Anyone attempting to follow the early careers of bop musicians will find sinister gaps in many of their working lives, during which time they were confined, as drug addicts, in sanatoriums and state prisons. In many cases, their addiction led to death. Even the great Charlie Parker was in the life-wrecking grasp of heroin. The alcoholism that occurred among a minority of early jazzmen took its toll more slowly.

Despite the sufferings and vicissitudes of the bop pioneers, the music became more popular and a large number of white musicians became interested in the challenging new style. The precursors of the active white bop players were a spate of highly proficient white pianists who began playing the new style impressively enough to become members of otherwise black bands. They included Al Haig, George Wallington, Dodo Marmarosa and Joe Albany.

Most of the white brass and saxophone players who became bop musicians were already working professionally in big bands. The enthusiasm of these musicians for the new music was a big factor in changing the style of those big bands that had retained the sounds of the Swing Era long after it had ended.

Woody Herman, and most of his sidemen, were among the first white musicians to respond actively to the new sounds. Herman, who began leading a big band in 1936, has always kept abreast of jazz developments. His band, affectionately named The Herman Herd by writer George T. Simon, made a record called 'Caldonia' in 1945. In the recording studio it was decided to insert a short bop-inspired passage arranged by Neal Hefti. The effect was no more than a sprinkling of bop seasoning, but it made the record one of the most talked-of big-band issues of the period. Bands led by Claude Thornhill, Boyd Raeburn, Charlie Barnet and George Auld began including 'modern' arrangements in their performances, much to the delight of their musicians.

Few of the established black big bands made obvious efforts to use bop arrangements. For a time, young modernists thought the bands of Count Basie, Jimmie Lunceford, Lucky Millinder, Andy Kirk and Lionel Hampton were old-fashioned, though Hampton's Band was in fact a veritable nursery of modern jazz talent, producing many fine jazz stylists, including one of the first tenor-sax players to master bop, Dexter Gordon, trumpeters Clifford Brown and Benny Bailey, and two amazingly facile improvisers, trombonist Jimmy Cleveland and tenor-saxophonist Johnny Griffin.

Duke Ellington was held in awesome respect by all jazz musicians no matter which style they followed. The timelessness of Duke's creativity, and his immense musical talents, kept him out of the verbal war that developed between the followers of old and new style jazz. He was immune from the spiteful insults that rival jazz fans traded; the shout of 'dirty bopper' was countered with 'moldy fig' (directed at the traditionalists). Jazz critics were as divided as the fans and new magazines started that dealt with only one style of jazz.

The popularity of bop grew more swiftly on the East Coast of America than on the West Coast. An all-star bop band featuring Dizzy Gillespie, Charlie Parker and vibraphonist Milt Jackson failed miserably with the general public in late 1945 during a booking at Billy Berg's Club in Los Angeles. That same club was where a local jazz fan, Norman Granz, organised a series of momentous jam sessions during the early 1940s. The crowd's reactions encouraged him to become a full-time jazz promoter. In 1942, he began organising concerts at the Philharmonic Auditorium in Los Angeles. At first they were musically amorphous, but Granz soon arrived at a format which featured seven or eight top jazz musicians engaging in an on-stage jam session.

Granz had the happy knack of assembling groups of highly individualistic jazzmen, with widely varying styles, and somehow encouraging them to produce high quality jazz. He did not accept the prevalent view that there was total incompatibility between the old and the new styles. All of his line-ups were multi-racial. By July 1944, the events were being recorded live on stage. Granz's method of mixing musicians meant that Dizzy Gillespie might be accompanied by Benny Goodman's pianist, Mel Powell and that Basie's star trumpeter, Buck Clayton, worked alongside Charlie Parker. The method of presenting these 'Jazz At The Philharmonic' concerts (later shortened to JATP) became internationally successful for over thirty years. Granz was often criticised for the adventurous permutations of musicians, and for the vociferous reactions of the audiences at JATP. He was accused of rabble-rousing, despite the fact that slow ballads were always part of the programme. To be sure, some of the long drum solos, and some of the high register trumpet-playing seemed designed more for the gallery than for posterity, but none of the musicians' improvising skills were ever fettered. Tenor-saxophonist Illinois Jacquet's high-note work came in for particular abuse but they were only one facet of the playing technique of a magnificent jazzman, who was still proving his immense worth three decades later. Besides the fine music played at the concerts, JATP made the public more aware of racially mixed jam sessions and during the late 1940s they became part of the musical life of almost every North American city.

By 1947, popularity polls organised by jazz magazines showed a total decimation of traditionalists among the winners. The poll-winners of that year assembled to make a celebratory record were: Dizzy Gillespie on trumpet, Bill Harris on trombone, Flip Phillips on tenor-saxophone, Nat King Cole on piano, Billy Bauer on guitar, Eddie Safranski on string-bass, Buddy Rich on drums and Buddy De Franco on clarinet. Pianist Nat King Cole gained his first professional experience in Chicago, before moving to California. His trio, consisting of himself, a string-bassist, and a guitarist, gained considerable popularity. One of his occasional vocals was recorded and as a result he rapidly achieved fame as a singer, but he never let this success affect his ability to play superb jazz piano.

Buddy De Franco was a rarity – a bop-playing clarinettist. The clarinet, which had once been thought essential for a jazz ensemble was rarely used in bop bands although occasionally, talented jazzmen like Tony Scott, Jimmy Giuffre and Stan Hasselgard made individual contributions to the new music without changing the general lack of interest in the instrument.

Several established tenor-saxophonists like Charlie Ventura, Lucky Thompson, George Auld and Budd Johnson incorporated bop in their own personal styles. By the mid-1940s, young tenor-saxophonists who had begun their jazz careers playing bop began to make their mark. One of them was Gene Ammons, the son of the famous boogie-woogie pianist Albert Ammons. At the same time, a number of inventive bop baritone-saxophonists came to the fore. All of them were Charlie Parker disciples, and they had the difficult task of transferring their idol's speedy alto-sax fingering on to the larger baritone-sax. The most brilliant of them was a white Bostonian, Serge Chaloff, followed by Pepper Adams and Leo Parker.

A wordless style of scatting known as 'bop singing' enjoyed temporary popularity in the late 1940s, along with bop expressions such as 'Go, Man, Go', an exhortation for the musician to continue playing. Most of the jargon was as transient as the Swing Era's killer-diller talk, but some bop expressions such as 'hip' and 'cool' passed into the language. Several young singers who emerged during the early days of bop were still jazz favourites in the 1970s, including Sarah Vaughan and Carmen McRae, both of whom were also competent pianists.

By 1947, the work of every young big-band soloist was bop-orientated, but bop had still not achieved widespread popularity with the ballroom crowds, who accounted for the major part of a big band's income. Even sympathetic band-leaders often had to ask for a more broad-minded approach from their musicians. In 1948, drummer Buddy Rich, then only thirty-one, felt he had to make drastic changes in his band for stylistic reasons. 'It's not that I dislike bop,' Rich explained, 'but there are lots of other things I want to play. These fellows want to play bop, and nothing else. Let's make it clear I'm not going commercial, everything that isn't bop is not necessarily commercial.' Dizzy Gillespie took his own exciting big band on tour in 1945, but was soon forced to disband. He tried again, a few years later, but this venture also ended in disappointment. Soon afterwards, in 1949, he said: 'Bop is part of jazz, and jazz music is to dance to. They don't hear those four beats. They're not particular about whether you're playing a flatted fifth, or a ruptured 129th, as long as they can dance. I think George Shearing is the greatest thing that's happened to bop in the past year. Anybody can dance to Shearing's music, he has made it easier for me, and for everybody else who plays bop.'[2]

Shearing was something of an odd-man-out on the American bop scene. He was a blind, expatriate Englishman who heard bop live for the first time when he visited New York in the mid-1940s. He soon moved to the USA permanently, and there developed a style of 'locked hands' playing (each hand moving parallel on the keyboard), which was similar to a technique developed by Milt Buckner. Shearing's original American quintet consisted of piano, vibraphone, guitar, drums and bass. The whole accent of the group was on mellow sounds, which it presented with impeccable rhythm. It was a pleasant jazz side-water, but not one that was to prove important.

One of the biggest ballroom successes of the 1940s played neither bop nor dixieland. It was a highly versatile quintet known as Louis Jordan's Tympany Five, which featured the leader's humorous vocals, and jumpy alto-saxophone playing. Much of the quintet's material consisted of urban blues and the style of Jordan's music (and of other similar groups) was called rhythm-and-blues. R-and-b, as it became known, was to maintain and supplement the big following it gathered during the 1940s.

Big-band leader Stan Kenton believed that the future of jazz lay in concert-hall presentations. When asked if his band was good for dancing he proudly replied: 'Definitely not.'[3] His musical experiments were based on sound-blocks and tone colours rather than rhythms, though he did sometimes incorporate Cuban rhythms into his orchestrations. Two other big-band leaders featured experimental line-ups during the 1940s – the Boyd Raeburn Orchestra, which consisted of eight brass, seven saxophones, four rhythm, two french horns and a harp, and Claude Thornhill, who used twenty-two musicians. Big bands playing modern arrangements developed an enthusiastic following among bop musicians who realised that the bop jam session was in danger of being enmeshed in a series of clichés that were as repetitive as those of the swing ensembles that they had usurped.

Neither Charlie Parker nor Dizzy Gillespie worked exclusively with set instrumentations, each recording with various line-ups, including orchestras with string sections. Gillespie was always trying to locate inspiring musical companions and one of his keenest interests in the mid-1940s was attempting to link bop improvisations with Cuban music. Twenty-five years later, in an interview with British journalist, Max Jones, Gillespie recalled the Cuban percussionist, Chano Pozo: 'He was a trail-blazer in the class of Charlie Parker. I'm picking up now, on some of the things he did, and he's been dead since 1948.'[4] At the time of his collaborations with Pozo, Gillespie said: 'If the kids get so hip they frown on everything that isn't out-and-out bop, we're going to wind up with a sad bunch of musicians ten years from now.'[5]

Gillespie need not have worried. A number of young musicians born between 1925 and 1930 were re-shaping bop, and the first significant fruits of their efforts came from a recording group led by trumpeter Miles Davis. Davis, born into a middle-class black family in Alton, Illinois, spent his teenage years listening to the broad-toned trumpeters that near-by St Louis was noted for. He was particularly impressed by Harold Baker's sound, and by the speed and clarity of Clark Terry. His other early musical hero was a Cleveland trumpeter, Freddie Webster. By the time he was fifteen, Davis was working in local bands and three years later he was good enough to sit in with Billy Eckstine's Band when it visited his home town. After finishing high school he went to New York intending to study at the Juilliard School of Music but he spent most of his time visiting clubs to hear Charlie Parker, Gillespie and Thelonious Monk play. Each of these men personally helped Davis to develop his already expansive knowledge of harmony. Davis gained experience in Benny Carter's Band before joining Billy Eckstine's Band for a few months. He then settled in New York, and worked regularly with Charlie Parker (who was now generally referred to by his nick-name 'Bird' – a contraction of an enigmatic sobriquet 'Yardbird'). Bird and Davis made many recordings together during this period. The effect on many is that of master and pupil, simply because of the chasm between Parker's vast technique and that of Davis's, which was still developing. There was less disparity between the two musicians' creative ideas. Parker recognised that Davis had genuine individuality, which was then at a premium. Many bop trumpeters were making sizeable reputations by slavishly copying Dizzy Gillespie's solos.

The turning-point in Miles Davis's career came in 1948. Claude Thornhill's Band had the services of a brilliantly individual arranger, Gil Evans. Some of Thornhill's sidemen suggested that Evans wrote some small-band arrangements which utilised the tone colours and scoring that he had written for the big band. The Capitol Record Company became interested in the project, and as a result an informal committee consisting of Gil Evans, John Lewis, an important young black pianist, baritone-saxophonist Gerry Mulligan and trumpeter John Carisi from Thornhill's Band, met to discuss the instrumentation and personnel to be used on the session. The alto-saxophonist selected was Lee Konitz who was also in Thornhill's Band and a devotee of the Chicago teacher-pianist Lennie Tristano. Miles Davis seemed the obvious choice to play the jazz trumpet solos.

Davis dominated the initial rehearsals, and assumed leadership of the band. During the early months of 1949, Davis assembled the group in the recording studio on two occasions and each time they recorded four tunes. The band only ever played in public for a few weeks but, nevertheless, its meagre recorded output was to influence a whole new school of jazz musicians. Passionate intensity and prolific instrumental techniques were the hallmarks of bop. They were superseded by a gentler playing approach which was full of understatement and used more subtle harmonies and tone colours. The heat of bop was replaced by a less fiery approach and the new jazz style became known as the 'cool school'.

Recommended Reading

Dance, Stanley (ed.) *Jazz Era – The Forties* (Detailed selection of outstanding records), Macgibbon and Kee, London, 1961

Gitler, Ira *Jazz Masters of The Forties* (A survey of the bop era's leading musicians), Macmillan, USA, 1966

Harrison, M., Morgan, A., Atkins, R., James, M. and Cooke, J. *Modern Jazz 1945–70* (Five critics' skilful advice on compiling a record library), Centurion Press, London, 1975

Horricks, Raymond (and others) *These Jazzmen of our Time* (Essays on important modernists), Gollancz, London, 1959

James, Michael *Ten Modern Jazzmen* (An appraisal), Cassell, London, 1960

Reisner, Robert *Bird – The Legend of Charlie Parker* (Reminiscences by Parker's contemporaries), Citadel Press, USA, 1962

Russell, Ross *Bird Lives* (Biography of Charlie Parker), Quartet Books, London, 1972

10 Theory (2) new harmonic and rhythmic developments introduced

As bands became bigger, they required more musical organisation. In early jazz, most bands relied on 'head arrangements'. This meant that a sequence of events and solo order was discussed (and perhaps rehearsed), but nothing in the way of a notated arrangement was written down. A typical 'plot' for a jazz-band number of the 1920s might be:

4 bars	Piano introduction
32 bars	Ensemble, trumpet leading
14 bars	Clarinet solo
2 bars	Trombone break
16 bars	Trumpet solo (clarinet and trombone holding long notes in the background)
14 bars	Ensemble, trumpet leading
2 bars	Drum break
16 bars	Ensemble, trumpet leading
4 bars	A worked-out ending that served as a coda.

This type of planned format was ideal for a small band, but it was impractical for large units unless they were prepared to spend an enormous amount of time at rehearsals. The answer was to have the 'plot' put in musical notation by an arranger; the chords used by the soloist for his improvisations were also utilised by the arranger to ensure cohesion between the musicians' written parts. The notes of a C major triad could be used for harmonising a brass section consisting of two trumpets and a trombone:

G	First trumpet (lead)
E	Second trumpet
C	Trombone

Or for three saxophones

G First saxophone (alto)
E Second saxophone (tenor)
C Third saxophone (alto)

Sometimes, a short, repetitive background figure was sketched out by the arranger for the band to play as accompaniment for a soloist. These figures became known as 'riffs'. A riff consists of a two- or four-bar phrase which is usually composed to fit the tonic chord, but devised so that it can be played over subsequent chord progressions with the minimum of adjustment (figure eight).

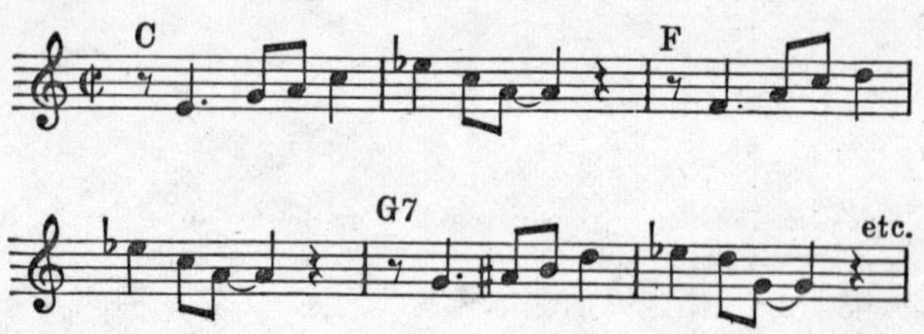

Figure 8 A riff

Jam sessions were the breeding-ground of many of the best riffs. There the riff was born of necessity, since a line-up of three trumpets, five saxophones, two trombones and a rhythm section all attempting collective improvisation usually produces cacophony. Riffs brought a degree of orderliness, and often they stimulated the soloist. Some riffs were tuneful enough to be developed into full-length compositions, the 'One O'Clock Jump' being a prime example.

Big-band arrangements (or charts as they were also called) became more elaborate during the Swing era. Arrangers were continually trying new ways of blending the tone colours of various instruments, and altering the way they 'voiced' the written parts in efforts to produce fresh sound textures. A baritone-saxophone harmonised with two trombones produces a rich, robust sound; to create an eerie effect a clarinet plays in close harmony with three tightly-muted trumpets. No arranger was more adept at producing original tone colours than Duke Ellington, though Glen Miller produced a fine example of successful experimentation in arranging a new sound for his reed section. Instead of having an alto-saxophone playing the melody with the other saxophones playing lower harmony parts as was usual, Miller gave the melody part to a clarinet and arranged for a tenor-saxophone to play the melody also, an octave down. He then wrote parts for the other three saxophones to harmonise within the interval of an octave (figure nine).

With the coming of big swing bands, collective improvisation virtually disappeared for almost a decade. Good arrangements became vitally important for a band's success, improvisation was minimised and even a band's star soloist found his work restricted. If musicians wanted to extend themselves they usually did so at a jam session. Some young musicians found no enjoyment in playing at these – they found no stimulation in the continual repetition of a small number of tunes that were jam session favourites, and they were bored with the constant replaying of old, clichéd riffs. They began experimenting with new ways of interpreting, and creating, chord sequences. Their efforts were to produce a completely new style of jazz playing, which eventually became known as bop.

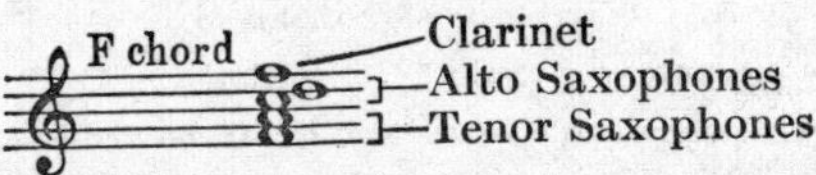

Figure 9 A Glen Miller arrangement

Bop was well and truly formed before it received a permanent name. At first the style was called 'modern jazz'; it became 're-bop' and then 'be-bop' which was eventually shortened to bop. The new jazz style gained its first widespread publicity in the mid-1940s, but inklings of its sounds had been heard years before in the playing of Lester Young, Coleman Hawkins, Art Tatum, Roy Eldridge and Henry Allen, all of whom were exploring new harmonies, and fresh ways of phrasing their solos during the 1930s. But none of the phrases that Charlie Parker played could be directly attributable to any previous jazz musician. At first, his playing antagonised fellow musicians because it did not fit in either harmonically, with what his front-line colleagues were playing, or rhythmically, with the accents of orthodox drumming. Similar stylistic clashes occurred later at New York jam sessions when boppers and veterans improvised together on standard tunes like 'I Got Rhythm'. The basic difference between the two jazz styles, old and new, was that the youngsters were adding more notes to the chords on which they based their improvisations.

Many of the chords used in early jazz were simple triads that is, three-note chords such as C major, consisting of the notes C, E and G. The biggest chord that early soloists had to deal with was a ninth chord, which was a C seventh chord (C, E, G and B flat) plus the note that was nine scale steps up from the tonic (in this case the 9th is a D). To the modernists, a ninth chord was basic and they thought nothing of improvising on harmonies that were symbolised C thirteenth flat ninth – which consisted of the notes C, E, G, B flat, D flat, F and A (the top note A being thirteen scale steps up from the tonic). Many of the boppers' improvisations were on extended chords, which are chords that contain notes that are beyond an octave above the tonic.

If the soloist based his improvisations on such a large selection of notes he needed accompaniment that could skilfully resolve extended harmonies. Fortunately for the progress of the new style, pianists who were able to follow the bop soloists were on hand to provide suitable backings.

The early bop jam sessions were like musical workshops; ideas were freely exchanged, and new approaches readily attempted. Drummer Kenny Clarke developed a method of playing that changed the function of drum equipment, and of drumming. The bass drum had formerly been used as a time-keeping device, either being struck twice or four times each bar in regular patterns. Its role was now transformed so that it became used for playing short, punctuating accents, sometimes on the beat, sometimes off. Long rolls on the snare-drum were rarely played and were replaced by snappy, sporadic snare-drum interjections. A snare-drum is a small side-drum with a turnable switch which tenses a series of coiled-wires against the skin of the drum. The clamped coils vibrate crisply when the drum is struck. The sound of the cymbals came to the fore and were used for indicating the pulse of the tune. The drummer beat out the tempo on them, usually in eight-to-the-bar patterns; this sound linked with the hi-hat cymbals which were used for playing positive off-beats. The lower sound frequencies became the exclusive domain of the string-bass, whose pulseful four-in-a-bar patterns replaced the heavy use of the bass drum.

Bop pianists ignored the stride style of earlier eras, and, because of the bassists' more dominant role they could develop a method of accompaniment which became known as 'comping' (said to derive from 'complementing' the soloist). It consisted of the sparse playing of intricate harmonies, a laying down of sporadic harmonic signposts which guided a soloist through a labyrinth of chords, allowing him to improvise freely, without being distracted by the pianist playing a busy counter-melody.

The overall effect of changing the functions of the piano, bass and drums was to take away the boom-boom-boom-boom, four-in-a-bar, pulsations of the pre-bop rhythm sections, where often each player duplicated the same patterns as his colleagues. This rhythmic feel was replaced by a looser sound in which the bass and the cymbals emphasised the beat while the piano and drums played phrases that filled the gaps that occurred in the soloist's improvisations. Charlie Parker summarised the change: 'The beat in a bop band is with the music, against it, behind it. It pushes. It helps it. It has no continuity of beat, no steady chug-chug.'[1] A rhythm guitar was featured on some early bop recordings, but it was soon realised that the most satisfactory role that a guitar could fulfil in a bop band was in playing an amplified single-note style, acting as one of the front-line.

The rhythms used in bop made listeners aware of a triplet rhythm 'feel', which gave the impression that each of the four beats in a bar was sub-divided into three even parts. This 'feel', which had been hinted at in many earlier jazz performances, caused classical musicians to argue (without success) that any example of jazz should be written with a twelve-beats-in-a-bar time signature (12/8).

Yet with all the differences between the old style and the new it was still plain to hear that Charlie Parker could play the blues superlatively, with power and emotion. The twelve-bar blues sequence was probably the most accommodating chord progression for any session which mixed boppers with veterans, but even then there were differences in harmonic approach.

The basic blues sequence shown in figure ten was altered by the harmonic sophistry of bop into a complex progression. There were many variations, one of which is shown in figure eleven.

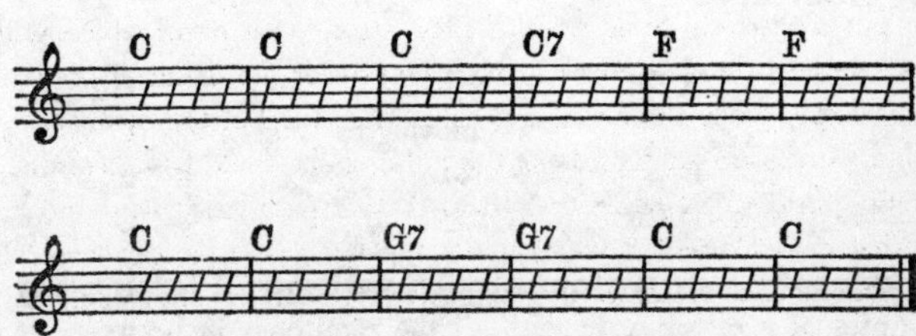

Figure 10 The basic twelve-bar blues

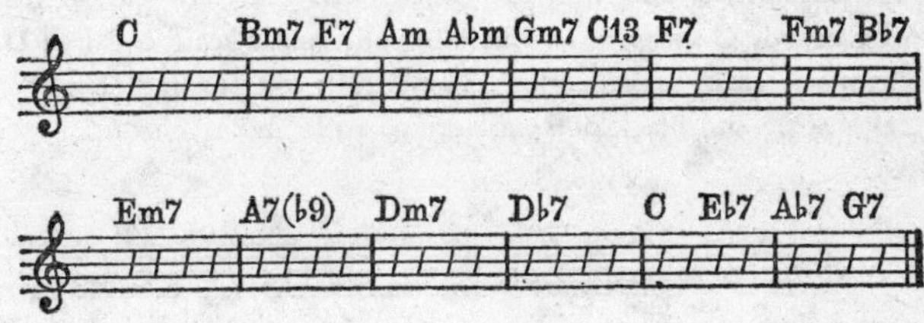

Figure 11

Modernists discouraged the old 'free-for-all' attitude of the 1930s' jam sessions. They wanted to experiment to the maximum, unhampered by older players. It has been suggested that they deliberately played odd-sounding chords and used unusual keys, and very fast tempi, in order to discourage interlopers. A rift developed between boppers and non-boppers (partly stimulated by the musical press), and it soon became rare for old and new stylists to be heard playing side by side.

In bop harmonisation there was prevalent usage of what were known as substitute chords. Instead of a chord progression resolving itself smoothly in the direction that the listener's ears were expecting, surprising chromatic chords were dramatically substituted. Chromatic chords include one or more notes not in the ordinary scale of the prevailing key. If we take C, the ordinary (or diatonic) scale is C, D, E, F, G, A, B, C. Therefore, C sharp, D sharp, F sharp, G sharp and A sharp will be chromatic notes. The use of a chromatic chord such as a D flat seventh to C movement often replaced the G seventh to C ending which had long been the commonest ending for tunes. So instead of:

F		G
D		E
	moving in conclusion to	
B		C
G		G

there occurred:

B		C
A flat		G
	moving to	
F		E
D flat		C

A chromatic scale is constructed on semitones. It is formed by combining the notes of a major scale with all the semitones in between. It consists of twelve different notes which proceed alphabetically, C, C sharp, D, D sharp, E, etc. In an ascending chromatic scale the added semitones are referred to as sharps; when descending they are called flats. They are the same notes on a piano keyboard, C sharp in an ascending chromatic scale is called D flat when the chromatic scale is descending. In the following example, white notes are the major scale and black notes are added to form the chromatic scale (figure twelve).

Figure 12 The chromatic scale

A chromatic run is an excerpt from such a scale, for instance: G, G sharp, A, A sharp, B, C or G, G flat, F, E, E flat, D.

A chromatic chord progression is one that moves by semitones, in this example, F, E, E flat which in musical notation is shown in figure thirteen.

Figure 13 A chromatic chord progression

Here the melody note at the top remains unchanged, while many of the harmony notes alter chromatically.

In a way, the boppers' use of chromatic scales and chords was slightly reminiscent of the work of several modern classical composers who, early in the twentieth century, created music that treated all twelve chromatic notes as being of equal importance, no set key note ever being established.

Mention of one aspect of bop harmonies seemed to enter every controversy sthat the new style created. This was the flattened or flatted fifth, arrived at by selecting the fifth note in a major scale, then flattening it by a semitone, G flat being the flatted fifth of C. During the 1920s, arrangers such as Don Redman had occasionally used the dissonant device effectively but by the end of the 1920s it was being written of as a possible ingredient for jazz improvisations.[2] For bop players it became an essential blue note, as important as the minor third and minor seventh. A scalic run in bop might contain three blue notes: C, D, *E* flat, F, *G* flat, A, *B* flat, C.

Using the chord progressions of standard tunes like 'How High The Moon', 'Blue Skies' and 'All The Things You Are', bop musicians composed tunes that incorporated their rhythmic ideas, and their melodic ideas (which featured what were then thought of as unusual intervals). Most important of all, they grafted their own extended chords and substitutions on to the tune's existing progression. Parker said that a harmonic revelation occurred to him one night in 1939 when he was playing a standard tune, 'Cherokee', in a jam session at Dan Wahl's Chilli House in New York City. Parker discovered that by using the higher parts of an extended chord he could re-harmonise an existing melody. His regular colleague at those jam sessions was guitarist William (Biddy) Fleet, who recalled: 'Bird and I were usually the first to arrive. It was an after-hours spot for musicians. Bird and I worked on chords, voicings, inversions, etc., until the other cats came. It was the same as what went on at Monroe's Uptown House and Minton's Playhouse later on.'[3] Parker had discovered that if a chord is extended far enough its top notes can take on the characteristics of a different chord. A bop extension might include a ninth, an augmented eleventh (the eleventh note from the tonic raised a semitone – literally a flatted fifth played an octave higher), and a thirteenth. The complete chord would contain: C, E, G, B, D, F sharp, A. The top four notes of the extension, B, D, F sharp and A, also form the basis of a B minor chord, with a seventh note added, symbolised B minor seventh. So the top part of the extended chord suggests one chord, while the lower notes suggest another.

The basis of Parker's future style was clearly apparent by the time he began recording in 1941. The story was quite different with his one-time colleague Dizzy Gillespie. Dizzy was a Roy Eldridge copyist when he began recording in 1937, but he was soon on a path of steady exploration, which can be followed on recordings he made between 1937 and 1945. An early sign of his penchant for including unexpected notes in his solos was his use of runs based on whole-tone scales. There are only two whole-tone scales which between them utilise every note between one C and the C an octave above. They literally use every white and black note on a piano, but instead of using them chromatically they use them in patterns in which all the notes are a tone apart.

C, D, E, F sharp, G sharp, A sharp, C.
C sharp, D sharp, F, G, A, B, C sharp.

Dizzy's formidable technique enabled him to play double-time phrases with absolute ease (when an improviser deliberately plays part of his solo at twice the rhythm section's tempo he is said to be playing in 'double time'. Done in moderation it creates excitement). A challenging feature of bop sessions was the regular featuring of 'four-bar chases' (or 'four-bar exchanges') where two, or more, players took it in turn to improvise four-bar interludes.

Parker was the titan of the new style. Pianist Lennie Tristano said in 1952: 'If Charlie Parker wanted to invoke the plagiarism laws he could sue everyone who's made a recording in the last ten years.'[4] Tristano, who coached many fine jazz musicians including Lee Konitz and Warne Marsh, steeped his players in Parker's music. Warne Marsh spoke of Tristano's method: 'One must learn Charlie Parker solos by ear from the record, and learn to sing them in one's head, then learn to sing them, and finally to learn to play them on one's instrument.'[5] When this training had been applied to the work of several important jazz players, Tristano encouraged his pupils to seek originality. His comments about plagiarism aptly described saxophone players who learnt Parker's solos note for note and then repeated them in parrot-like fashion, even including the 'quotes' that the originator had included. Quoting is the insertion of a short, instantly recognisable, phrase from one tune into the improvisations being conceived on another tune. The soloist may be taking a chorus on 'What Is This Thing Called Love' when he suddenly plays the theme of 'Take the A Train'. The manœuvre might have been pre-planned or it could have been subconsciously conceived during the flight of improvisation. The only rule is that the inserted quote is harmonically appropriate. Sometimes players deliberately insert an inapt quote to create a light-hearted, or even comic, effect. Quoting occurred occasionally in the 1920s and 1930s – Louis Armstrong included part of 'Lady Be Good' in his solo on 'Dinah' – but it was not a widespread practice before the bop era. Charlie Parker was a master of the genre. Some of his quotes can be deduced instantly, others are very obscure. His inclusion of a phrase from Louis Armstrong's solo on 'West End Blues' in one of his own solos show what an expansive listener he was.

Initially Miles Davis's harmonic approach was similar to that pioneered by Parker and Gillespie, but he soon developed from being a straightforward bop player into an individualistic improviser, harmonically, melodically and in phrasing.

On Miles Davis's early recordings it is often apparent that his trumpet technique was not capable of transmitting the ideas he had conceived. He often fluffed notes and mis-fingered the valves, but gradually he developed a style that precluded hesitancy and ambivalence. Davis's approach to trumpet playing was quite different to Gillespie's; it was nothing like as spectacular, he used very little vibrato, and rarely played ultra-fast, or in the upper register.

On the 1949 recording of 'Jeru' (arranged and composed by Gerry Mulligan), all of Davis's work, except for one short phrase, is in the middle register. On 'Move' the whole solo (except for two notes) is within an octave. The basis of Davis's early style is understatement and the conveying of a musical idea was the primary object. The overall sound of his 1949 ensemble was virtually vibratoless. The inclusion of a french horn and a tuba provided interesting tone colours, particularly as the tuba was used as a facile lower-register voice and not as a rhythm instrument.

During the 1940s new stylistic devices were continually being incorporated into big band repertoires. For example, great use was made of the increased range of trumpet players. In the 1920s, Louis Armstrong had showed that it was possible to produce a good sound right up to the instrument's top G (figure fourteen).

Figure 14 Top G on a trumpet

In the 1930s, many players followed Louis's example, and some bold individuals like Roy Eldridge, Tommy Stevenson, Sonny Dunham and Erskine Hawkins extended the range still further. By the 1940s, a whole army of trumpet players could produce notes in the instrument's extreme range, some of them able to hit a double top C, which is an octave above what had been thought the practical range twenty-five years before. William (Cat) Anderson and Maynard Ferguson were two particularly skilful exponents of stratospheric playing. Big-band arrangers, ever willing to try out new tricks, saw the possibilities of scoring a whole trumpet section in the higher register. Whereas a three-man trumpet team of the 1920s would play as in figure fifteen.

Figure 15

The five trumpeters of a late 1940s' big band might be greeted with parts as shown in figure sixteen.

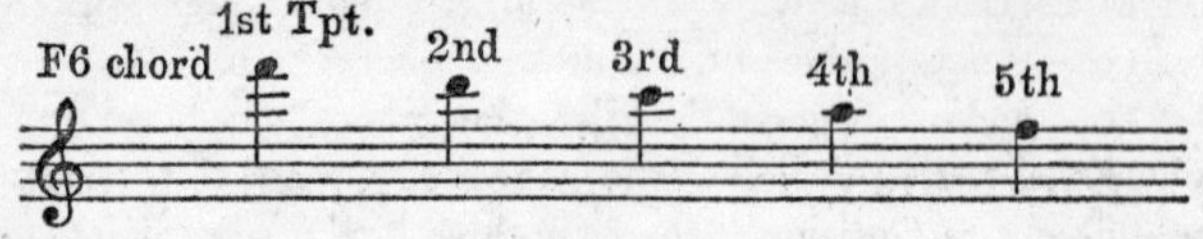

Figure 16

Trombone sections, on the contrary, tended to move lower in register with the adoption of a bass-trombone. The bass model had the same slide action as the ordinary tenor model, but the coils of tubing that hung over a player's shoulder enabled him to produce much lower notes. This was in accordance with the basic principle of music which is that the longer the distance the sound has to travel within an instrument the lower the note will be. Before J. J. Johnson developed his amazingly fast technique, the trombone had always been thought of as the slow-moving member of the brass family. Soon every big-band trombonist was playing faster, as if Johnson had broken through the musical equivalent of the four-minute mile. This newly-found speed enabled trombonists to join in with (and keep up with) the fast-moving bop arrangements that had previously been the domain of the trumpet and saxophone line-ups. During the 1950s it was rare to hear anyone playing the valve-trombone. A young eclectic from Kansas City, Bob Brookmeyer, was a notable exception.

In the late 1940s, a new harmonic approach to arranging was developed which enabled orchestrators to write parts that allowed sections to phrase together more smoothly. Reed player-arranger Jimmy Giuffre first introduced the style for a saxophone section on his arrangement of the tune 'Four Brothers' for Woody Herman's Second Herd. The style applied a different chord for each and every note in a fast-moving passage. It not only created a new sound, it also allowed each player in a section to have a part that moved in exact contours with his partners. The technique did not replace the previously accepted method of scoring, but it did become another useful addition to an arranger's armoury. But arranging-devices, no matter how skilful, are (or should be), only showcases for highlighting the skill of the jazz soloist.

Recommended Reading

Baker, David *Jazz Improvisation* (a comprehensive method), USA, 1971

Baker, David *Techniques of Improvisation*, Maher, USA, 1971 (Four volumes)

Collier, Graham *Jazz* (A Student's and Teacher's Guide), Cambridge University Press, London, 1975

Feather, Leonard *Inside Be-Bop* (A musical summary of bop, also contains biographies and historical background), Robbins, USA, 1949

Tanner, P. and Gerow, M. *A Study of Jazz* (Definitions and backgrounds of all jazz styles, complete with musical examples, and a sample record), William C. Brown, USA, 1975

11 Modern jazz cools down, and gains popularity

Small, refined bop groups, many of them with unusual instrumentations, achieve huge record sales; reacting against the polite approach of this 'cool school' young modernists re-introduce fire and vigour to their improvisations, the new style becoming known as 'hard bop'; several non-American jazz musicians gain international recognition; traditional jazz and 'mainstream' (an amalgam of jam-session music and swing) gain popularity.

In the USA, most of the verbal acrimony that had existed between various jazz schools dissolved during the early 1950s and jazz co-existence developed; in other parts of the world bitter feuds over jazz styles were to continue for years.

During the 1940s, while the controversy between modernists and traditionalists raged, the big-band leaders, who had established themselves in the 1930s, continued to work regularly, almost impervious to the rows over jazz styles. But at the beginning of the 1950s, big bands suffered a recession, and even Count Basie was temporarily forced to cut down to a smaller line-up. Worst hit were the new big bands who were trying to introduce bop to ballroom audiences. Dizzy Gillespie's third valiant attempt to maintain a regular touring big band ended in the summer of 1950.

The most successful big-band leader of the period was Stan Kenton who took a large ensemble, complete with a full string section, out on tour. The unit, billed as 'Innovations in Modern Music', did good business, both at the box office and through record sales. Kenton's strategy in persuading his record company to concentrate on getting America's disc-jockeys to play his records, instead of spending their money on press and poster advertising, was greatly responsible for his successes in the early 1950s.

After working as a pianist in big bands and club groups in California, Kenton began leading his own big band in 1941. After a transitional period, he recorded some highly distinctive music, which had its roots in the big, swing-band traditions, but which also deliberately introduced nuances of dissonance. The early Kenton Bands featured well-drilled saxophone sections, brash trombones, and daringly high-register scoring for the trumpets, the playing of which demanded panache, skill and confidence. An early sign of the leader's penchant for dissonance was the band's 1947 version of 'The Peanut Vendor'. Kenton's music became known as 'progressive jazz'. The young public took to its sounds, and Kenton confidently used even more grandiose arrangements, many of the new compositions that he commissioned being closer to modern classical music than to jazz. The band's individuality was based on its library of written arrangements, more than its soloists, but nevertheless Kenton gave employment and encouragement to many young white jazz musicians including Art Pepper, Kai Winding, Frank Rosolino, Bud Shank, Bob Cooper and Shelly Manne.

Kenton's musical pretentiousness could be irksome, but the most persistent critics of the band maintained that it did not swing, that the band's rhythmic stiffness remained despite personnel changes. Kenton ignored his critics, and moved implacably on through a whole series of stolid, pseudo-classical works, before returning to more orthodox big-band music. Despite several bouts of serious illness, Kenton continued to lead a successful big band into the late 1970s. As a spokesman, Kenton had a far-sighted candour. Commenting on the future of modern jazz in 1948, he said: 'We must have a synthesis of Louis Armstrong, and modern musicological development.'[1] He was quick to utilise instrumental precocity, and made full use of Maynard Ferguson, a young Canadian trumpeter whose accuracy and command in the high register was remarkable, and which later brought widespread success to the brass-player's own band.

In California during the early 1950s several ex-Stan Kenton alumni became co-founders of a new jazz movement, which was broadly based on the style of Miles Davis's 'cool school' group, amalgamated with the precision of Kenton's Band. It soon became known as 'West Coast Jazz'.

The term West Coast Jazz served to describe a style that was well-executed, clean-cut and full of understatement; the soloists' playing was almost devoid of vibrato, and rarely given to wild abandon. Most of its leading exponents were studio musicians. A highly individual tone, or an intense, personal vibrato are the last things required for the lucrative anonymity of session work. Individuality was rare and the sounds of Miles Davis and Lester Young echoed in practically every new band formed in California during the early 1950s. Davis summarised this by saying: 'All those West Coast tenor players sound alike to me.'[2] Many of the alto-saxophonists aped Lee Konitz's playing, who was himself a Lester Young admirer. The West Coast arrangements demanded precision, but the need to attain this seemed to affect the soloists' improvisations. Neatness, rather than excitement, was the order of the day.

One of the principal figures in West Coast Jazz was trumpeter Milton (Shorty) Rogers, who left Stan Kenton in 1950 and soon organised his own recording band, prior to joining a group led by another ex-Kentonian, bassist Howard Rumsey. Rogers's own recordings, and those he made with Rumsey, benefited by being issued on the newly adopted microgroove process (with playing-speeds of 33 or 45 revolutions per minute). These long-playing innovations soon totally replaced the breakable 78 r.p.m. discs. The new product proved a boon for extended jazz performances. The three-and-a-half minute maximum of the 78 r.p.m. record often presented a false picture of bands who sometimes played arrangements which lasted for ten minutes.

Clifford Brown was a young trumpeter who might have fulfilled Stan Kenton's forecasting of the perfect modern jazzman, had he not suffered a premature death in a car crash. Brown had five prerequisites which make a great jazz player; a finely developed sense of rhythm, range, tone, instrumental facility and imagination. Shortly before his untimely demise, Brown gave his reactions to the music he heard while touring California: 'The type of jazz they like out there, the kind being played by Shorty and Chet, is more on the cool side. So naturally, the West Coast audience is cool too, there's nothing for them to get excited about.' Referring to the group that he co-led with drummer Max Roach, he continued: 'Our own policy is to aim for the musical extremes of both excitement, and subtle softness. Their material is more prepared, a little more formal, and less spontaneous.'[3]

As a reaction to the criticism that West Coast jazz was stereotyped, many small bands in California tried out unusual instrumentations. The 'Chet' referred to by Clifford Brown was Chesney Baker, a trumpeter raised in California, who, after service in the US Army, joined a novel-sounding, pianoless quartet led by baritone-saxophonist, Gerry Mulligan. Mulligan, who had been a member of Miles Davis's 1949 Band, moved to California in 1952. The other two members of the original quartet were bassist Bob Whitlock and black drummer Chico Hamilton. Chet Baker patterned most of his solos in the lower register of the trumpet. His mellow tone, played almost without vibrato, contrasted strongly with the verve and gruffness of Mulligan's saxophone-playing. The melodic counterpoint that was the group's speciality might well have displeased those who conduct formal musical examinations, but the enthusiasm with which it was presented pleased those jazz fans who wanted to feel part of an experimental music without suffering any aural hardships. Although short-lived, the group gained an international following. Their first album sold 30 000 copies, a colossal figure for jazz groups in that era.

After leaving Mulligan, drummer Chico Hamilton formed his own West Coast group, which also featured unusual instrumentation. It typified the eternal search for new jazz sounds, consisting of Buddy Collette on flute, clarinet and saxes, Fred Katz on cello, Jim Hall on guitar, Carson Smith on string-bass, and the leader on drums. The new blend of tone colours intrigued the public, and Hamilton's group enjoyed widespread success. His policy of giving prominence to young jazzmen gave Jim Hall, Gabor Szabo, Charles Lloyd, Arthur Blythe and Eric Dolphy their first national publicity.

Conversely, the West Coast's biggest success of all featured a highly conventional line-up: piano, alto-saxophone, string-bass and drums. Such instrumentation would not have been out of place at a 1930s tea dance but with it the Dave Brubeck Quartet became one of the world's most popular musical attractions. Pianist Dave Brubeck began playing at the age of four. He majored in music, and went on to study with the French composer, Darius Milhaud. Brubeck's original band consisted of eight pieces, but in 1951, he recruited alto-saxophonist Paul Desmond, and formed the quartet. Whether Brubeck would have ever gained public acclaim without utilising Desmond's talents is debatable. The pianist rarely hit wrong notes, yet he seemed to the unpartisan listener, to play in a heavy-handed, quasi-dramatic manner that rarely swung. Desmond, in contrast, was the epitome of melodic gracefulness. Light in tone, he used minimal vibrato to produce pithy phrases which suggested a latter-day Frank Trumbauer. Brubeck and Desmond worked with a series of talented drummers and bassists, the most memorable being white drummer, Joe Morello, and black bassist Eugene Wright, who together achieved a crisp, swinging unity. The group's individuality emanated from the musical interplay between Brubeck and Desmond, and the use of unusual time-signatures (the number of beats in each bar). Their best-known recording featured Paul Desmond's composition in five-four, 'Take Five'. Brubeck also experimented with classical form (the system whereby each section in a piece of music is interrelated). He continued to explore improvisation in different time-signatures, and extended form, during the 1970s. After Desmond's death in 1977, Brubeck toured with a group that featured his own three sons' musical performances.

Commercially successful though they were, neither Brubeck nor Desmond had any decisive effect on jazz developments, and the same can be said of the Modern Jazz Quartet, a group whose lifespan almost paralleled that of Brubeck's group. The enigma of the MJQ's music-making was that each individual member could improvise with an exciting vibrancy but *in toto* the group specialised in genteel baroque counterpoint. All four members were black and three of the original personnel were prominent during the early days of bop, pianist John Lewis, Milt Jackson (vibraharp) and drummer Kenny Clarke. The bassist, Percy Heath, was younger than his colleagues, but he too had spent years playing in robust bop groups.

The MJQ's approach to jazz attracted promoters who sponsored 'jazz packet' concerts during the 1950s. One show consisted of several contrasting groups. The MJQ were ideal participants because no other group sounded like them. They provided a visual contrast as well, being attired in black jackets and pin-striped trousers. The group played as many blues as they did fugues, but the result was tantalising when one considered the hard-swinging potential of each individual player. Their best-selling record, 'Django', typified their neo-classical approach to polyphony. Kenny Clarke left in 1955 to settle in Europe, and was replaced by the versatile Connie Kay. This personnel stayed together until the group disbanded in 1974, rarely changing the formula that brought them success.

Kenneth (Red) Norvo, one of the first vibraharp players in jazz, enjoyed continued success throughout the 1950s. By then, Norvo was travelling light, using a trio consisting of vibes, guitar and bass. Virtuoso string-bassist Charles Mingus worked regularly with Norvo during the early 1950s and then, during the period 1951–55, he worked with several leaders with contrasting jazz styles, including Duke Ellington, Louis Armstrong, Lionel Hampton, Kid Ory and Stan Getz. Mingus decided to use his vast experience in a practical way by becoming a bandleader. His initial efforts as a leader showed the gentle approach of the West Coast school, but soon Mingus was composing themes and formulating ideas that were to place him in the forefront of jazz innovators. Mingus's goal was jazz which allied modern techniques with the earthiness and vigour of early black American folk music. The energetic force of Mingus's music alarmed casual listeners, but he retained an uncompromising attitude and, despite a troubled personal life which sometimes kept him away from active music-making, he was able to exert a strenuous influence on the jazz of the 1960s.

Miles Davis was one of the other leading innovators of the decade. He continually re-shaped a trumpet style that was already highly individual, and his tone became more poignant, moving even further away from the brassy pyrotechnics of bop playing. Gil Evans, one of the most visionary arrangers in jazz, saw the possibilities of showcasing Miles Davis's individuality in a series of recordings which presented him as a soloist accompanied by a twenty-piece orchestra. Some of the material used was a mixture of standard tunes (like Gershwin's 'Porgy and Bess') and such pieces as 'Sketches of Spain', most of which were specially composed and presented like miniature concertos. The gamut of trumpet-sounds that Davis could produce (which included wistful muted effects), was augmented when he began doubling on flugelhorn.

The Gil Evans–Miles Davis collaborations were recording-studio projects. Miles continued to work with his own small group, which usually consisted of himself and a saxophonist, with piano, bass and drums. For a time his band had what was considered to be one of the best rhythm sections of the era: Red Garland on piano, Paul Chambers on string-bass and Philly Joe Jones on drums. Later, an outstanding white pianist, Bill Evans, worked briefly with Davis's group. Evans's playing with his own trio later brought him widespread acclaim, his forte being the playing of slow tempo ballads, but this was only one aspect of a very talented jazz improviser, whose considerable technique and rhythmic ingenuity on well-known tunes first attracted a number of new listeners to jazz. Miles Davis, never effusive with praise, said of Evans: 'He plays the piano the way it should be played.'

On his recordings Davis often worked with top-class saxophonists, including Lucky Thompson, Sonny Rollins, Jackie McLean, Julian Adderley and Hank Mobley. One of Miles's tenor-saxophonist colleagues of the 1950s, John Coltrane, developed into one of the most influential of all jazz musicians. Coltrane gained a great deal of knowledge from working regularly with Miles Davis, and his stylistic and harmonic development owed much to the innovations that Davis formulated. By 1955, Davis was experimenting with a form of improvising based on modes – the note patterns used by the Ancients long before the system of scales was devised. Coltrane was an instinctive musician and developed a style that combined modal playing with a highly advanced chordal system. In 1958, Miles Davis's Sextet, featuring Coltrane and Julian Adderley, made an album called 'Milestones', which contained the embryos of many of the jazz innovations which developed during the 1960s.

Not all the modern jazz groups of the 1950s based their styles on the cool school; several groups came into being that had direct links with the fervent style pioneered by Charlie Parker and Dizzy Gillespie. As a direct reaction to the mellow sounds of West Coast jazz, the new groups exaggerated the harshness and vigour of bop. This approach was soon realistically named 'hard bop'.

One of the new style's principal exponents were The Jazz Messengers, a cooperative black group whose figurehead was drummer Art Blakey. Blakey is also known as Abdullah Ibn Bulhaina, being one of many jazz musicians who adopted the Muslim faith. Blakey wanted to convey the vigour and excitement of bop to new listeners, and also to add complicated changes of tempo, and more exotic rhythm patterns. He, like other jazz musicians of his generation, felt a need to return to what were called the roots, which incorporated the study and practice of pure African rhythms. Blakey pioneered a technical approach which lifted jazz drummers out of their customary role of accompanists. They were encouraged to play 'in with', rather than behind the soloist. For tyro jazz listeners a dialogue between a front-line player and a drummer could seem relentless, but the rhythmic exitement engendered converted many people to hard bop, at the expense of West Coast jazz. An important aural difference between the two schools was that the hard bop tenor-saxophonists used a fuller tone and harder-sounding approach – more akin to tonal qualities developed by Coleman Hawkins, Chu Berry and Ben Webster. Most of the hard-bop trumpeters followed a stylistic line that had its origins in Dizzy Gillespie's playing. The Jazz Messengers featured several trumpeters who became important jazz players in their own right during the 1960s, including Donald Byrd, Lee Morgan, Freddie Hubbard and Bill Hardman.

Horace Silver, The Jazz Messengers' original pianist, became a renowned jazz composer, whose own group enjoyed great success during the 1960s and 1970s. Silver was one of the originators of a style of playing known as 'funk', which consisted of the intertwining of early ethnic harmonies with catchy melodies which were played over an emphatic rhythm. Akin to this were the popular 'soul sounds' made famous by the Adderley Brothers (Julian on alto-saxophone and Nat on cornet), which had their roots in gospel music. This style was ingeniously linked with melodies that seemed inspired by Charlie Parker phrases.

The 1950s saw the gradual rise to eminence of one of jazz's most subtle composers, pianist Thelonious Monk, who had been part of the early bop clique. He had an early compositional success with 'Round Midnight'. It was not long before jazz musicians realised that Monk's tunes were ideal vehicles for their improvisations. Monk's composing had little to do with the use of melodic tricks which feature in pop songs, and, in his selection of notes and rhythms, his work was more like a jazz solo of masterful ingenuity. As a soloist, Monk continued deliberately to eschew any display of technique, his object being to reach his listeners with stark melodic lines. The guidance and inspiration that he has given to numerous jazz musicians has made him a father figure of the post-bop era.

During the 1950s many jazz musicians who had made their recording début in the previous decade continued to establish their international reputations without becoming part of any partisan group or revolutionary school. The outstanding example was the Canadian pianist Oscar Peterson, who throughout the decade undertook worldwide tours featuring his trio, which included, at one time or another, several other jazz perennials: guitarists Barney Kessel and Herb Ellis, drummer Ed Thigpen, and one of the most accomplished of all jazz bassists, Ray Brown.

Tenor-saxophonist Stan Getz, was another who blossomed into an international jazz star during the 1950s. A list of bandleaders for whom Getz worked, early in his career, reads like an all-star jazz cast: Jack Teagarden, Stan Kenton, Jimmy Dorsey, Benny Goodman and Woody Herman. All his work in the 1950s was with small groups. Originally, Getz was one of many gifted Lester Young disciples. He developed his own highly individual style, and became one of the most expressive ballad players in jazz. He also used his instrumental technique to produce effortless, interesting improvisations at the fastest tempi. During the early 1960s, his fame increased through recordings that he, and guitarist Charlie Byrd, made of Brazilian tunes. This blend of jazz and Latin American rhythms became known as 'bossa nova'. During the 1970s, Getz's cautious, but successful, experiments with the electrically amplified saxophone did not diminish his popularity.

Another tenor-saxophonist, John (Zoot) Sims, steadily built his reputation during the 1950s. His unfailing ability to swing, combined with the ease with which he played with contrasting stylists, meant that he was justly regarded during the 1970s as one of the great white sax-players. From 1955 onwards he enjoyed a close working partnership with tenor-saxophonist Al Cohn. Their double saxophone line-up was only one of many small groups which featured front-line duos of musicians playing the same instrument, one of the most dynamic groups being the Jay and Kay Quintet, which featured two superb trombonists, J. J. Johnson and Kai Winding. Valve trombonist Bob Brookmeyer, who worked frequently with Gerry Mulligan during the 1950s, later formed a very agile working duet with an ex-Duke Ellington brassman, Clark Terry, possibly the most versatile of all jazz trumpeters.

During the 1950s a happy stage came into jazz appreciation, whereby people listened to players whose work they liked, undisturbed by the fact that their favourites were not trying to originate a new school of jazz. Trumpeters Art Farmer and Emmett Berry, pianists Hampton Hawes, Tommy Flanagan and Hank Jones, and trombonists like Urbie Green, Frank Rosolino and Jimmy Knepper all benefited from this more broad-minded approach. The great jazz loss of the decade was the death at the age of thirty-four of the arch innovator Charlie Parker, who after a lifetime of wild excesses, died from a heart attack in New York in 1955. Bird left behind him a whole army of musicians who plagiarised his work, but he also inspired several alto-sax players who developed jazz individualism. They included Sonny Stitt, Eugene Quill, Phil Woods, Julian Adderley and Jackie McLean.

Many skilful guitarists and vibes players consolidated their reputations for playing satisfying jazz during the 1950s. Terry Gibbs, Marjorie Hyams, Teddy Charles and Cal Tjader on vibes, and guitarists Tal Farlow, Kenny Burrell and Wes Montgomery, were all superb instrumentalists, but none of them were jazz trail-blazers. Something in the physical nature of the instruments seems to preclude vibists and guitar players from influencing the main course of jazz development.

One of the jazz vocal favourites of the decade was Dinah Washington. Other singers who had originally found fame in the 1940s continued to make artistic advances including the svelte stylists Peggy Lee, the ex-Stan Kenton band-singer June Christy, and the poised vocal improviser Anita O'Day, who was one of the stars of a fine documentary film *Jazz On A Summer's Day*. Two noted female singers of the 1930s, Maxine Sullivan and Helen Humes, were, during the 1950s, half-way through careers that were to carry them triumphantly into the late 1970s. Perhaps the most interesting vocal developments of the 1950s came from a trio comprised of Dave Lambert, Jon Hendricks and Annie Ross. These three singers formed a group that specialised in harmonising jazz instrumental numbers, and adding lyrics; their recreations of Count Basie's best numbers revealed their ingenuity and their uncanny grasp of the jazz soloist's phrasing. The divine sound of the gospel singer Mahalia Jackson was seldom heard accompanied by jazz, but in 1958 she consented to make an album with Duke Ellington's Orchestra, with memorable results.

Ray Charles, whose superb voice presented an amalgam of gospel music and urban blues, seemed at his best when using jazz accompaniment. He originally made his name working in the swiftly-growing rhythm-and-blues circuits, which featured small groups, usually septets or octets, whose insistent beat came from amplified guitars, and drummers who solidly emphasised off-beats (the second and fourth beat of each bar). The principal soloists in r-and-b were the raucous-toned tenor-sax players, who concentrated on re-enforcing the band's beat rather than playing melodic subtleties.

Rhythm-and-blues was a style that revived public interest in dancing to live music. It was succeeded in terms of mass popularity by its country cousin, rock-and-roll. When Bill Haley's record of 'Rock Around The Clock' began to sell in millions, it heralded the fact that popular music was entering a new phase, one that was bitterly criticised by some jazz musicians. Count Basie, who had re-formed his big band, saw the bright side of the situation: 'Rock-and-roll started the kids dancing again – that's certainly a blessing for us.' Basie's new band, like its forerunner, set great store in the blues, and included many in its repertoire. Its new vocalist, Joe Williams, served his musical apprenticeship in the Chicago clubs that were the spawning grounds of rhythm-and-blues. Jimmy Witherspoon, who had also been singing with r-and-b bands (in California), began enjoying success as a solo artist. All the soloists in Basie's new band were well versed in both the blues and bop. They included trumpeter Joe Newman, trombonist Henry Coker, and two reed-players, Frank Foster and Frank Wess.

All the big bands benefited from the dancing boom of the 1950s. Some of them presented programmes that were heavy with nostalgia, but eventually every big-band leader who had pretensions to featuring jazz introduced arrangements that had some facet of bop in them. Elements of the style were also featured in the musical writings of the men who arranged background music for films and television. This was a positive indication of how a jazz style could, eventually, seep through into the ears of mass audiences.

The success of the documentary film *Jazz On A Summer's Day*, which featured the participants at the 1958 Newport Jazz Festival, has been mentioned. An earlier movie, *Jammin' The Blues*, made in 1944, also presented a fruitful marriage of imagery and jazz improvisation, but in general the film industry has failed miserably to take advantage of the cinematic potential of the music. Many, many films have included jazz interludes; as nostalgia most are delightful, but as examples of jazz performed under authentic circumstances few can be recommended. *Jazz In The Movies*, a book compiled by David Meeker (published in 1977), is a guide to the pitfalls, and pleasures, of the subject.

In the thirty-year period from 1919 to 1949, the world outside the USA produced only one jazz musician whose playing could be measured alongside that of the finest American jazzmen. This was the self-taught Belgian gypsy guitarist Django Reinhardt. Reinhardt played with a most unorthodox fingering style as a result of an accident that lost him the use of two fingers on his left hand. He lived in France for most of his life, and became the only European jazzman of his era to influence American jazz players. His remarkable gift for melodic invention was exemplified in his rhapsodic single-string playing. Django, together with the French violinist Stephane Grappelli, was part of the Quintet of the Hot Club of France, which was one of the most original-sounding jazz groups of the 1930s.

By the 1950s, a whole legion of top-class jazz improvisers had emerged from many places all over the world. They included trombonist Albert Mangelsdorff from Germany, sax-player Bobby Jaspar from Belgium, pianist Bengt Hallberg from Sweden, pianist Toshiko Akiyoshi from Japan, and multi-instrumentalist Victor Feldman from Britain. The last two named moved to the USA permanently; others remained resident in their own countries, visiting the USA to play in the growing number of jazz festivals organised there during the 1950s.

American jazz musicians benefited from reciprocal offers to play at overseas jazz festivals. The 1950s produced a format whereby a single jazz concert package did tours which spanned several countries. One of the most persistent travellers on these jaunts was Louis Armstrong, who was always delighted to be welcomed at diverse airports by bands playing in a style similar to the bands he heard during his youth. The similarity was only passing, but it showed how widespread the appeal of New Orleans jazz had become.

By the early 1950s, the traditional jazz revival was in full swing in most European countries and throughout Australia. Coincidental to the emergence of Lu Watters's Band in California, a band with a similar line-up, George Webb's Dixielanders, was formed in England during the early 1940s (one of the band's early trumpeters was Humphrey Lyttelton, who became a revered figure in European jazz). Simultaneously, pianist Graeme Bell's Band, which also featured two trumpets and a tuba among its members, was being assembled in Australia. Originally, each of these three bands were unaware of the other's existence but they shared a passionate desire to recreate a style of music that they felt was in danger of extinction in the land of its origin. At about the same time, The Dutch Swing College Band (which is still in existence) was formed, and in France, soon after the end of the Second World War, dozens of 'revival' bands were formed. Two of Lu Watters's sidemen, trumpeter Bob Scobey and trombonist Melvin (Turk) Murphy became successful small-band leaders. Murphy became something of an institution on the West Coast of America, enjoying considerable localised fame.

The revival of interest in traditional jazz never swept the USA as it did most other parts of the world. In the USA, there were pockets of staunch devotees, but not enough regular venues to support more than a few full-time touring jazz bands. Some clubs in New York continued to cater exclusively for traditional jazz fans; among them were Eddie Condon's, and Jimmy Ryan's, where a band formed by Wilbur and Sidney De Paris enjoyed a long residency. Interest in live jazz in New Orleans, which had long remained dormant, except for a small number of visiting enthusiasts and local historians, began to develop. The central figure was George Lewis, formerly the clarinettist in Bunk Johnson's Band. His successes in New Orleans during the early 1950s helped to rekindle interest, and led to him being booked in California, then in Europe and Japan. Another ex-Bunk Johnson sideman, trombonist Big Jim Robinson, was one of several veterans who benefited from the renewal of interest in their playing.

In Europe, hundreds of jazz clubs mushroomed during the 1950s, some functioning every night of the week and these clubs formed the basis of a convenient touring circuit for visiting American jazzmen. Several famous jazz players, including Sidney Bechet, Albert Nicholas, Don Byas, and trumpeter Bill Coleman (one of the most melodic of all jazz improvisers) moved to Europe to take permanent advantage of playing regularly to worshipping fans.

Dizzy Gillespie, Coleman Hawkins, Lester Young, Rex Stewart, Henry Allen, Buck Clayton, Roy Eldridge and many other fine jazz players undertook successful international tours during the 1950s, some of which were sponsored by the American Government. The styles of most of these men changed little in the ten years from 1946 to 1956. Their work fell into the 'mainstream' of jazz – a term first used in the 1950s by writer Stanley Dance. It indicated a middle-of-the-road style, that was more closely related to the sounds of a late 1930s jam session, than to Dixieland or bop.

The usual mainstream arrangement consisted of one chorus of melody played by the ensemble, which was followed by a string of solos (some accompanied by riffs); a few four-bar chases might take place, and then the band repeated the opening theme. Standard tunes (or original compositions based on them) and blues themes formed the basis of a mainstream programme, all played over a four-in-the-bar rhythm. In the mid-1950s, several recording-companies issued mainstream records played by specially assembled 'all star' bands. The most successful of the genre were those organised by trumpeter Buck Clayton, featuring as they did permutations of musicians who had made their names in pre-war bands, including ex-Jimmie Lunceford trombonist James (Trummie) Young, ex-Fletcher Henderson trombonist Benny Morton, bandleader Woody Herman on clarinet and ex-Count Basie drummer Jo Jones. A relative newcomer to the jazz scene, trumpeter Ruby Braff, was also featured.

Braff was an anachronism. Unlike most other young jazz musicians of his age he chose not to take part in any bop experiments, and from an early age propounded the merits of Louis Armstrong, Lester Young and Billie Holiday – sometimes to semi-hostile listeners. He played in dixieland sessions in his native Boston during the early 1950s, but was stylistically much more at home in mainstream surroundings. The popularity of mainstream recordings was sufficient to warrant 'follow-up' releases, but not substantial enough for anyone to form a regular touring unit of established stars.

The two poles of interest that concerned the jazz world in the late 1950s were, firstly, whether revival jazz would gain popularity, and secondly, if a new style would replace hard bop and funk as the main interest of erstwhile young jazz musicians. Still no black youngsters took any part, or interest, in the traditional or mainstream movements.

Traditional jazz did become more popular in the 1960s, and during the same period a group of young black musicians emerged who completely transformed the existing ideas on jazz improvisation. Two news items published within weeks of each other in late 1959 augured the forthcoming events. A British jazz band, led by trombonist Chris Barber, was booked to play a concert at the New Orleans Municipal Hall. In New York, saxophonist Ornette Coleman and trumpeter Don Cherry were photographed at a recording session that spearheaded the new style of jazz improvising.

Recommended Reading

Cole, Bill *Davis, Miles* (A bio-discography), William Morrow, USA, 1974

Dance, Stanley *The World of Duke Ellington* (Lengthy interviews with musicians who worked with Duke Ellington), Scribner's, USA, 1970

Delaunay, Charles *Django Reinhardt* (Biography and discography), Cassell, London, 1961

Easton, Carol *Straight Ahead* (The story of Stan Kenton), William Morrow, USA, 1973

Goldberg, Joe *Jazz Masters of the Fifties* (Essays on the important jazzmen of the decade), Macmillan, USA, 1965

12 Avant garde and trad. become twin poles of jazz

Young musicians pioneer a new style of non-chordal improvisation that becomes known as 'free jazz'; many young black jazzmen adopt a political stance; the incorporation of Oriental instruments and musical ideas into jazz continues to increase; many jazz veterans undertake world-wide tours.

During the late 1950s, a surge of the restlessness which regularly affects jazz occurred, and from a maelstrom of new ideas there came a form of jazz that was revolutionary. Rules of jazz improvising, thought to be sacrosanct, were swept away. Soloists no longer were expected to observe chorus lengths and pre-ordained harmonies. An alternative method evolved in which improvisations could contain any notes that the soloists felt appropriate, those notes to be played for a duration of time chosen by the performer. The musicians who pioneered this style of playing did so in the face of widespread opposition from jazzmen of every previous school.

Ornette Coleman and Don Cherry, two of the new music's leading practitioners, have already been mentioned. Other key figures in the 'free jazz' movement (as it became known) were pianists Cecil Taylor and Sun Ra, together with reed players Albert Ayler, Eric Dolphy and Archie Shepp. Charles Mingus was one of the first to experiment with free jazz concepts, but he did so in a highly personal way that was reminiscent of the way in which Duke Ellington worked alongside different jazz movements without becoming enmeshed.

At the onset, the experimental music was called either 'the new thing', 'the new wave' or 'avant garde jazz'. These descriptions were later abandoned in favour of 'free jazz'. Originally this led to confusion, as Ornette Coleman found out at one of his early concert appearances when people reading the advertising posters assumed that admission to the hall was free. The term free jazz implies freedom from the stylistic rules which many young improvisers felt had restricted the self-expression of earlier jazz musicians. Free jazz musicians rarely improvised on standard tunes. Usually they used their own themes (or those of their colleagues) as the basis of their work.

Ornette Coleman, unlike the leading figures of previous jazz schools, did not have a wide, practical experience of playing earlier jazz styles. He had worked with a rhythm-and-blues band, and taken some commercial dance-band jobs, but had not been part of a fully-fledged jazz group during his early playing years. While gaining general musical experience, he began developing a most unorthodox method of improvising – one that did not fit in with what his colleagues were playing. It was to be some while before Coleman found a compatible front-line partner. Eventually, he joined up with trumpeter Don Cherry, who was to be a regular associate during the late 1950s. Their first engagement together took place in 1957. Cherry recalled: 'It was Ornette's first jazz gig, and he was really beautiful.'[1]

Many jazz musicians had harsh words to say about Coleman's music. The more abusive comments came from men who had been young modernists in the early 1940s. One famous player of the Swing Era tried to make a joke of it all by asking a group of free jazz musicians to take him to their leader, mockingly indicating that he thought they were playing the music of the planet Mars. Utter disbelief would have reigned if the detractors had been told that by 1972 Coleman's compositions would be performed in London's Albert Hall by a vast symphony orchestra.

Some established musicians listened carefully and sympathetically to the new style. Pianist John Lewis, wrote of Coleman: 'I first heard him one afternoon in 1959 in San Francisco and was greatly impressed both with his playing and with what he had to say about the future of music.'[2] Charles Mingus spoke of the paradox of Coleman's music: 'Now aside from the fact I doubt he can even play a C scale in tune, the fact remains that his notes and lines are so fresh. I'm not saying everybody's going to have to play like Coleman, but they're going to have to stop copying Bird.'[3] Saxophonist Julian (Cannonball) Adderley found Coleman's playing unintelligible on first hearing, but later realised that it contained a wealth of constructive originality. Many listeners, preconditioned to hearing jazz solos that related to accompanying harmonies, remained permanent sceptics.

Canadian pianist Paul Bley summarised the importance of Coleman as a musical revolutionary: 'You see Ornette solved, in a single swoop, a problem that had been accumulating for ten years. Bird was a virtuoso of chord changes, and there were dozens of virtuoso players after Bird. There was nothing left to play on songs.'[4]

Initially, critics castigated Coleman for his lack of technique on the alto-saxophone. He explained that he was not interested in acquiring a legitimate technique and that he thought each note on his saxophone possessed a vocal quality of its own. Each was an individual, independent ingredient that was available for use in improvised sound patterns. The timbre of Coleman's playing could be related to the sounds produced by previous jazz saxophonists, but his rhythmic approach to improvising was highly individual. It was this exciting, and novel, way of playing that first attracted serious attention to Coleman's playing. Charles Mingus said: 'It gets to you emotionally like a drummer.'[5] During a three-year sabbatical, from 1962 until 1965, Coleman taught himself to play the violin and the trumpet. On both his playing was just as uncompromisingly individual as his work on saxophone.

General acceptance of Coleman's originality was very slow to develop during the late 1950s. In fact, the majority of jazz listeners were distinctly hostile. Bassist Charlie Haden, who worked regularly with Coleman at that time, has said that both East and West Coast listeners were equally unsympathetic:

> 'They didn't understand what he was doing. It was the same when we first came to New York. People thought we didn't know how to play our instruments, didn't know anything about music, and all that. The first night we opened at the Five Spot in September 1959, I guess every jazz musician in town was there, and most everybody came back. Coltrane used to come and hear us every night. He would grab Ornette by the arm soon as we got off the band-stand, and they would go off into the night talking about music.'[6]

John Coltrane's reputation was firmly established by the time Ornette Coleman's first recordings were issued. His apprenticeship (which included working in bands led by Johnny Hodges, Earl Bostic and Miles Davis), was as extensive as Coleman's was sparse, yet he was no less of a revolutionary. In terms of gathering active disciples Coltrane's playing style was more influential than Coleman's. Coltrane linked modal playing with complex harmonies, such as those used in modern classical music and his solos were presented with a speed of execution, and energy, that had never been heard before in jazz. This ferocious projection often caught listeners unaware, and he, like Ornette Coleman, was to suffer from the backlash of a confused public. Writer Martin Williams described Coltrane's approach to rhythm as 'speeding up time', and another writer, Ira Gitler, in attempting to convey the impact of the tenor-saxophonist's cascading notes, likened them to 'sheets of sound'. Coltrane, or Trane, as he was generally referred to, saw this intensity as being directly linked with his African ancestry.

Coltrane's stamina was awesome. It was not uncommon for him to play duets with drummer Elvin Jones for half an hour; on some solos he blew continuously for over an hour, often at a very fast tempo. Jones had the energy, and the technique, to keep up with Coltrane during these marathons. He was able to complement the sax-player's involved phrases by playing compatible rhythms, or by embellishing a superimposed time signature, which might have five beats in the bar against the three in a bar being played by Coltrane. The effect was like a web of interconnected rhythms.

In 1960, Coltrane began doubling on soprano-saxophone, an instrument on which Sidney Bechet had been the principal specialist. Other veterans, notably Johnny Hodges, had played the instrument with finesse, and younger players such as Steve Lacy specialised on it before Coltrane began playing it. However, Coltrane's skills on the instrument inspired countless young players to attempt to play soprano-saxophone. Coltrane virtually re-introduced the instrument back into jazz, and indirectly made it one of the most prevalent reed sounds in jazz of the 1960s and 1970s.

As the years passed, Coltrane became increasingly fascinated by the metaphysical nature of his music. One by one, his early colleagues dropped out of the group, either because they were disenchanted by the direction of Coltrane's experiments, or because they were disinterested in restless musical exploration. By the mid-1960s, Coltrane's musical individuality had earned him a global reputation, but by then he was suffering consistently from ill health. After a 1966 tour of Japan he returned to New York and began a series of musical experiments, involving vast teams of percussionists, which typified his turbulent spirit. We shall never know how Coltrane's music would have developed because his illness was diagnosed as a severe liver ailment from which he died in June 1967. Since his death, his widow Alice, herself a musician, has supervised the release of a great deal of unissued recorded material by her late husband.

Theodore (Sonny) Rollins, the tenor-saxophonist, was one of the most revered jazz improvisers of the 1960s, who co-existed with John Coltrane without adopting his ideas or copying his phrases. He was three years younger than Coltrane, but their professional experience began at about the same time. Like Coltrane, Rollins was a big-toned tenor-sax player and he too originally made his name as a bop player. He then temporarily became part of the hard bop movement, before developing a rich vein of individualism. Despite having an international following, Rollins has on several occasions given up playing in public, and recording, in order to re-group his thoughts and theories on improvisation. During the 1960s, he occasionally worked with players who were heavily involved in free jazz, but he never became a mainstay of the movement. For much of the 1960s he worked in a group that consisted of himself, string-bass and drums. One of his many innovative ideas was the inclusion of tunes inspired by the music of Caribbean Islands (his parents were originally from the West Indies).

Pianist Cecil Taylor is often spoken of as the third man in the triumvirate which revolutionised jazz in the 1960s (along with Coleman and Coltrane). Taylor received extensive Conservatory training on piano and in composition, and his knowledge of modern European composers led him to listen with interest to two white jazz pianists, Dave Brubeck (who had also studied in similar musical areas) and Lennie Tristano. Taylor soon realised that he would only find the inspiration he needed in the work of fellow black musicians.

Taylor's playing in the 1960s has been cited as being the most atonal (belonging to no set key) in early free jazz. This harmonic freedom, and the percussive use of intricate rhythms made his work difficult for the public to understand, because they were used to regarding a light touch as an attribute. Bookings were scarce. Many of the free jazz pioneers spent long periods without musical work and none suffered more for possessing an uncompromising attitude to improvisation than Cecil Taylor. Eventually, the energy of his music made an impact via recordings. Those that gave close attention realised that his playing was not formless as had been suggested. There are inner structures within his improvisations, but no sooner are these structures established than they are replaced by completely different outlines. With the complexities involved, it is not surprising that Taylor's most successful musical liaisons are with players who have worked with him for long periods.

Saxophonist Archie Shepp summarised his experience of playing with Taylor:

> 'With Cecil, because there's no steady pulse going, you have to be really conscious of what's going on rhythmically. Cecil plays the piano like a drum, he gets rhythm out of it like a drum, rhythm and melody. In a way it's more of a throwback rather than a projection into some weird future. A throwback in the the direction of the African influences on the music. In a way, it's a rebellion against the ultra-sophistication of jazz. The Negro musician is a reflection of the Negro people as a social and cultural phenomenon.'[7]

An increasing number of black musicians were taking a political stance. The ferocity of free jazz caused its detractors to brand it as a music of hate although John Coltrane emphatically denied this. Nevertheless, free jazz reflected violent times, and also a smouldering anger directed towards racial injustices. Archie Shepp was a leading exponent of the new style, and also one of its most coherent spokesmen. During his teens he played local jobs in Philadelphia with rhythm-and-blues bands. After finishing drama and literature studies he went to New York, and eventually worked there with Cecil Taylor. Shepp's tone, similar to the saxophone sounds of the Swing Era, set him apart from his contemporaries who favoured the harsh tonal approach and his occasional use of a heavy vibrato added to his individuality.

In the mid-1960s, Shepp gathered together for recording sessions an imposing roster of young free jazz talent, including trumpeter Tommy Turrentine, and trombonists Roswell Rudd and Grachan Moncur III (the son of a distinguished jazz bassist). Roswell Rudd, had an unusual pedigree for free jazz. He was white, and his early musical experiences were in dixieland bands. One of Shepp's close colleagues, Bobby Hutcherson, became one of the first exponents of playing free jazz on the vibraphone and on the marimba. Shepp established a modus operandi for the 1970s, by presenting a programme that combined tributes to jazz giants of the past, with his own bold, experimental sorties. When not touring he teaches as a college professor.

Eric Dolphy was another saxophonist who moved back and forth between orthodoxy and experimentation. Before he was twenty he had worked in several 'name' bands in California. He moved to New York in 1960, and worked in turn with Charles Mingus in 1960, with John Coltrane in 1961, and with Ornette Coleman in 1962. Playing alto-saxophone, bass-clarinet and flute, Dolphy rejoined Mingus for an overseas tour in 1964. Finding the social climate in Europe more amenable, Dolphy settled there and worked with some of the growing number of young European musicians who were dedicated to free jazz. He was taken ill in Berlin, and died there in June 1964. Dolphy was the most eclectic of free jazz pioneers, equally fluent when playing ballads, free jazz, blues or hard bop. His search for new sounds led him to follow the rendering of a Swing Era theme like 'The Jitterbug Waltz' with a series of instrumental bird-call imitations. His growing skills on the bass-clarinet might well have led him eventually to specialise on that jazz rarity.

Reed-player Rahsaan Roland Kirk also experimented with a wide variety of sounds which included the playing of three wind instruments simultaneously, saxophone, manzello and stritch. Most of Kirk's best-known work was within the framework of orthodox jazz, but he could also play telling solos in free form. He was equally at home on saxophone, flute or clarinet, and was one of the first jazzmen to develop circular breathing, a technique which enables musicians to inhale through their noses while improvising, allowing them to play longer phrases. Harry Carney had previously used the effect for holding dramatic long notes in Duke Ellington's orchestrations, but the technique was known to Indian musicians centuries ago.

There were several tragic deaths among the forerunners of the free jazz movement. In late 1970, saxophonist Albert Ayler's body was found in New York's East River under circumstances which have never been clarified. Controversy surrounded his name in death, as it did throughout his professional life.

Ayler, one of a musical family, was born in Cleveland, Ohio in 1936. He played conventionally throughout his teen years, and did summer tours with rhythm-and-blues bands (a common starting-point for many free jazzmen). While serving in the US Army Band, he began experimenting with ways of producing new tonal effects on the saxophone, and exploring non-chordal improvisation. He was attracted by both Ornette Coleman's playing and John Coltrane's. Concentrating on the tenor-saxophone he began using the hardest reeds available, which produced a harsh but tremendously powerful sound.

He settled temporarily in Europe and made his record début in Scandinavia in 1962. Ayler's love of martial music coupled with his belief in complete freedom for improvisers produced some stark sounds. His habit of blowing a long series of notes of indeterminate pitch alarmed tender ears. When he did this while playing the theme of a well-known tune the effect usually produced derision, for it seemed, by the existing method of analysis, that he was woefully out of tune. Little of his work swung in the previously accepted way; he preferred to establish rhythmic excitement by punching out notes in irregular rhythmic patterns. He was a true iconoclast. He said 'he wanted to play music that people could hum', and many of his themes were like the simplest of folk themes, or rudimentary nursery songs. Conversely he developed a rough, brutal sound on tenor-saxophone, and his re-pitching of standard tunes seemed to be decidedly unhummable.

In the last few years of his short life, Ayler was constantly trying to simplify his improvisations. He was encouraged by a record company to make recordings that harked back to his days in r-and-b bands but the disappointment was that these records contained many clichés that musicians with less imagination than Ayler would have avoided. Ayler remains an idiosyncratic part of the early free jazz movement; almost always he imbued his music with great vitality, but beneath this there seems a poignant, troubled melancholia. During the 1970s, Albert's brother Donald established himself as a bold experimentalist on trumpet.

Probably the most enigmatic figure in free jazz – or perhaps in any jazz era – is the bandleader-pianist known as Sun Ra. He began life as Herman Blount in Birmingham, Alabama, *circa* 1912. His early jazz interests were in the big bands led by Fletcher Henderson and Duke Ellington. He eventually settled in Chicago and began playing with such jazz luminaries as Coleman Hawkins and Stuff Smith; for a time he played piano in Fletcher Henderson's Band while the leader conducted.

Early in the 1950s, Sun Ra, as the pianist now chose to be called (taking his name from an Egyptian God), augmented the quartet he was leading into a big band, which he called The Arkestra. It was one of the first, if not the first, regularly assembled big bands to explore the possibilities of free improvisation. The musicians adopted a life style that pre-dated that of rock groups. They rehearsed and experimented with their music in commune, under the stern direction of Sun Ra, who composed many of the themes that they worked on. At one point during these musical conclaves, Sun Ra announced to a sceptical jazz world that the music that he and his sidemen-disciples were making was being transmitted to them from outer space. A little later he said that it was 'inter-galactical' music. Several important free jazz musicians had become deeply involved in esoteric philosophies, but this, in the parlance of the 1960s, was 'something else'.

Wherever Sun Ra's music comes from, it is seldom less than startling. His early recordings, which were issued in small numbers by obscure companies, sowed the seeds for the Sun Ra cult. Concerning one recorded in 1956, he said: 'My aim is to educate as many people as I can so far as the appreciation and enjoyment of good jazz is concerned.'[8] Sun Ra was accused of being a charlatan, but he achieved spectacular success in producing a cohesion of intention among his musicians, some of whom, like John Gilmore, Pat Patrick and Marshall Allen, stayed with him for over twenty years. Saxophonist Marion Brown, an eminent performer himself, said of Sun Ra that he was greater than Stravinsky or Bartok.

Sun Ra's publicity became more bizarre in the 1960s. Wearing gold lamé head-gear, which he described as an Egyptian space helmet, he directed his fifteen-piece band (which usually featured five percussionists, and a whole team of dancers) with success at many venues throughout the world. The most appropriate description of Sun Ra's Arkestra presentations came from German critic, Ekkehard Jost, who said they contained 'the pomposity of a latter-day Paul Whiteman, combined with the blues power of a Chicago Jump Band'.[9] The histrionics tended to detract from the merit that Sun Ra's innovatory efforts deserved. He had created some unusual new voicings for saxophone sections; he was among the first jazz group leaders to encourage his musicians to use electronics (one of his sidemen was featured on an electric bass in 1956) and, later, he became an early advocate for the synthesiser (a sophisticated electronic device for producing musical notes). He also urged all his musicians to play percussion instruments so that they could play counter-rhythms alongside the regular drummers. Who can say what the effect would have been had he simply said that his music came out of black America, rather than from outer space. In the mid-1970s, Sun Ra's solo piano playing at an American Festival moved many of those who had come to mock.

Both Miles Davis and Charlie Mingus were often inactive during the 1960s due to ill health. When they did appear in public, or made records, they still exerted an influence over imaginative young musicians. When Davis was in good health he undertook international touring, and was particularly successful in Japan. His band gave wide exposure to several young jazz musicians who became famous in the 1970s, including drummer Tony Williams, whose stupendous technique and rhythmic adventurousness took him into Davis's Band at the age of seventeen. Other young sidemen were pianist Herbie Hancock, bassist Ron Carter and saxophonist Wayne Shorter. As the sixties ended, Miles seemed to be increasingly engrossed in effecting a musical marriage between jazz and rock music. His interest in the new possibilities was commendable but unfortunately it had a dramatic effect on the lucidity of his improvisations. He tended to play only sporadically, leaving huge gaps in his solos. By adding an electronic device to his trumpet he changed a once unique sound into something which seemed to replicate a twanging guitar. Even so, the recordings sold well, and like all of Miles Davis's earlier recordings, they had a 'time-bomb effect' in stimulating young players.

Inspiration came to Charles Mingus from many sources but three were vital, and ever-present in his work during the 1960s: gospel music, the blues and the work of Duke Ellington. Mingus made no secret of his admiration for early jazz composers. In some ways, the verbal shouting, the semi-hokum interludes, and the beautiful coalescing of the timbre of various instruments, which were featured on Mingus's recordings, reflected his liking for Jelly Roll Morton, who had used these effects in the 1920s. The interludes where Mingus urged his entire band to improvise simultaneously were early landmarks in the history of free jazz. Mingus's encouragement of individuality was praised by John Handy III, who played alto-saxophone in one of the bassist's bands: 'He urged me to play whatever came into my head, and to stop falling back on Charlie Parker as a crutch.'[10] The same player shared Mingus's eclectic approach: 'Mingus and I got along together so well musically. It's very necessary to know the history and be able to play a reasonable amount in all idioms. If they laugh at blues, I think they're showing their stupidity. The blues are very beautiful, very valid, and very necessary.'

The emphasis in this chapter on the emergence of free jazz is not meant to indicate that the creation of other sorts of jazz (traditional, mainstream and bop) completely ceased during the 1960s. On the contrary, Mingus's idol, Duke Ellington, was consistently busy and creative throughout the decade. He continued widespread touring throughout Europe, the Near and Middle East, Japan, Australia and South America, presenting new works that were inspired by his travels. The death in 1967 of composer Billy Strayhorn, who had been Duke's closest writing-associate since 1939, greatly affected Ellington, but he continued to produce music of amazing breadth. Many of the musicians who travelled with Ellington in the late 1960s had been with him for over thirty years, and even the so-called youngsters of the band, like the highly individual tenor-saxophonist Paul Gonsalves, were approaching twenty years' service. The loyalty of the musicians was a tribute to the creative genius of an employer, whose talent seemed inexhaustible. Cecil Taylor summarised the entire jazz world's feelings about that remarkable, composer, band-leader and pianist: 'There's one constant, Duke Ellington.'

Louis Armstrong also undertook rigorous itineraries during the 1960s and his globe-trotting earned him the honorary title of Ambassador Satch (Satch being a variant on Louis's early nick-name Satchelmouth). Most of the music played at concerts by his six piece All-Star unit consisted of material that had been part of Armstrong's programmes for some years, but the power and inspiration with which he re-introduced these numbers continually won him new admirers. The obvious showmanship and well-drilled comedy routines of the All Stars irritated some critics, but Louis never let stagecraft ploys restrict the emotional content of his playing or singing.

After a period of well-paid semi-obscurity, playing mainly in clubs, Louis's ex-colleague, pianist Earl Hines, stepped back into the limelight during the mid-1960s. A 1966 tour of Russia marked the beginning of a decade of ceaseless activity at concerts and festivals all over the world. Benny Goodman also took his band to Russia in the 1960s. Goodman toured Europe on several occasions in the 1960s and 1970s; on some visits, he brought only a few key musicians, and recruited the rest of his personnel in Europe – a sure sign that transatlantic standards were rising. Because of the increase in international offers of work for American jazzmen, European, Japanese or Australasian local musicians could learn directly from the Americans without leaving their own country. Arranger–composer George Russell, who played a big part in educating musicians in the techniques of modal improvisation, found many eager pupils when he moved temporarily to Scandinavia. From the mid-1950s onwards, many jazz groups from America toured Africa, some of these tours being sponsored by the American Government.

Several American exponents of free jazz, finding that the reaction to their music overseas was consistently more encouraging than in their homeland, moved abroad. The standard of musicianship had risen to the point where the visitors' accompanists were not only keen and willing, but also able and inventive. Some of the more brilliant European jazz musicians made their way to America and joined groups that were the best of their kind in the world. The travellers included pianist Joe Zawinul from Austria, who was with Julian Adderley's group from 1961 until 1970, and British bassist Dave Holland, who joined Miles Davis as soon as he reached New York. Another European bassist, Denmark's Neils-Henning Orsted Pedersen, had such a reputation with American jazz musicians that he could, when he felt like it, commute to and from Copenhagen for recordings in the USA.

Both Holland and Pedersen specialised on string-bass, an instrument which lost some popularity in the 1960s to the electrically amplified bass-guitar, a solid creation that was soundless when not amplified. During that decade, an increasing number of instruments used in jazz were being amplified by a direct electronic attachment. Many of the experiments were dismissed as gimmickry, but if the amplified instrument was in the right hands the effects it produced could enhance some numbers, as the veteran saxophonist Sonny Stitt was one of the first to prove.

However, the timbre of an instrument, no matter how skilfully it is projected, artificially or otherwise, is only one factor of jazz. The most important aspect is the musical line that the improviser creates. Many young jazz musicians, wary of the encroachment of mechanically aided techniques, became increasingly interested in the methods that Oriental musicians used in their improvisations. The Indian master-musician, sitar-player Ravi Shankar, was listened to and admired by a wide circle of jazzmen. Early in the 1960s, a West-Indian, alto-saxophonist Joe Harriott, had experimented spasmodically with an Indo-Jazz fusion in Britain without achieving a significant breakthrough. In 1968, Shankar himself gave his views on the free jazz movement: 'I have heard enough of the new thing . . . it is a very tortured and disturbed sound.'[11]

The harshness and restlessness of the new music accurately reflected the troubled 1960s in musical form. It mirrored black people's disappointments and frustrations. Many senior jazzmen, and the majority of those interested in earlier jazz, only gave the new style a cursory hearing. Nevertheless, free jazz developed and the improvisations of many young musicians throughout the world began to reflect its revolutionary sounds.

Recommended Reading

Cole, Bill *John Coltrane* (A study of Coltrane's music, life and ideals), Schirmer, USA, 1976

Ellington, Duke *Music is My Business* (Autobiography), Doubleday, USA, 1973

Ellington, M. and Dance, S. *Duke Ellington in Person* (A son's biography), Hutchinson, London, 1978

Hawes, Hampton and Asher, D *Raise Up Off Me* (A portrait of pianist Hampton Hawes), Coward, McCann and Geoghegan, USA, 1974

Jewell, Derek *Duke* (A portrait of Duke Ellington), Elm Tree Books, London, 1977

Jones, Leroi *Black Music* (Essays on jazz of the 1960s), William Morrow, USA, 1967

McRae, Barry *Jazz Cataclysm* (A summary of post-bop jazz), A. S. Barnes, USA, 1967

Simosko, V. and Tepperman, B. *Eric Dolphy* (A musical biograph and discography), Smithsonian Institute, USA, 1974

Simpkins, C. O. *Coltrane* (A biography), Herndon House, USA, 1975

Spellman, A. B. *Four Lives in the Bebop Business* (A detailed study of the life-styles, works and aims of Ornette Coleman, Herbie Nicholas, Jackie McLean and Cecil Taylor), Pantheon Books, USA, 1966

Thomas, J. C. *Chasin' the Trane* (The music and mystique of John Coltrane), Doubleday, USA, 1975

Williams, Martin *Jazz Masters in Transition 1957–69* (Essays of the leading jazzmen of the post-bop period), Macmillan, USA, 1970

Wilson, John S. *Jazz – The Transition Years 1940–60* (A summary of two decades of jazz), Appleton Century, USA, 1966

13 Theory (3) an outline of modal jazz, and the principles of free jazz playing

During the 1950s collective improvisation again became a feature of small-band jazz, and many contemporary groups became obsessed with the possibilities of improvised counterpoint. It was not the pulsating, intense polyphony of early jazz, which sometimes tended to ignore harmonic rules, but a more formal contrapuntal style, closer to Johann Sebastian Bach than to King Oliver. This was not surprising, considering that many of the young jazz practitioners of the 1950s had been students of formal European music.

The fascination with European classical music also led musicians to experiment with the possibilities of improvising in different time signatures – using five beats to each bar, or three beats, or any number. Superimposed time signatures were also utilised. This meant the simultaneous use of two or more rhythmic pulses: a soloist might be playing four beats to each bar while his accompanists were playing rhythm that emphasised three beats in each bar. Benny Carter, Fats Waller and others had improvised in 3/4 (waltz-time) during the 1930s, but no pre-1950 jazz groups experimented in 5/4 (five beats to the bar). The use of this time signature in jazz was introduced to the general public in 1959 by Dave Brubeck with his huge selling record 'Take Five'. Max Roach and Leonard Feather had premiered earlier works in 5/4, but it was Brubeck who showed the masses that they could tap their feet to jazz even though there were an uneven number of beats in each bar.

Stravinsky is the classical composer who has most consistently interested jazz musicians. Bix Beiderbecke was fascinated by the *Firebird Suite*, and Coleman Hawkins said that the composer's work had played an important part in his musical education. During the 1950s, when interest in atonal jazz was growing, Stravinsky's *Petrushka* (written in 1911), was often cited as an inspiring example of how two keys could be implied simultaneously. It was Stravinsky's use of harmonies rather than rhythms which interested jazz musicians; in 1946, when the composer wrote 'Ebony Concerto' for Woody Herman's Orchestra, the results were monumentally disappointing.

A whole series of experimental orchestral works that attempted to link contemporary music with jazz were composed and premiered during the 1950s and early 1960s. The general name for these hybrid liaisons was Third Stream Music. During the same era, a number of young jazz musicians came to the conclusion that it was more satisfying to re-examine the roots of earlier jazz than to explore ideas that European composers had yawned over decades earlier. They felt there was a need to develop a form of collective improvisation that was not restricted by the polite familiarities of West Coast jazz. They wanted polyphony that combined the spirit and individuality of early jazz with modern developments and they found their champion in Charles Mingus.

The funk and soul movements grew alongside Mingus's work. Many soul tunes employed harmonies such as might be found in a Baptist hymn book. There was a particular emphasis on the chord progression that moved from the fourth note of the tonic scale on to the tonic (technically called a plagal cadence). In the key of C this would involve an F chord moving to a C chord. This return to more simplistic harmonies was achieved with a degree of slickness, and the high-lighting of insistent rhythms, constructed in easily repeatable patterns which greatly appealed to dancers. Soul music sounded particularly effective when played on the organ, and during the 1950s a large number of players who specialised on electric organ came to the fore, including Jimmy Smith, Bill Davis, Bill Doggett, Shirley Scott and Richard Holmes. Many electric organists worked unaccompanied. They provided their own bass notes (similar to those played by a double-bass) by manipulating foot pedals.

The most decisive jazz development of the 1950s came from a series of recordings made by Miles Davis. Literally ten years after he had formulated the guidelines of a new jazz style he again instigated highly effective ideas for new methods of improvising. He stopped using complicated chords and instead based his solos on modes similar to those used by the Ancient Greeks. He did this at a time when many bop musicians were beginning to feel that extended chords had become so complex they were restricting a soloist's ideas. An improviser interpreting the harmonies of a chord containing seven or eight notes could easily end up by simply playing (up and down) the notes of the chord, creating something that sounded more like a printed exercise than an impassioned solo.

Centuries before the devising, and adoption, of the major and minor scales which formed the basis of all European compositions from *circa* 1600, there existed a highly organised system of note patterns called modes, typical examples being shown in figure seventeen.

During the late 1950s, Miles Davis made increasing use of the modes in his improvisations. Sometimes he included modal interludes in what were otherwise orthodox chord-observing performances, but gradually he abandoned the use of popular songs for his improvisations and concentrated on modal themes. Improvisations based on the playing (up and down) of chordal patterns became known as 'vertical' improvisations, while solos based on scalic-patterns, or modes, became known as 'horizontal' or 'linear'. During the 1960s, the horizontal approach became increasingly popular.

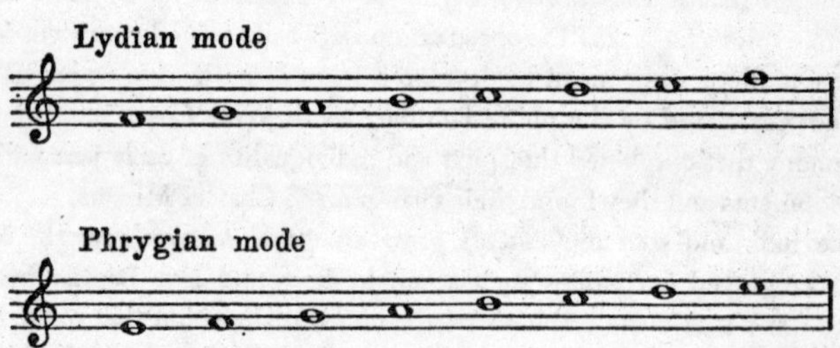

Figure 17 The Lydian and Phrygian modes

Davis not only changed his method of improvisation, he also changed the actual sound of his trumpet playing, which became even more vocalised. He also began doubling on the flugelhorn, and was largely responsible for its subsequent popularity. The flugelhorn has the general shape of a fat trumpet with a large bell; it uses the same three-valve system and tuning but its wider tubings gives it a mellower sound than the trumpet. It was used occasionally in the 1930s, but it was Davis's individual prowess which showed hosts of players the instrument's possibilities. Clark Terry, Art Farmer, and later, Chuck Mangione, all became master players on the instrument, and by the 1970s it had developed into the standard 'doubling' instrument for trumpeters.

Ornette Coleman's development of new concepts of jazz improvisation coincided with Davis's explorations, but he used a vastly different, more revolutionary approach. The angry reactions that greeted Charlie Parker's initial forays into the jam sessions were like shouts of welcome compared to what greeted Ornette Coleman's early attempts to share a bandstand with established jazz musicians.

> 'I remember once,' he told writer Michael Bourne in 1973, 'I was in California with Clifford Brown, Max Roach, Kenny Drew, and I think it was Sonny Rollins on tenor sax. I asked them to let me sit in, this was in the early 1950s, and they started playing "Donna Lee" and "Back Home in Indiana". I knew the changes and I started playing along, and finally I couldn't play, because I didn't want to stay on that same pattern. So I started playing the way I'm playing to-day. And they walked off the bandstand on me.'[1]

This reaction became typical for some while, for Coleman's method of free improvisation was revolutionary. All previous jazz styles had featured the improviser playing within a framework of harmony and rhythm: he utilised the chord sequence of the tune, and constructed his solo in units that lasted as long as individual choruses of the melody. Free jazz dispenses with both restrictions; the accompanying chords need not be adhered to, and there are no enforced measurements of solo time. If a soloist feels like playing a solo for half a minute, or for half an hour, then that is his prerogative. The free jazz player continues until he feels that he has expressed himself. He then plays a pre-arranged motif that tells his colleagues that the solo is about to conclude. Sound, mood and energy became more important criteria than adherence to musical formalities and rules.

For a time it seemed that the words free jazz and Ornette Coleman were synonymous, but there were in fact several other practitioners of free playing in the late 1950s. By the mid-1970s, the term free jazz spanned the work of many dissimilar stylists, the one description covering all of their work. Early jazz had also suffered from a restricting nomenclature. It was talked of as being a single stylistic approach, but people who used the expression as a blanket term for jazz of the 1920s often forgot that it covered sounds as disparate as the dainty cornet playing of Red Nichols and the rasping earthy work of trombonist Ike Rodgers.

Coleman's early career was filled with a restlessness which resulted from being confined to set-length choruses, and having to observe established key signatures (which meant he regularly had to return to a musical base – the tonic chord). He devised a style of improvising that by-passed these restrictions. He defined his intentions and method by saying that each and every one of the notes that he could play on his alto-saxophone had a separate, non-connected, existence – each could be played in any order, in any rhythmic pattern. Coleman totally rejected the long-established jazz practice of improvising on popular songs. He said: 'I think basically that I try to stay with the traditional concept of being an improviser without having to rely upon Tin Pan Alley structures.' (Tin Pan Alley was being used here as a general term for the publishers of popular songs.) Coleman felt that improvising on popular songs of the twentieth century automatically brought restrictions since so many of them were constructed on similar harmonic patterns. He suggested that the main failing of bop was that most of its themes and harmonies (and the improvisations on them) were too closely connected with commercially contrived material. He spoke of John Coltrane as 'the most successful instrumentalist of all', but he also said, of Coltrane's record albums, that 'most of them were filled with Tin Pan Alley songs'.[2]

Coleman does not base his improvisations on harmonic progressions, nor does he believe in the musical rules that apply to formal European music.

However, he often temporarily grants a particular note a place of eminence in his improvised phrases, which seems to become almost a tonal centre (similar to establishing a key signature); but this note is peremptorily discarded and replaced by another axis note which in turn is swiftly replaced. None of these developments are announced by a modulatory passage (indicating that the key is being changed) which was thought essential in previous forms of jazz. Coleman said: 'I believe freedom is totally unmagnetised by harmony or melodic line. To me, free is not a style. It's a personal ability. Playing free is not having to have a style.'[3]

Coleman's idea that each individual note that he played had its own character also allowed for the possibility that the character of each of those notes changed in different circumstances. The note A played in a slow ballad might take on dissimilar tonal qualities when used in a dynamically exciting passage. The player would deliberately attempt to project an entirely different sound, even if he used exactly the same fingering on both occasions.

Analysing Coleman's note selection on the previously established method of summarising jazz solos by chords, we hear that he might start using a G note as a tonal centre, but suddenly this G becomes the third note of a newly created tonal centre (in chord symbol language he moved from a G chord to an E flat chord). This move is transitory and the original G now becomes the seventh note of a passage in the key of A. The whole effect means that no hard-and-fast key note (or home base) is ever established. Within one part of a solo, lasting for perhaps thirty seconds, a free soloist might well use ten different tonal centres. This requires extremely quick aural reactions from the other musicians in the unit, who have to listen intently to the soloist's line of improvisation in order to follow him through the complex patterns.

Such a revolutionary as Coleman must have aides. Billy Higgins and Edward Blackwell were two important drummers who often worked with Ornette Coleman and Don Cherry and both provided sympathetic, but exciting percussion sounds that complemented, rather than accompanied, the wind-players' improvised lines. Blackwell, from New Orleans, provided a discernible link between heritage and modernity. He was as technically adventurous as any of his colleagues, but he also respected the drum sounds that had previously been created by Baby Dodds, Paul Barbarin and Zutty Singleton.

For decades, jazz drummers had indicated the important landmarks of a tune's contours by playing rhythmic phrases that signified the end of the first eight bars, the end of the second eight bars, etc. On a blues sequence they always marked the beginning of a new twelve-bar chorus. Drummers in free jazz had no need to concentrate on this system of rhythmic punctuation; they devoted their entire attention to linking their playing to the shifting ideas of the soloist. The freedom allowed them to provide 'straight pulse without number' leaving the rhythmic field entirely open.

Bassists who worked with Ornette Coleman found that they too were expected to join the front-line as a deep-voiced melody instrument rather than act as providers of metronomic rhythm patterns. Charlie Haden, bassist with Coleman's group when it first went to New York in 1959, said:

> 'Technically speaking it was a constant modulation in the improvising . . . I learned more about listening, playing with Ornette, than I ever learned in my life from anyone, because to play with him you have to listen completely to everything he plays, every note he plays; sometimes he modulates from two and three keys at a time to other keys.'[4]

Jimmy Garrison, the bassist who followed Haden into Coleman's group, stressed the educational possibilities of working with Coleman:

> 'I came up in the bebop school, so working with Ornette certainly changed my way of thinking about music, and approaching the instrument. Ornette wanted the bass to be part of the front-line. When I joined the group, that's where I stood – right between Ornette and the trumpet. Knowing that any note can be part of a whole spectrum you train yourself to think in that manner; as a result you come up with melodies you didn't know existed.'[5]

The technical dexterity of string-bassists improved enormously during the 1960s. Ideas that had been thought startlingly difficult to perform, like producing chords by improvising simultaneously on two or more strings, became almost commonplace. Some groups chose to use two bassists, one as a rhythm-maker, the other for providing low-register tonal effects.

Lennie Tristano's group of musicians were among the first jazz musicians to attempt free improvisations. As early as 1949, they made a recording (called 'Intuition') in which none of the participants were forewarned about the key, the chords, or the tempo of the piece; they were to rely on a mixture of telepathy and trained reaction. But these musicians were part of a clique who assembled regularly, and all of them had absorbed Tristano's methods. Within a second, mutuality and empathy guided them into contrapuntal patterns similar to those that they had played together before. One of the group, tenor saxophonist, Warne Marsh, looked back during the 1970s on this period: 'In the 1940s, Lennie, Lee Konitz and I experimented with playing free music, and I think our first attempts were the most successful, the more we played the more difficult it seemed to be.'[6]

Bassist Charles Mingus was a true pioneer of what became known as free jazz, but as a bandleader he chose to use the style as a part of his presentations, rather than as a method that affected everything he and his sidemen improvised on. Alto-saxophonist Jackie McLean spoke of a revealing experience that occurred while he was working with Mingus: 'I turned to Charlie one night when he taught me a new tune and asked, "What are the chord changes?" He said there were no chord changes. I asked "What key am I in?" He said "You're not in any key".'[7]

Mingus was a devout eclectic. The roots of his music can be found in Gospel hymns, Mexican carnival music, the sound of a New Orleans street parade, the solos of Charlie Parker and Fats Navarro, and the compositions of Ravel, and of Jelly Roll Morton. Mingus's classical training endowed him with the compositional technique to blend seemingly alien music styles. In doing this he produced exciting jazz themes, on which veterans and youngsters could create inspired improvisations side by side. He rarely wrote out a fully arranged part for his musicians. Usually he taught them aurally by playing the composition to them on the piano, explaining the mood of the piece and the emotions that he wanted conveyed to the listeners. Thus the players are able to reflect the composer's feelings, not only in their solos, but also in the improvised ensembles.

These 'jazz workshops', as they became known, brought to mind the interaction of an early New Orleans ensemble. Mingus deliberately chose soloists who came from widely differing musical backgrounds; a rugged blues specialist like tenor-saxophonist Booker Ervin might play alongside a light-toned musician who was principally interested in modern European music. Mingus welded these disparates together, and continually stimulated his musicians' interests by introducing sudden changes of tempo, and linking together unlikely sound combinations. Dozens of future jazz stars passed through his bands, the one constant being drummer Dannie Richmond. The bonus in listening to a Mingus group is to hear the leader's own contribution on string-bass. Long recognised as a virtuoso, he was capable of projecting dozens of varying tonal effects, ranging from gentle flamenco-like guitar sounds, to something that is akin to the thunderous roll of a kettle-drum. He was also a magnificent, orthodox, four-in-the-bar bassist.

Saxophonist John Coltrane was also a true virtuoso, with an instrumental technique that was prodigious. Through recordings, his career can be followed right from his days as a bop player. Some of these early efforts were captured on 'air shots' which are tape recordings taken from concerts and radio shows, and not recorded in a studio. Whenever the young Coltrane was given the opportunity to extend a solo beyond one chorus he always experimented, and the glimmerings of his future style show through.

By the mid-1950s, Coltrane, like many other young jazzmen, was finding that the extended bop chords were becoming rigidly systematic. The set-pattern chords, and the pre-destined chorus lengths seemed increasingly restrictive. A flight of imagination which might have taken the soloist away from the established confines had to be disregarded, no matter how tempting the prospect. Inevitably, players with sufficient imagination sought ways of playing jazz that by-passed the restrictions. John Coltrane was among their vanguard. Unlike Ornette Coleman, Coltrane did not sweep away all the previous rules; he saw freedom in improvisation as offering the soloist the choice of improvising on many differing musical systems; European, African and Asian.

Listening to Coltrane's early recordings with Miles Davis, one becomes aware that he is improvising in a way that no saxophonist had ever tried before. His very sound seems different. Basically he had started his professional life as a big-toned player, using a sound that had been originally created by Coleman Hawkins. Latterly he developed a way of projecting notes that was startingly energetic, like a hoarse, passionate shout. This sound was soon known as the 'angry tone'. Coltrane's instrumental range was superlative (he had direct tuition from Earl Bostic, a master of high-note saxophone playing) and his control in the extreme register allowed him to improvise freely on the high notes, playing them with great strength. But it is the shape and content of the man's phrases rather than their power that made his work so individual.

In 1958, Miles Davis's Sextet, which included Coltrane, recorded a piece called 'Milestones'. It did not have a chord sequence but, instead, it was structured in two distinct sections, each employing a different mode. The first section used the Dorian Mode as the basis for the improvisations as shown in figure eighteen.

Figure 18 The Dorian mode

The second section, which continually alternated with the first section, used the Aeolian mode as in figure nineteen.

Figure 19 The Aeolian mode

For Coltrane it was the perfect occasion to implement ideas that he had been developing. Modal playing was only one aspect of his extensive studies. He was particularly engrossed by the use of harmonics, which are the overtones that ring off any musical note. Besides the initial vibrations of the fundamental note, a whole series of vibrations occur which produce subsidiary notes at a higher pitch. These are called harmonics. Most of the time no direct attention is paid to them and we automatically ignore the subsidiary sounds and concentrate on listening to the note from which they emanate. A simple experiment will make any listener directly aware of them.

If a low C (figure twenty) is played on a piano with the sustaining-pedal

Figure 20

pushed down, a whole pattern of higher notes will form as soon as the vibrations emanating from the initial note reach the other strings on the piano. The striking of the first note thus produces waves of sound. Analysed, these overtones, as they are called, are as shown in figure twenty-one.

Figure 21 Harmonics

Coltrane's well-developed musical ear, and his control of the higher register of his saxophone, enabled him to include the extreme harmonics in his improvisations, no matter how fast the tempo. Coltrane's rigorous practice schedule developed his technique to virtuoso standards. During his early professional days he could play Charlie Parker solos note-for-note at extreme speed; ten years later his playing was considerably faster. He said: 'I found there were a certain number of chord progressions to play in a given time, and sometimes what I played didn't work out in eight notes [eight notes in a bar], or sixteenth notes, or triplets [three linked notes of equal value]. I had to put the notes in uneven groups like fives and sevens in order to get them all in.'[8] Coltrane was constantly striving to achieve both bi-tonality (whereby a phrase could have more than one key note) and advanced polyrhythmic playing (where two or more time signatures, or pulses, were simultaneously operative).

He commented on his work with Miles Davis:

> 'Miles was once interested in chords for their own sakes, but now it seemed that he was moving in the opposite direction, using tunes with fewer chord changes, and free-flowing melodic lines. This approach

allows the soloist the choice of playing chordally [vertically] or melodically [horizontally]. I now found it easier to apply the harmonic ideas that I had. I could stack up chords – say on a C seventh, I sometimes super-imposed an E flat seventh up to an F sharp seventh down to an F. That way I could play three chords on one.'[9]

All these notes might cascade out within the space of four beats. It was comparable to an ingenious system of hyphenating loosely connected words into intricate coherent sentences. The effect, however, was not totally cerebral, sometimes the notes would explode with all the vigour of an African kraal song.

Coltrane, like many other saxophonists of the 1960s, was ceaselessly experimenting with the possibilities of playing more than one note at a time, he said: 'Monk was one of the first to show me how to make two or three notes at one time on tenor. It's done by false fingering and adjusting your lips, and if it's done right you get triads.' This was a complete breakthrough, for it enabled one wind instrumentalist to blow simultaneously the three notes of a chord. Like many other innovations in jazz, it is impossible to say who was the first player to perfect the idea. Several trombonists also worked along similar lines, producing more than one note at a time. In the 1970s, Dewey Redman introduced a dramatic effect into the repertoire of saxophone sounds by singing notes in his throat that were of a different pitch to those he was playing on his instrument.

By 1960, John Coltrane was doubling on soprano-saxophone, showing a technique that was even more impressive than his playing of the larger, easier to play, tenor model. The soprano-saxophone is notoriously difficult to play in tune throughout its registers but, by endless practice and self-determination, Coltrane overcame the technical problems. In his hands it seemed capable of producing many tone colours, some reminiscent of an oboe, others of an Indian shenai. He could even coax an imitation of a bagpipe chanter from it.

Coltrane was a self-doubting perfectionist, who was continually trying to broaden the scope of his improvisations by analysing non-jazz music forms. At one time his prime interest was in modal music. Then followed a period in which he undertook intensive studies of Indian *ragas* and this stimulated an analysis of Balinese music. For a time it seemed as though Eastern music would become the most important factor in Coltrane's music; he began using two string-bass players simultaneously, to create the droning effect of an Indian *tamboura*. But his 1961 recording 'Chasing The Trane' showed another area of inspiration, being a blues-type composition which contained Debussy-like phrases. By the mid-1960s, his improvisations were a compound of African rhythms and tones, European classicism, and Oriental music.

In 1960, Ornette Coleman had organised a recording session which featured two separate groups playing against, with, and for each other at different moments. It was, in effect, a complex free jazz debate, not between individual musicians but between two groups of musicians. In 1965, as Coltrane moved nearer to the centre of the free jazz movement, he too organised a large gathering of young musicians in the recording studio, all of whom were active in the new music. They included Marion Brown and John Tchicai on alto-saxophones, Dewey Johnson and Freddie Hubbard on trumpets, Pharoah Sanders and Archie Shepp on tenor-saxophones. Coltrane also took part in the recording, as did his regular musicians McCoy Tyner on piano, Elvin Jones on drums and Art Davis and Jimmy Garrison on string-basses.

The work that the ensemble recorded was called 'Ascension', and it was to prove one of the most influential releases of the decade. It alternated between two modes (the Phrygian and the Aeolian); the transition between them was made dramatic by the simultaneous use of rhythmic changes. The piece showed how masterfully Coltrane could steer a large ensemble of collective improvisers into musical areas that produced dense tone colours, and by his own exciting example encouraged the players to attempt continual rhythmic interplay.

In the last two years of his life, Coltrane paid increasing attention to the exploration of tone colours within his group, occasionally featuring a gong, cowbells, and an African tintinnabular *zanza*. Often he played bass-clarinet and flute alongside his new colleague Pharoah Sanders, who played most of the woodwind family. When the two men duetted it was not like a jam-session 'carving match'; it was more a dialogue in which each musician's role was to contribute sounds that had a different 'vocal' quality to his partner's phrases. Latterly, Coltrane also created an effect that resembled a musical dialogue with himself. He would switch from the top register of his instrument to the bottom notes with great speed, going restlessly back and forth, playing counter motifs that seemed to hark back to the African call-and-answer tradition.

Coltrane's erstwhile sideman Eric Dolphy was just as eclectic as his leader. He was ever-willing to look in any direction for musical ideas. Sometimes he attempted to imitate the songs of birds on his flute or saxophone, pointing out that they contained many graduations of pitch more minute than the smallest measurement in European music, which is a semitone. He stressed that Indian fretted instruments allowed players to include in their improvisations many intervals that were a quarter of a tone apart, or less. Dolphy firmly believed that the incorporation of these graduations of pitch would widen the dimensions of jazz improvisations. During the 1970s there was an ever-increasing interest in the jazz usage of these microtones, as they are called.

During the 1960s, composer Gunther Schuller contended that Sonny Rollins added 'new dimensions to jazz improvisation, chiefly by using the technique of thematic variations'.[10] The format of early jazz featured the statement of a theme followed by each soloist's variations, but the restrictions imposed by the short-playing records often allows us only an inkling of a player's potential.

With greatly increased time at his disposal, coupled with an extremely fertile musical imagination, Rollins developed a style that regularly demonstrated his powers of thematic development. He would often return to a phrase that had been formed early on in his solo, and develop this into an impressive variation. Then this variation would itself become a secondary theme, liable to development. Rollins was an architect of jazz themes, and presented his improvisations with a combination of musical logic and passionate creativity. His was a reverse procedure to that used by some jazz soloists who present their listeners with a swiftly changing succession of fragmentary ideas, rather like a 'musical stream of consciousness'.

Often Rollins presented his variations unaccompanied. This was not an innovation as Coleman Hawkins recorded 'Picasso' unaccompanied in 1949. In contrast, Rollins' solos lasted for much longer, yet he rarely lost the listener's interest because of his strong respect for the main theme. For this reason, his duets with drummers were also highly popular, being sign-posted with reassuring references. During the 1960s he sometimes worked with players who were heavily involved in free jazz, but he never became a mainstay of the movement himself. Though a major influence more on the jazz of the 1960s than of the 1970s, he remains one of the most vibrant figures in the music.

The majority of the leading figures in the development of free music have been saxophonists: Ornette Coleman, John Coltrane, Eric Dolphy, Albert Ayler, Archie Shepp, Jackie McLean and Anthony Braxton. Pianist Cecil Taylor and trumpeter Don Cherry are two major exceptions.

Don Cherry's role in the early 1960s was that of a subsidiary partner to Ornette Coleman, occupying a position that was similar to the part Miles Davis played on the early recordings with Charlie Parker. But, as the 1960s passed, Cherry was increasingly recognised as an innovator in his own right. He was usually featured playing a small 'pocket' trumpet (each part made in miniature). In his latter-day improvisations he has made regular use of the modal scales that form the basis of Arabic and Turkish music. He has also developed an interest in Indian *ragas* and Indian plain song, learning various Oriental instruments, and transferring nuances of their sounds first into his trumpet work, then into his compositions. He continually strives to bring the sounds and rhythms of the Third World into jazz. In the mid-1970s there was increasing evidence that the free jazz movement had two distinct sectors, one containing players who were continually experimenting with the potentials of the natural timbre of instruments, and the other having players whose principal interest was in using electronics to produce sound variations.

Pianist Cecil Taylor remains the most controversial of all contemporary free jazz players. He has occupied a position of eminence in the movement for over ten years, yet even the mere mention of his name can spark off a controversy. None of his performances links with existing jazz definitions, which his supporters say is due to the paucity of the language applied to today's improvisations. He consciously tries to amalgamate the technique and harmonies of modern European composers with the energy and rhythms of early Afro-American music. He has said: 'I have within my mind a conception of how Black Tom played'[11] (see chapter one). The frenzied tremolos and the swift parallel runs, where both hands move together at enormous speed, are juxtaposed with displays of astonishing ambidextrousness and mental agility which produce two completely independent musical lines. Note-clusters spill out with all the percussion of a drum roll. There is little to reassure listeners who wait for the sound of a simple motif. Taylor has been called the architect of sounds to come. His own hope is to make listeners aware that 'the thing that unites all is the developing of one's senses to respond to sound'. This could be the creed of the new generation of musicians emerging in the late 1970s who want to convey their emotions via improvised sound patterns without having to overcome the prejudices of listeners conditioned to accept only one particular school of jazz.

Recommended Reading

Buddes, Michael J. *Jazz in the Sixties* (An analysis of musical resources and techniques), University of Iowa Press, USA, 1978

Jost, Ekkehard *Free Jazz* (A lucid and well-written analysis of the work of the free jazz pioneers, complete with musical examples), Universal Editions, Vienna, 1975

Russell, George *The Lydian Concept of Tonal Organization for Improvisation* (An exposition of the potentials of tonal resources – suitable for those with a sound knowledge of musical theory), Concept Publishing, USA, 1959

14 Homogeneous jazz survives

Traditional jazz, mainstream, big bands, bop and free jazz all have their devotees; Avant garde musicians organise their own outlets by giving mini-concerts in lofts and studios; electronic instruments are used on many jazz recordings but conversely the interest in using ancient instruments in jazz grows; a fusion of jazz and pop develops; jazz groups with multi-national personnel thrive; jazz slowly becomes an international music.

During the 1970s, nostalgia played a big part in jazz listening – and in jazz record buying. Retrospection affected the appreciation of all styles, including free jazz, some of whose followers yearned for a recurrence of the drama that accompanied Ornette Coleman's first gladiatorial entrance into the jazz arena.

The ease of world-wide jet travel meant that jazz heroes of yesteryear, or in some cases, of past decades, were able to perform in person for their foreign fans with the minimum of inconvenience. Septuagenarian jazzmen from New Orleans did tours which spanned the Earth, astounding audiences with the vigour and charm of their music. Other jazz veterans, like drummer Tommy Benford, trumpeter Doc Cheatham, violinist Joe Venuti, and trombonist Clyde Bernhardt, all of whom had taken part in 'classic jazz' recordings during the mid-1920s, were internationally active fifty years later.

Several of the stars of Bob Crosby's band of the 1930s, including bassist Bob Haggart, trumpeters Yank Lawson and Billy Butterfield, and tenor-saxophonist Eddie Miller, played in a highly mobile group called The World's Greatest Jazz Band. In 1971, Dizzy Gillespie, Thelonious Monk, Art Blakey and Sonny Stitt, doyens of bop, took leave from their own groups and did a global tour that recaptured the spirit of the early 1940s' small bands.

In the USA, vocalist Dave Wilborn, an original member of one of the leading black big bands of the 1920s, became part of a successful *New* McKinney's Cotton Pickers. Several of the big bands originally formed in the Swing Era continued to work regularly, including those led by Count Basie, Woody Herman, Harry James, Stan Kenton, Lionel Hampton and Buddy Rich. Some of the musicians who made their names working in these bands such as Maynard

Ferguson, Louis Bellson (perhaps the most versatile of all drummers) and Gerald Wilson, were by the mid-1970s long established big band leaders themselves. Thad Jones and Mel Lewis co-led their own big band with great success. For big band jazz lovers, the biggest loss of the 1970s was the death of Duke Ellington in 1974. The Duke's last years were filled with accolades, and new odysseys, including a tour of Russia in 1971. After his death, his trumpet-playing son Mercer took over the band and continued to present Duke's music.

Quincy Jones, who led a big band in the 1960s, later consolidated his position as a leading composer of film and television themes, occasionally re-assembling a big touring band. A big band featuring trumpeters Pee Wee Erwin, Joe Newman, and Jimmy Maxwell, did extensive touring playing a programme that was a posthumous tribute to Louis Armstrong (who died in 1971). It featured Louis's solos orchestrated by Dick Hyman for a trumpet section playing in harmony. Supersax featured a similar idea; they had alto-saxophonist Med Flory leading a saxophone section that recreated Charlie Parker's solos. A small group known as Soprano Summit, featuring Bob Wilber and Kenny Davern on soprano-saxes, and clarinets, did much to remind listeners of Sidney Bechet's important role in shaping jazz. Even the pioneers of free jazz occasionally indulged in nostalgic get-togethers, as happened at the Newport Jazz Festival in 1977, when Ornette Coleman, Don Cherry and Dewey Redman enjoyed a creative reunion.

The spirit of the 1970s was more one of consolidation than of daring advances into a musical no-man's land. Jazz musicians who had been completely iconoclastic saw there was no shame in acknowledging tradition, and many players who had seemed set in styles that were derived from bop adopted a freer, less chord-bound approach to jazz improvisation, notably saxophonists Cecil Payne, Charlie Mariano and Art Pepper. As in past jazz history, New York and Chicago were the key centres of jazz developments. In both cities there existed established coteries of free jazz musicians who did not rely on the patronage of promoters, or of record companies, to present their music to the public. They did it themselves, by organising their own performance outlets in such unlikely venues as house-lofts, basement studios and disused warehouses.

In New York, the 'loft' scene as it became known, vaguely resembled the Harlem 'rent parties' of the 1920s, when people were charged admission to hear jazz in private surroundings so that the host, or the hostess, could raise money for the rent. In the 1970s the gatherings were organised by the musicians themselves; the money collected helped them to survive without having to compromise their music.

The term 'loft jazz' was first used in the early 1960s, but it was ten years before it became general jazz parlance. During that time, saxophonist-composer Sam Rivers established himself as one of the central figures in the movement;

in 1971, he opened his own studio to the public. Rivers gained wide experience in rhythm-and-blues bands, and in hard bop units, before working with Miles Davis, Andrew Hill, McCoy Tyner and Cecil Taylor. Rivers's playing reflects his concept that the free jazz of the 1970s should be a fusion of black jazz of the 1940s, 1950s and 1960s. He has commented on his eclecticism: 'People hear me playing the blues, and say – hey, you, shouldn't be doing this, you're an avant-garde such-and-such. And I guess I am. But I also do all the other things. I guess I was inspired by the freedom of Ornette Coleman. I probably would have been a traditionalist to-day, if it hadn't been for what somebody else did.'[1] Rivers has given his own cryptic view on the loft scene: 'The music here is based on a life-style, and that is black.'[2]

In the lofts there was much experimentation with the acoustics of exotic wind-instruments. The work of the percussionists was also full of exploration; drummers in free music, eager to try out new sound effects, incorporated ancient percussion instruments into their drum-kits, and paid extra attention to the tuning of their more recently manufactured accessories, spending hours tightening and slackening the stretch of the drum heads. The prominence of the drummer's role in jazz, which had developed throughout the hard bop era, became more sharply defined. Players like Milford Graves, Sunny Murray, Andrew Cyrille, Charles (Bobo) Shaw and Rashied Ali, created multi-directional rhythmic debates with their band partners. The idea that drummers should doggedly follow the front-line soloist's train of thought no longer applied. Some groups employed two percussionists, one to keep a pulse going, the other to embellish the ensemble with cohesive poly-rhythms. It was an atavistic move, as Milford Graves pointed out: 'Drummers had taken the drum too far from Africa.'[3]

Sam Rivers had a long wait for recognition, so too did Chicago pianist Muhal Richard Abrams. Abrams became a professional musician at eighteen and his wide experience in jazz is reflected in his playing, which shows traces of such diverse stylists as James P. Johnson and Bud Powell. Like Rivers, and most other important figures in free jazz, Abrams composes much of the material that he improvises on. His founding of the AACM (Association for the Advancement of Creative Musicians) in 1965 served to aid and guide many young Chicago musicians, including reed-player/composer Anthony Braxton, Roscoe Mitchell on reeds/percussion, Lester Bowie on trumpet/percussion, Leroy Jenkins, brilliantly innovative on violin, and percussionist Jack De Johnette. De Johnette symbolised the new status that drummers were accorded in the 1970s. In pre-bop days, a drummer who doubled on any other instrument was a rarity, a drummer who composed and arranged was less likely. By 1978, most young drummers were as well versed in musical theory as their fellow instrumentalists. De Johnette composed, arranged and performed adeptly on saxophone and piano.

Anthony Braxton, one of the early AACM members, felt that the word 'jazz' was an unsuitable description of free music, and preferred the use of the phrase 'creative music'. To expect one word to describe sounds as different as dixieland and hard bop was asking a lot, but 'jazz' is no more restrictive than the word 'literature'. Miles Davis concurred with Braxton's viewpoint. He said: 'I don't like the word jazz that white folks dropped on us.'[4]

Davis's playing opportunities were severely restricted after he was involved in a serious car crash in 1972. During the three-year period before that he had only recorded occasionally. The results of those sporadic sessions stirred controversy, for Davis seemed determinedly reluctant to let his improvised solos flow. Nevertheless, his presence seemed cataclysmic and the ability of young musicians who worked alongside Davis seemed to vault dramatically. Several of his sidemen became famous players of the 1970s, including drummer Billy Cobham, pianist Keith Jarrett, pianist Chick Corea and guitarist John McLaughlin. Miles himself gave a laconic explanation of his influence: 'Our music changes every month.' Davis also absorbed the music of his young sidemen. His ex-bassist Ron Carter dwelt on this: 'People often assume that everyone learns from Miles, but they never reverse the situation, that Miles learns from the players he hires.'[5] Davis's album 'Bitches Brew', made in 1969, inspired a spate of recordings featuring young jazz musicians' attempts to marry jazz solos to rock sounds and rhythms. This policy became an important feature of the widespread success of trumpeters Freddie Hubbard, Donald Byrd, and of the group Weather Report (featuring Joe Zawinal and Wayne Shoster) who chose their name to suggest that their music, like the weather, was ever-changing.

During the 1970s, many established jazz players incorporated electronics into their music-making. Synthesisers, transmitting electronic signals into audible sounds, became commonplace in live performances, as well as in recording studios. They fulfilled a dual role. They could create new tone colours, and they could be programmed to imitate the sounds of orthodox instruments. The early synthesisers had keyboards which were restricted to producing one note at a time but they were superseded by designs that could create chords. Electric pianos were often used in place of the traditional model, which was increasingly referred to as an 'acoustic piano'. In many groups it became standard procedure for the pianist to alternate between electric and acoustic pianos, as well as doubling on electric organ. A reaction occurred in the mid-1970s, when several leading keyboard players reverted to specialisation on acoustic pianos. Many new sound-making devices came into jazz via the world of 'popular' recordings. Giant record companies, ever eager to find new sounds that might boost record sales, gave pop musicians ample licence, and big advances in royalty monies, to experiment. Young jazz musicians incorporated any of these tone colours that seemed interesting.

The borrowing from pop was not one-sided – during the 1970s, several best-selling records were tinged with the jazz sounds of the 1960s. This followed an established pattern whereby new jazz ideas underwent a long incubation period before they reached the general public on popular records, or on film sound-tracks. This lease-lend of musical ideas became known as jazz–rock fusion, or simply 'cross-over'. Some groups like Chicago, and Blood Sweat and Tears, enjoyed the best of both musical worlds to such a degree that it was difficult to place them emphatically in one category or the other. One problem with the success of the fusion was that it placed several jazz musicians on a treadmill that was well known to those pop stars who *had* to find a successful follow-up album in order to survive. A few promising jazz groups disintegrated under the pressures of trying to please their record companies and devoted jazz fans.

An area of significant experimentation with fusions developed from the jazz musicians' quest for a deeper understanding of Asian, African, Middle-Eastern and South American music. Ex-John Coltrane pianist, McCoy Tyner, who has been cited by many musicians as being one of the most influential performers of the 1970s, summarised a growing open-mindedness among jazz players. They acknowledged the African-American basis of their music, but they also saw that future jazz might well be a conglomerate of musical influences from many parts of the world. Tyner visualises an improvised music based on sounds from 'Africa, India, good European classical music, anything'.[6] Some musicians were engrossed with the work of twentieth-century European composers. Pianist Roger Kellaway said: 'My influence doesn't come from jazz to-day, it comes from Stravinsky, Messiaen, and Varese.' Herbie Hancock's choice coincided, but he added the names of Stockhausen and John Cage.[7]

An interest in the music of India, which, for many jazz musicians was inspired originally by Ravi Shankar's sitar playing, developed for a minority into full-scale studies of the intricacies of the music of Northern and Southern India. British guitarist John McLaughlin, who emigrated to the USA in 1968, was involved enough to adopt the Indian name Mahavisnu for several years. During that period he defined his passionate interest by saying: 'Indian music uses pulse. Western music is either four beats in a bar, or total craziness.'[8]

A more broad-minded attitude to jazz instrumentation developed. The hide-bound convention that jazz performers had to be accompanied by a rhythm section was often ignored. Wind instrumentalists like Jimmy Giuffre, Sonny Rollins, Anthony Braxton, John Klemner and Roscoe Mitchell played concerts as solo artistes, as did violinist Leroy Jenkins (who also made records accompanied only by Rashied Ali on drums). Braxton performed with three other saxophonists without percussion. German trombonist Mangelsdorff was one of several brass-players who gave solo concerts. He, like a number of other trombonists, explored the possibilities of producing more than one note at a time by singing a harmony with the throat while blowing an ordinary note. For a time,

Mangelsdorff was also part of an interesting European group called Mumps, along with British saxophonist John Surman, and he also took part in a large international aggregation of free jazz musicians who appeared under the name of Globe Unity.

The long-held belief that the USA was the only country capable of producing world-class jazz improvisers gradually disappeared. During the ten-year period from 1965 to 1975, many jazz trend-setters emerged who were not born in the USA including pianist Jan Hammer from Czechoslovakia, violinist Jean-Luc Ponty from France, saxophonist Jan Gabarek from Norway, pianist Dollar Brand from South Africa, trumpeter Kenny Wheeler from Canada and guitarist Derek Bailey from England.

Tenor-saxophonist Leandro (Gato) Barbieri, from the Argentine, came to jazz prominence in the mid-1960s when he often worked with trumpeter Don Cherry. Subsequently, he became deeply involved in linking free jazz improvisations with the rhythms and form of South American music. He has spoken of his efforts to interrelate two ethnically dissimilar kinds of music: 'The rhythm comes from Africa; in Argentina, Chile, Bolivia and Peru the folk music is more from Indian origins.'[9]

Prejudice against female jazz players diminished in the 1970s. In the 1940s, Toshiko, Marian McPartland, Beryl Booker and Melba Liston were rarities: women who earned their living playing jazz. They followed on from the female jazz-pioneers of the 1920s, Lil Hardin, Lovie Austin and Mary Lou Williams, all of whom were piano-players, arrangers and composers. Musicians reminiscing about those early days sometimes speak of female brass and saxophone players who were fine jazz players; they could not, however, work professionally because of sexual discrimination. Happily, by the 1970s these restrictions had all but disappeared and many women, including the outstanding composer-pianist Carla Bley, were able to contribute to jazz unimpeded by archaic custom.

Jazz educational facilities improved greatly during the 1970s, particularly in the USA. In 1975, Charles Suber, publisher of the magazine *Down Beat*, estimated that there were 500 000 part-time students of music in the USA, and a good proportion of them specialised in jazz. An increasing number of jazz musicians became part of the teaching faculties at colleges, including Mary Lou Williams, trumpeter Bill Dixon, saxophonist Jimmy Lyons, pianist John Lewis and percussionist Max Roach. The enlistment of these jazz luminaries counteracted an uneasy situation which had developed wherein young jazz students were having difficulty in understanding that all jazz styles are interconnected.

Two of the great pioneers of free jazz, Charles Mingus and Ornette Coleman, did not take up formal teaching posts. Both chose to transmit inspiration by performing. No sooner was Mingus described as conventional, than he surprised the jazz world by working with Colombian drum accompanists. Ornette

Coleman also continued to intrigue the jazz world; one of his albums of the 1970s featured interludes where he seemed to be paying direct homage to his early heroes, the Texan blues tenor-sax players. This was a passing reversion and Coleman continued to be a paragon of free improvisation.

One very practical education aid, the Jazz Mobile (a vehicle equipped to present jazz concerts in the open air) gained popularity in the 1970s. The travelling unit, which toured New York City, was organised by pianist Billy Taylor and drummer Dave Bailey.

Few big bands of the 1970s were experimental but trumpeter Don Ellis's Band was a notable exception. Ellis continued his work of the 1960s, in exploring the use of complex time signatures, experimenting with electronics, and connecting jazz with non-European music. Ellis believed that the time signatures of Western European music were divorced from the rest of the world's rhythmic varieties. A big band led by Toshiki Akiyoshi and saxist-flautist Lew Tabackin presented several new blendings of orchestrated tone colours which were creatively presented in a series of extended works that avoided pretentiousness.

Great orthodox jazz soloists, with the priceless gifts of originality and creativity, continued to display their talents. Long after trumpeter Roy Eldridge had celebrated his fifty years as a professional musician he continued to blow jazz that was fiery and inventive. Other senior jazz trumpeters like Dizzy Gillespie, Harry Edison and Clark Terry seemed unaffected by the passing of time. A plethora of individualistic tenor-saxophonists continued to bring pleasure to uncommitted jazz listeners, including Arnett Cobb, Eddie Davis, Dexter Gordon, Bud Freeman, Scott Hamilton, Jimmy Heath, Eddie Miller, Flip Phillips, Zoot Sims, Sonny Rollins, Buddy Tate and Warne Marsh. Marsh's one-time colleague alto-saxophonist Lee Konitz, led a much-praised nine-piece band, based in New York City.

A category known as mainstream-modern developed. It included young players who had taken stock of jazz developments before selecting a mixture of swing and bop for the basis of their improvisations. Bill Watrous, a trombonist with an amazingly facile technique was one example. Another trombonist, Carl Fontana, sounded equally at home playing in dixieland bands or in hard-bop units. Pianist Monty Alexander from Kingston, Jamaica, consistently produced swinging, eclectic improvisations. Some young musicians like trumpeter Woody Shaw were equally adept playing orthodox jazz, or working in free form. A single jazz solo lasting for an hour was less common; the trend was for improvisations that were more direct and concise. Tenor-saxophonist Stanley Turrentine made the point that if you cannot say it in two choruses you might as well give it up.[10] The 1970s could be noted for the prominence given to the growing number of multi-instrumentalists, two of the most remarkable of whom were Ira Sullivan, who played saxophone, trumpet, flute and percussion supremely well, and Howard Johnson, whose versatility enabled him to perform expertly on baritone-saxophone, tuba, flugelhorn and clarinet.

The role of the vibraphone remained generally unchanged during the 1970s. The technique of playing with four mallets, which had been perfected by Gary Burton, was gradually adopted by all vibes-players and it gave them opportunity to play four-part harmonies. Most vibes-players worked within the broad mainstream-modern field, but in free jazz some players attempted to eliminate the instrument's mellow qualities replacing them with a percussiveness that was reminiscent of an African *marimba*.

The virtuosi guitarists Barney Kessel, Herb Ellis, Joe Pass, Jim Hall, Tiny Grimes, Al Casey, Tal Farlow and Jimmy Raney remained constantly popular with fans of orthodox jazz. One versatile guitarist, George Benson, achieved a popularity that was like that of a pop super-star, his big-selling records being regularly heard on radio and television. His success was exceptional; the dilemma that plagued most young jazz musicians was that their work was rarely given mass media exposure. Jazz, of any sort, was seldom played on widely-heard radio shows. Hardest hit were those who played free jazz and many of the music's finest practitioners were virtually unknown to the general public. The ragtime revival of the early 1970s was a perfect example of the selling power that repeated radio plays could create for unfamiliar sounds – in this case Scott Joplin's tune 'The Entertainer'.

Two of the main factors that popularised early jazz – vocals and organised dancing – have not developed to any degree in the free jazz movement. Their absence has undoubtedly slowed down the general public's awareness, and possible acceptance. The innovators of the new music have taken the sound of contemporary jazz further and further away from Tin Pan Alley song structures, but most of their potential listeners have been bombarded by Tin Pan Alley tunes, via the media, since the day that they were born. Nevertheless, those who organise, and play within, the loft scene are encouraged by the open-mindedness of their audiences.

Undoubtedly, the internecine controversies about the merits of various jazz styles have dissipated the number of potential jazz followers. Too often, people trying to take their first steps in jazz appreciation are confused, and scattered, by the sectarian bickerings. Jazz listening and impartiality have rarely gone hand-in-hand, and some of the printed criticisms have been absurdly biased. If in literary criticism it was said that no books were worth considering if they were written before 1930, or alternatively, after 1960, everyone would instantly realise that such a creed was ludicrous, yet, to this day, similar view-points are expressed by some musicians and critics. These same people want jazz to be considered an art form, yet they apply the critiques of the fashion industry.

Mercifully, many of today's jazz listeners are learning to trust their own emotional reactions to a music that has many unique qualities. Jazz gives immense scope to individual musicians. Listeners who are new to jazz can soon recognise the unmistakable traits of various improvisers, and those hearing it for the first time often respond immediately to both its rhythmic stimulation and to the excitement of hearing phrases created *and* performed within a fleeting instant. The very ethos of the music is that its creators often produce rhythmic and melodic patterns that exist only in jazz improvisations. One recorded phrase from a great improviser can, at the same moment, inspire listeners in many different lands. Jazz has slowly become an international music whose sounds can bridge differences of class, creed and language. Its unpredictability will probably preclude it from ever gaining mass popularity, but as long as listeners respond to a jazz performance, from any era, the music will survive.

Recommended Reading

Carr, Ian *Music Outside* (Contemporary jazz in Britain), Latimer New Dimensions, London, 1973

Coryell, Julie and Friedman, Laura *Jazz-Rock Fusion* (The People, the Music), Marion Boyars, London, 1978

Taylor, Arthur *Notes and Tones* (Interviews with important black jazz musicians), Arthur Taylor, Liege, Belgium, 1977

Wilmer, Valerie *As Serious As Your Life* (A summary of free jazz and its creators), Allison and Busby/Quartet Books, London, 1977

Glossary

Atonal Music that has no established key, or tonal centre.

Boogie-woogie A style of piano playing in which the left hand continually repeats a series of bass patterns while the right hand improvises incisive, varying phrases. It is usually performed on a twelve-bar blues, the left-hand patterns producing an effect that suggests eight beats in each bar.

Bossa Nova A fusion between Brazilian rhythms and jazz improvisations which achieved popularity in the early 1960s.

Break A short interlude, usually lasting for two bars, where all accompaniment ceases, allowing a soloist to improvise a short unaccompanied phrase.

Chase When two or more jazz musicians take consecutive turns at improvising on short sections of a tune, they are said to be indulging in a 'chase'. The usual length of a chase is four bars. Soloist A plays four bars, then soloist B improvises on the next four bars, soloist A takes the next four bars, soloist B the next four, etc. If more than two musicians are involved the pattern would be: soloist A four bars, B four bars, C four bars, D the next four bars, and so on, eventually returning to A and then following the previous pattern. Occasionally, all of the wind instrumentalists take it in turn to play a chase with the drummer. Soloist A plays four bars, the drummer then plays four bars, soloist B plays four bars, which is followed by four bars of drumming, and so forth.

Circular Breathing A technique whereby a musician trains himself, or herself, to breathe in through the nose while expelling air from the mouth into a musical instrument. Thus the flow of long musical phrases is not interrupted by the need to take in more air through the mouth.

Double-time An effect created when a jazz soloist temporarily plays at twice the tempo of his accompanists. While they are completing one bar at the original tempo he plays two bars of improvisation at twice the speed. *Doubling-up* occurs when everyone in a band, at a given signal, accelerates the tempo to a speed which is exactly double the tempo that they have just left.

Harmonics When a musical note is played it gives off vibrations. Besides the vibrations of the fundamental note there occurs a whole series of vibrations which produce subsidiary notes (or overtones) of a higher pitch; these are called harmonics. Most of the time, the listener pays no direct attention to them, and listens only to the note they emanate from. The term *natural harmonics* is increasingly used to describe this process. The word *harmonics* is increasingly used to describe the notes in the extreme high register of any non-keyboard instrument. Some saxophonists, by devising a new system of fingering, can produce notes that were formerly thought to be beyond the instruments' potential range. These high notes are often referred to as *harmonics*.

Jam Session Informal gathering where jazz musicians improvise without using any sort of arrangement – written or verbal. The tunes to be played, and their duration, are chosen solely by the participants.

Microtone Any interval smaller than a semitone, i.e. two notes whose distance apart would be smaller than the sound of two adjoining notes on a piano keyboard.

Modes The ancient scale-systems that were used prior to the development (*circa* 1600) of the major and minor scales which form the basis of European music.

Ostinato A musical figure, or phrase, that repeats itself over and over again – as in boogie-woogie.

Pizzicato The plucking of a stringed instrument that is usually bowed. Occasionally, a jazz violinist will temporarily cease bowing and pick at the strings with his finger-tips. Conversely, a jazz string-bassist gets his sound by plucking the strings, but occasionally uses a bow to produce notes (he is then said to be playing *arco*).

Polyphony Occurs when two or more instruments simultaneously play parts that are different both in melody and rhythm.

Riff A two-bar or four-bar phrase that is constructed in such a way as to allow it to be played throughout all the chord progressions of a particular tune with the minimum of note alteration. Riffs are usually played as background accompaniment to a soloist's improvisations, but occasionally a melodic riff becomes a tune in its own right as in 'One O'Clock Jump', 'My Guy's Come Back', etc.

Scat A vocal style where the singer improvises wordless syllable patterns. Apocryphally it is said to have come into being when Louis Armstrong dropped a sheet of lyrics while recording a vocal and for continuity sang rhythmic sounds instead of words.

Sidemen Employees of a bandleader.

Snare-drum A small side-drum with a turnable switch which tenses a series of coiled wires against the skin of the drums. The clamped coils vibrate crisply when the drum is struck.

Stride piano A style in which the pianist provides his own bass accompaniment by firmly playing (with his left hand) a single bass note on the first and third beats of each bar (which are usually called the strong beats), and follows this by playing a bass register chord (also with his left hand) on the second and fourth beats (usually called the weak beats). Another speciality of the stride pianist is the playing of tenths whereby the left hand spans the keyboard and plays two notes that are ten notes apart.

Synthesiser A machine which transmits electronic signals into audible sounds the pitch of which can be controlled to produce musical notes. The timbre of these notes can be adjusted to sound like orthodox musical instruments.

Tonic The first note of a major or minor scale. Also the note that establishes the key (or tonal centre) of a piece of music. Most tunes end on the tonic note.

Walking Bass A bass line that does not reiterate the same note consecutively but continuously moves up and down the notes of a chord.

Recommended records

Chapter two

Keppard, Freddie *Jazz Cardinals* (also has tracks by Sidney Bechet and Louis Armstrong), Fountain FJ 107

Morgan, Sam *Sam Morgan's Jazz Band*, VJM VLP 32

Morton, Jelly Roll *The Library of Congress Recordings* (eight volumes), Classic Jazz Masters 2–9

New Orleans Jazz *Various Bands* (three volumes), RCA Black and White 741107/7003/7127

New Orleans Ragtime Orchestra (featuring Bill Russell), Arhoolie 1058

Original Dixieland Jazz Band *Two volumes*, RCA Black and White 730/703–704

The Halfway House Orchestra *1925–28*, VJM VLP 32

The Sounds of New Orleans *Jazz Odyssey* (three volumes), Columbia C3L 30

Chapter three

Armstrong, Louis *Okeh recordings*, CBS VSOP 88001/2/2/3

Austin High School Gang *That Toddlin' Town 1926–28*, Parlophone PMC 7072/Swaggie S 1255

Chicago Jazz *1925–29* (two volumes), Biograph 12005/12043

Dodds, Johnny *1926–29* (two volumes), MCA Coral 7362 D 1/2

Dodds, Johnny and Ory, Kid *New Orleans Wanderers*, Columbia JLA 16004

Morton, Jelly Roll *Red Hot Peppers 1926–27*, RCA Black and White 731–059

New Orleans Rhythm Kings *1922–23* (two volumes), Milestone M 47020

Noone, Kimmie *1937–41*, Swaggie S 1226

Oliver, King *Creole Jazz Band 1923*, Herwin H 106

Ory, Kid *Sunshine Band*/and others, Arcadia 2001

Spanier, Muggsy *1920s in Chicago*, Fountain FJ 108

The Sounds of Chicago *Jazz Odyssey*, Columbia C3L 32

The Wolverines (complete) (Featuring Bix Beiderbecke), Fountain FJ 114

Chapter four

Jazz From St Louis *1924–26* (Fate Marable, etc.), Parlophone PMC 7157/Swaggie 1258

McKinney's Cotton Pickers *1928–31* (four volumes), RCA Black and White 1080/1088/1109/7059
Missourians *1929–30*, RCA Black and White FPM1 7017
Moten, Bennie *Kansas City Orchestra 1923–25*, Parlophone PMC 7119
Moten, Bennie *Count Basie in Kansas City*, RCA Black and White FXM1 7062
Rainey, Ma *1925–28* (two volumes), Milestone M 47021
Smith, Bessie *Complete recordings* (ten albums), CBS 66258/62/64/73 and 67232
Teagarden, Jack *King of the Blues Trombone*, Columbia JSN 6044
Territory Bands *1925–20*, Parlophone PMC 7082
Territory Jazz *1925–32*, RCA Black and White FXM1 7205
The Territories *Volume 2 1927–33*, Arcadia 2007

Chapter five
Allen, Henry *1929–31*, RCA Black and White FXM1 7060/7090/7192
Beiderbecke, Bix *The Young Man With The Horn*, CBS 88030
Ellington, Duke *1925–38* (ten double albums), Available on CBS
Henderson, Fletcher (Featuring Louis Armstrong (1924–25)), VJM VLP 60
Jazz in Harlem *Various Bands 1926–31*, Arcadia 20008
Johnson, James P. *Father of the Stride Piano*, Columbia CL 1780
Nichols, Red *1926–27*, Classic Jazz Masters CJM 24
Original Memphis Five *The Sounds of New York*, RCA Black and White 741 115
Scott Cecil/Johnson, Charlie and their Orchestras 1927–29, RCA Black and White 741 065/066
Small Bands (The Greatest of . . .) *From Chicago to New York* (Volume four), RCA Black and White 741 103
Swing Street *1933–45* (four volumes), Columbia JSM 6042
The Sounds of Harlem *Jazz Odyssey*, Columbia C3L 33
Venuti, Joe and Lang, Eddie *Stringing The Blues*, CBS 88142

Chapter seven
Basie, Count *Best of . . .* (two volumes), MCA 2–4050
Coleman, Bill *In Paris*, Pathé HTX 40328
Crosby, Bob *Big Noise From Winnetka*, MCA 2695
Dorsey, Tommy and his Orchestra, RCA Victor DPM 2026
Eldridge, Roy *Heckler's Hop 1935–40*, Tax M 8020
Ellington, Duke (Twenty separate albums covering years 1927–1945), Available on RCA Victor
Goodman, Benny *The complete years 1935–37* (four double albums), Bluebird AXM2 5505/15/32/37
Goodman, Benny *Carnegie Hall Concert 1938*, CBS 66202
Hampton, Lionel *The complete small groups*, RCA AXM 5536
Henderson, Fletcher *1936*, Bluebird 25507
Swing *Various Bands 1936–46*, RCA LPV 578
Tatum, Art *Masterpieces*, MCA 4019
Tatum, Art *Group Masterpieces*, Pablo 2625 706
The World of Swing *Various Bands*, CBS 88134
Waller, Fats (Complete recordings available on), RCA Black and White

Webb, Chick *Stomping At The Savoy*, CBS 52537
Young, Lester (also features Billie Holiday), CBS 88223

Chapter eight
Armstrong, Louis *Town Hall Concert 1947*, RCA Black and White 731 052
Bechet, Sidney (also features Bunk Johnson), Blue Note 81201/02
Bechet, Sidney *The Panassie Sessions*, RCA FXM1 7094
Condon, Eddie *Trombones*, London HMC 5007
Echoes from New Orleans (Various Bands of the 1940s (two volumes)), Storyville SLP 203/212
Freeman, Bud *Home Cooking (1933–40)*, Tax M 8019
Hodges, Johnny *Love in Swingtime 1938–39*, Tax M 8022
Johnson, Bunk *1944* (four volumes), Storyville SLP 128/202/205/152
Kirby, John *Boss of the Bass*, Columbia CG 33557
Newton, Frank *At The Onyx Club*, Tax M 8017
Original Boogie Woogie Sounds *1940s*, CBS (Fr) 80049
Ory, Kid *Tailgate (1944–5)*, Good Time Jazz L 12022
Shaw, Artie *Gramercy Five*, RCA Victor LSA 3087
Spanier, Muggsy *The Great 16*, RCA Black and White 731 061
Smith, Stuff (also features Jonah Jones), Collector's 12–12

Chapter nine
Chaloff, Serge *Blue Serge*, Capitol M 11032
Christian, Charlie *At Minton's*, Saga 6919/Everest FS 219
Christian, Charlie *Solo Flight*, CBS (Fr) 67233
Ellington, Duke *The World of . . . 1947–51*, CBS 88128
Garner, Errol *Concert By The Sea*, CBS 62310
Gillespie, Dizzy *When Be-Bop Met The Big Bands*, RCA Black and White 741095/731068
Gray, Wardell *Central Avenue*, Prestige PR 24062
Hawkins, Coleman *Body and Soul*, RCA FXM1 7325
Herman, Woody *The Thundering Herds*, Columbia C3L 25
Jazz at the Philharmonic *1946*, Verve 2610 020/024
Jordan, Louis *The Best of . . .*, MCA MCFM 2715
Navarro, Fats *Fat Girl*, Savoy SJL 2216
Parker, Charlie *Greatest Jazz Concert Ever* (also features Dizzy Gillespie), Prestige 24024
Parker, Charlie *The Definitive* (also features Miles Davis), Verve 2356 087
Powell, Bud *The Amazing . . .* (two volumes), Blue Note BST 81503/4
The Changing Face of Harlem *1944* (two volumes), Savoy SJL 2208
Thornhill, Claude *The Memorable* (two volumes), Columbia KG 32906

Chapter eleven
Adderley, Cannonball *Beginnings*, EmArcy EMS2 404
Basie, Count *Atomic Chairman*, Vogue VJD 517
Brown, Clifford *In concert* (also features Max Roach), GNP 18
Brubeck, Dave *All Time Greatest Hits*, Columbia 32761

Clayton, Buck *Swingin' Buck*, CBS 88031
Davis, Miles *The complete birth of the Cool*, Capitol M 11026
Davis, Miles *Sketches of Spain* (with Gil Evans), CBS 62327
Davis, Miles *Kind of Blue* (with John Coltrane), CBS 62066
Dickenson, Vic *Septet* (two volumes), Vanguard VRS 8520/1
Evans, Bill *Empathy*, Verve 2332 087
Getz, Stan *Moonlight in Vermont*, Vogue VJD 539
Jazz Messengers *Art Blakey with . . .*, CBS (Fr) 88060
Jazztime USA *Various Bands 1952–62*, MCA Coral MSP 806
Johnson, J. J. (and Kai Winding) *At Birdland*, RCA PL 42069
Kenton, Stan *Greatest Hits*, Capitol CAPS 1002
Lewis, George *1940s*, Storyville SLP 103/201
Mingus, Charles *Tiajuana Moods*, FXL1 7295
Modern Jazz Quartet *1950s*, Prestige PR 24005
Modern Jazz Quartet *The Last Concert*, Atlantic 60098
Monk, Thelonius *Genius of Modern Music*, Blue Note BST 81510/11
Mulligan, Gerry (with Chet Baker), Prestige 24016
Reinhardt, Django *Hot Club du France* (two volumes), Ace of Clubs ACL 1158/1189
Rogers, Shorty *Blues Express*, FXL1 7324
Silver, Horace *Best of . . .*, Blue Note BST 84325
Watters, Lu *Yerba Buena* (early 1940s), Goodtime L 12007

Chapter twelve

Ayler, Albert *At Saint Paul De Vence*, Shandar SR 10000
Bley, Paul *Barrage*, ESP 1008
Coleman, Ornette *Something Else* (with Don Cherry), Contemporary 57 551
Coleman, Ornette *At the Golden Circle*, Blue Note BST 84224/5
Coltrane, John *The best of . . .*, Atlantic SD2–313
Coltrane, John *Giant Steps*, Atlantic ATL 50 239
Davis, Miles *Bitches Brew*, CBS 66236
Dolphy, Eric *Memorial*, DJM 22041
Ellington, Duke *And His Mother Called Him Bill*, RCA LSA 3073
Kirk, Rahsaan Roland *Inflated Tear*, Atlantic 50233
Mingus, Charles *Town Hall Concert*, Fantasy JWS 9
Rollins, Sonny *Live at Montreux*, Milestone M 9
Rollins, Sonny *The Cutting Edge*, Milestone M 9059
Sanders, Pharoah *Karma*, Impulse AS 9181
Shepp, Archie *Attica Blues*, Impulse AS 9222
Sun Ra *Atlantis*, Impulse AS 9239
Taylor, Cecil *Looking Ahead*, Contemporary 7562

Chapter fourteen

Abrams, Muhal Richard *Things To Come*, Delmark DS–430
Alexander, Monty *Love and Sunshine*, MPS 68 043
Altschul, Barry *You Can't Name Your Own Tune*, Muse MR 5124
Art Ensemble of Chicago *Phase 1*, America 30 AM 6116
Barbieri, Gato *Alive in New York*, Impulse 8008

Braxton, Anthony *Duets with M. R. Abrams*, Arista 4101
Braxton, Anthony *The Complete . . .* (two volumes), Freedom FLPX 40112/3
Burton, Gary *Duets with Chick Corea*, ECM 1024
Cherry, Don *Brown Rice*, A and M SP 717
Coleman, Ornette *Crisis*, Impulse 8002
Coleman, Ornette *Dancing in your Head*, AM L5 722
Coryell, Larry *The Essential 1969–72*, Vanguard VSD 75
Coltrane, John *Ascension*, Impulse A 95
Ferguson, Maynard *New Vintage*, CBS 82282
Haden, Charlie *Closeness*, Horizon SP 710
Hancock, Herbie *The Best of . . .*, Blue Note BST 89907
Jarrett, Keith *Facing You*, ECM 1017
Jenkins, LeRoy *Duets with Rashied Ali*, Survival SR 112
Mingus, Charles *Changes*, Atlantic K 50202
New Orleans to Scandinavia *Veterans on tour*, Storyville SLP 232
Rich, Buddy *The Buddy Rich*, Sunset 505/6
Rivers, Sam *Fizzle*, Impulse IMPL 8025
Sanders, Pharoah *Elevation*, Impulse AS 9261
Taylor, Cecil *Indent*, Freedom FLP 41038
The New York Loft Scenes *1976* (five volumes), Wildflowers 1–5
Tyner, McCoy *Super Trios*, Milestone M 55003
Venuti, Joe *With Zoot Sims 1974*, Chiaroscuro CR 128
VSOP *The Quintet*, CBS 88273
Weather Report *Heavy Weather*, CBS 81775
World's Greatest Jazz Band (Two volumes), Atlantic K 60018

Further Reading

Balliett, Whitney *The Sound of Surprise*, E. P. Dutton, USA, 1959

Balliett, Whitney *Dinosaurs in the Morning*, Phoenix House, London, 1962

Balliett, Whitney *Such Sweet Thunder*, Macdonald, London, 1968

Balliett, Whitney *Ecstasy at the Onion*, Bobbs-Merrill, USA, 1971

Balliett, Whitney *New York Notes*, Houghton Mifflin, USA, 1976

Balliett, Whitney *Improvising*, Oxford University Press, USA, 1977
(All Mr Balliett's books are warmly recommended – contents consist mainly of reprints from *The New Yorker* magazine)

Berendt, Joachim (ed.) *The Story of Jazz* (Articles by specialist writers on jazz developments), Barrie and Jenkins, London, 1978

Berendt, Joachim *The New Jazz Book* (A history and guide), Peter Owen, London, 1964

Biagioni, Egino *Herb Flemming* (A jazz pioneer around the world), Micrography, Holland, 1978

Blesh, Rudi *Combo USA* (Biographical essays on well-known jazz figures), Chilton, USA, 1971

Blesh, Rudi Shining Trumpets (A general history with musical examples), Alfred Knopf, USA, 1958

Borneman, Ernest *A Critic Looks at Jazz* (Historical background and analysis), Jazz Music Books, London, 1946

Borneman, Ernest *Jazz Research/Jazz Forschung* (Contains Mr Borneman's 'Jazz and the Creole Tradition'), Universal Editions AG, Vienna, 1969

Borneman, Ernest *Jazz Research/Jazz Forschung* (Contains Mr Borneman's 'Notes for a History of American Negro Music'), Universal Editions AG, Vienna, 1970

Case, B. and Britt, S. *The Illustrated Encyclopedia of Jazz*, Salamander Books, London, 1978

Cerulli, Dom *The Jazz Word* (Essays covering various jazz eras), Dennis Dobson, London, 1962

Collier, James Lincoln *The Making of Jazz* (A brilliant, comprehensive history), Granada Publishing, UK, 1978

Condon, Eddie and Gehman, R. *Eddie Condon's Treasury of Jazz* (Wide-ranging essays from many writers), Dial Press, USA, 1956

Esquire *Esquire's World of Jazz* (A sumptuous production containing beautiful illustrations and interesting articles), Crowell, Thomas, USA, 1965

Feather, Leonard *The Book of Jazz* (A guide to the entire field), Arthur Barker, London, 1957

Feather, Leonard and Tracy, Jack *Laughter From the Hip* (Humorous anecdotes about jazzmen), Horizon Press, USA, 1963

Feather, Leonard *From Satchmo to Miles* (First-hand observations of a dozen jazz greats), Stein and Day, USA, 1971

Feather, Leonard *The Pleasures of Jazz* (Articles on star performers from various jazz eras), Horizon Press, USA, 1976

Finkelstein, Sidney *Jazz – A People's Music* (Analysis, and prognosis, of jazz), Citadel Press, USA, 1948

Fox, Charles (with photographs by Wilmer, Valerie) *The Jazz Scene* (Covers the whole spectrum of jazz concisely), Hamlyn, London, 1972

Fox, Charles *Jazz in Perspective* (A concise but authoritative history), BBC, London, 1969

Gammond, Peter (ed.) *The Decca Book of Jazz* (Essays from diverse hands on specialised aspects of jazz), F. Muller, London, 1958

Gleason, Ralph (ed.) *Jam Session* (Selected essays from all eras), Putnam's, USA, 1958

Gleason, Ralph *Celebrating the Duke* (Wide-ranging essays), Little Brown, USA, 1975

Goffin, Robert *Jazz – From Congo to the Metropolitan* (A general history), Doubleday, USA, 1945

Goldblatt, Burt *Newport Jazz Festival* (The illustrated History), Dial Press, USA, 1977

Green, Benny *The Reluctant Art* (Essays on Beiderbecke, Goodman, Young, Holiday and Parker), Macgibbon and Kee, London, 1962

Gridley, Mark C. *Jazz Styles* (An analysis of 60 years of jazz), Prentice-Hall Inc., USA, 1978

Grossman, W. L. and Farrell, J. W. *The Heart of Jazz* (A controversial evaluation of the traditional jazz revival), Vision Press, London, 1958

Hodeir, Andre *Jazz: Its Evolution and Essence* (Thoughtful analysis of the jazz improvisers' role), Grove Press, USA, 1956

Hodeir, Andre *Toward Jazz* (A musicologist's critical writings), Grove Press, USA, 1962

Harrison, Max *A Jazz Retrospect* (Thought-provoking essays on jazz and jazzmen), David and Charles, England, 1976

Hentoff, Nat *The Jazz Life* (An exploration of the social, economical, and psychological aspects of a jazzman's life), Dial Press, USA, 1961

Hentoff, Nat *Jazz Is* (Essays on famous jazz musicians), Random House, USA, 1976

James, Burnett *Essays on Jazz* (Erudite reprints from *Jazz Monthly*), Sidgwick and Jackson, London, 1961

Keepnews, O. and Grauer, B. *A Pictorial History of Jazz* (From New Orleans to Bop), Crown, USA, 1955

Langridge, Derek *Your Jazz Collection* (A comprehensive handbook on how to organise a jazz collection), Clive Bingley, London, 1970

Larkin, Philip Larkin *All What Jazz (A Record Diary 1961–68)* (A reprint of wide-ranging record reviews), Faber and Faber, London, 1970

Leonard, Neil *Jazz and the White Americans* (A study of the social and intellectual implications of white American's acceptance of jazz), University of Chicago, USA, 1962

Lyttelton, Humphrey *The Best of Jazz* (Illuminating essays on great jazz performances), Robson Books, London, 1978

McCarthy, A., Morgan, A., Oliver, P. and Harrison, M. *Jazz on Record* (A critical guide to the first fifty years), Hanover Books, London, 1968

Morgenstern, D. (text) and Brask, O. (photographs) *Jazz People* (An art production containing fine photographs and far-sighted writing), Harry N. Abrams, USA, 1976

Newton, Francis *The Jazz Scene* (A scholarly study of jazz, and its social phenomena), Penguin Special, London, 1959

Ostransky, Leroy *Understanding Jazz* (Deals with the problem of defining jazz; includes a chapter on musical elements), Prentice Hall, USA, 1977

Ostransky, Leroy *The Anatomy of Jazz* (A detailed discussion of the technical aspects of jazz), University of Washington, USA, 1960

Panassie, Hugues *The Real Jazz* (A list of recommended recordings), Smith and Durrell, USA, 1942

Panassie, Hugues *Hot Jazz* (A passionate summary of early jazz), Cassell, London, 1936

Pleasants, Henry *Serious Music – And All That Jazz* (Learned discussion about Afro-American music), Gollancz, London, 1969

Sargeant, Winthrop *Jazz: Hot and Hybrid* (An evaluation and comparison of jazz with other forms of art, with musical illustrations), Lowe and Brydone, London, 1959

Shapiro, N. and Hentoff, N. (eds.) *Hear Me Talkin' To Ya* (Fascinating accounts of jazz's development culled from magazine interviews with jazz musicians), Peter Davies, London, 1955

Shapiro, N. and Hentoff, N. (eds.) *The Jazz Makers* (Twenty-one articles by leading jazz writers), Rinehart and Co., USA, 1957

Stearns, Marshall *The Story of Jazz* (A general history), Sidgwick and Jackson, London, 1957

Summerfield, Maurice J. *The Jazz Guitar* (Its evolution and its players), Ashley Mark, UK, 1978

Tirro, Frank *Jazz – A History* (Wide ranging, and illustrated), W. W. Norton and Co., USA, 1977

Toledano, Ralph de *Frontiers of Jazz* (Reprints of interesting magazine articles), Oliver Durrell, USA, 1947

Townley, Eric *Tell Your Story* (Explanation of the meaning of esoteric jazz tune titles), Storyville, London, 1976

Traill, S. and Lascelles, G. (eds.) *Just Jazz* (four volumes) (Diverse essays):

I Peter Davies, London, 1957
II Peter Davies, London, 1958

III Four Square Books, London, 1959
IV Souvenir Press, London, 1960

Ulanov, Barry *A History of Jazz in America* (A detailed survey up to and including bop), Viking Press, London, 1952

Williams, Martin (ed.) *The Art of Jazz* (Essays on the nature and development of jazz), Oxford University Press, USA, 1959

Williams, Martin (ed.) *Jazz Panorama* (Essays reprinted from *The Jazz Review*), Crowell-Collier, USA, 1962

Williams, Martin *Where's The Melody* (A listener's introduction to jazz), Pantheon Books, USA, 1969

Wilmer, Valerie *Jazz People* (Illustrated essays on important jazz musicians), Allison and Busby, London, 1977

Wilson, John S. *Jazz: The Transition Years 1940–60*, Appleton, USA, 1966

Wilson, John S. *The Collector's Jazz* (An alphabetical selection of record recommendations), Lippincott, USA, 1958

Wilson, John S. *The Collector's Jazz – Modern* (Critical guide to jazz on microgroove), Lippincott, USA, 1959

Reference Books

Chilton, John *Who's Who of Jazz* (Over a thousand biographies of jazz musicians born before 1920), Bloomsbury Book Shop, London, 1970

Feather, Leonard *The Encyclopedia of Jazz* (contains biographies and assessments), Bonanza Books, USA 1960 and Quartet Books, London, 1978

Feather, Leonard *The Encyclopedia of Jazz in the 1960s* (An up-dated version of the previous entry), Horizon Press, USA, 1966

Feather, Leonard (and Gitler, Ira) *The Encyclopedia of Jazz in the 1970s* (Another up-dated and revised edition), Horizon Press, USA, 1976

Ferris, William *Mississippi Black Folklore* (A research bibliography and discography), University of Mississippi, USA, 1971

Gold, Robert S. *A Jazz Lexicon* (A dictionary of jazz jargon), Alfred Knopf, USA, 1964

Jepsen, Jorgen G. *Jazz Records 1942–68* (Discography in eleven volumes), Karl Emil Knudsen, Copenhagen, Denmark, 1970

Mecklenburg, C. G. H. zu *International Jazz Bibliography* (A detailed bibliography), Verlag Heitz, Baden-Baden, 1969 (1971–73 Supplement published by Studies in Jazz Research, Universal Edition AG, Vienna, 1975)

Meeker, David *Jazz in the Movies* (A detailed guide to 2500 films which contain jazz), Talisman Books, London, 1970

Merriam, A. P. and Benford, R. J. *A Bibliography of Jazz* (An impressive listing of book and magazine references up until 1950), American Folklore Society, USA, 1954

Panassie, Hugues *Dictionary of Jazz* (Selected biographies), Cassell, London, 1956

Rust, Brian *Jazz Records 1897–1942* (In two volumes: A–KAR and KAR–Z), Storyville, London, 1969

Stagg, T. and Crump, C. *New Orleans, The Revival* (A comprehensive listing covering records of the 1940s, 1950s and 1960s), Bashall Eaves, Dublin, 1973

Varley, Douglas *African Native Music* (An annotated bibliography), Dawsons of Pall Mall, London, 1970

Recommended Jazz Magazines and Periodicals (published in English)

Cadence (monthly) covers all styles. Rt. 1, Box 345, Redwood, NY 13679, USA

Coda (six issues a year) Covers all areas of jazz. Box 87, Station J, Toronto, Ontario, Canada

Crescendo (monthly) Mainly for performing musicians, but long articles on jazzmen are often included. 122 Wardour Street, London W1

Down Beat (fortnightly) Principally concerned with active jazz performers, it is sub-headed 'the contemporary music magazine'; also contains valuable technical advice. 222 W Adams Street, Chicago, Illinois, USA

Footnote (bi-monthly) Devoted to New Orleans music. 44 High Street, Meldreth, Royston, Hertfordshire

Jazz Index (quarterly) A bibliography of jazz literature in periodicals of various countries. Norbert Ruecker, Kleiststr. 39, Frankfurt/M 1, Germany

Jazz Journal International (monthly) Covers a wide spectrum. 7 Carnaby Street, London W1V 1PG

Journal of the Institute of Jazz Studies (occasional) A scholarly journal. Rutgers Institute of Jazz Studies, Transaction Periodicals Consortium, Rutgers University, New Brunswick, New Jersey, 08903, USA

Melody Maker (weekly) Now mainly devoted to pop music, but still carries detailed articles and record reviews on all aspects of jazz. 24–34 Meymott Street, London SE1 9 LU

Mississippi Rag (monthly) Summarises today's American traditional jazz but also has long articles on jazz veterans. 5644 Morgan Avenue South, Minneapolis, Minnesota, 55419, USA

Second Line (quarterly) Dedicated to the music of New Orleans, past and present. 1227 Webster Street, New Orleans, Louisiana 70118, USA

Storyville (bi-monthly) Devoted to 'classic jazz' from the pre-bop era, often contains rare photographs. 66 Fairview Drive, Chigwell, Essex

Notes to the Text

Chapter two

1. Dominic La Rocca: *Down Beat*, April 1937
2. Donald M. Marquis: Mr Marquis's book *In Search of Buddy Bolden – First Man of Jazz* (Louisiana State University Press, 1978) also contains biographical details of Buddy Bolden, February 1978
3. George Bacquet: *Down Beat*, 15 December 1940
4. Manuel Manetta: William Ransom Hogan Archive, Tulane University, New Orleans, interviewed 21 March 1957
5. George Bacquet: *Down Beat*, 15 December 1940
6. George Bacquet: *Down Beat*, 15 December 1940
7. Dr Leonard Bechet: *Mister Jelly Roll*, p. 96, Duell, Sloan and Pearce, USA, 1950
8. George Foster: *Pops Foster, New Orleans Jazzman*, p. 90, University of California, USA, 1971
9. Manuel Manetta: William Ransom Hogan Archive, New Orleans, interviewed 21 March 1957
10. George Bacquet: *Down Beat*, 1 January 1941
11. Tom Brown: *Second Line*, February 1951
12. Florian Lizana: William Ransom Hogan Archive, New Orleans, interviewed 18 May 1966
13. Richard Holbrook: *Storyville*, Issue 50 (December 1973–January 1974)
14. A wealth of information on the ODJB's work in Chicago and New York is contained in Jean-Christophe Averty's two-part summary of the band's history which appeared in *Les Cahiers du Jazz*, Issues 3 and 4, published in Paris, 1961

Chapter three

1. Paul Whiteman: *Jazz*, p. 138, J. H. Sears, USA, 1926
2. Percy M. Bergman: *A Chronological History of the Negro in America*, p. 396, Harper and Row, USA, 1969
3. Mutt Carey: *Hear Me Talkin' To Ya*, p. 53, Peter Davies, London, 1955
4. Bob Shoffner: *Down Beat*, 18 January 1962

5. Muggsy Spanier: *Down Beat*, 26 June 1958
6. Gene Krupa: *Down Beat*, 14 March 1974
7. *Metronome*: February 1928
8. *Metronome*: May 1929
9. Jelly Roll Morton: *Mister Jelly Roll*, p. 64, Duell, Sloan and Pearce, USA, 1950

Chapter four

1. Tony Catalono: *Down Beat*, May 1938
2. Louis Armstrong: *Swing That Music*, pp. 52–54, Longmans Green, London, 1937
3. William Ridgley: William Ransom Hogan Archive, New Orleans, interviewed 7 April 1961
4. Walter Page: *Jazz Review*, November 1958
5. Allen R. Carter (Chairman, Charleston Dance Committee): quoted on record sleeve Charleston NR 6386–1
6. James P. Johnson: *Jazz Review*, July 1959
7. John W. Work: *American Negro Songs and Spirituals*, p. 32, Bonanza Books, USA, 1940

Chapter five

1. Charters, S. and Kunstadt, L.: *Jazz, A History of the New York Scene*, p. 55, Doubleday, USA, 1962
2. Garvin Bushell: *Jazz Review*, January 1959
3. James P. Johnson: *Jazz Review*, July 1959
4. Don Redman: *Jazz Review*, November 1959
5. Abel Green: *New York Clipper*, 14 June 1924
6. Paul Whiteman: *Jazz*, p. 242, J. H. Sears, USA, 1926

Chapter seven

1. *Chicago Defender*: p. 7, 21 January 1933
2. Benny Goodman: *Hear Me Talkin' To Ya*, p. 308, Peter Davies, London, 1955

Chapter eight

1. Jelly Roll Morton: *Down Beat*, August 1938
2. Jelly Roll Morton: *Record Changer*, 15 December 1942
3. Bill Russell: *HRS Rag*, October 1940
4. Kid Ory: *Down Beat*, 8 January 1959

Chapter nine

1. Coleman Hawkins: *Melody Maker*, 28 April 1934
2. Dizzy Gillespie: *Down Beat*, 7 October 1949
3. Stan Kenton: *Down Beat*, 14 January 1948
4. Dizzy Gillespie: *Melody Maker*, 25 April 1970
5. Dizzy Gillespie: *Down Beat*, 17 November 1948

Chapter ten

1. Charlie Parker: *Down Beat*, 9 September 1949
2. *Metronome*: July 1929
3. William Fleet: Letter to the author, dated 18 October 1977

4. Lennie Tristano: *Down Beat*, 11 January 1952
5. Warne Marsh: *Coda*, December 1976

Chapter eleven

1. Stan Kenton: *Down Beat*, 14 January 1948
2. Miles Davis: *Down Beat*, 7 August 1958
3. Clifford Brown: *Down Beat*, 4 May 1955

Chapter twelve

1. Don Cherry: *Down Beat*, 21 November 1963
2. John Lewis: Foreword to L. Feather's (*Encyclopedia of Jazz in the Sixties*), Horizon Press, USA, 1966
3. Charles Mingus: *Down Beat*, 26 May 1960
4. Paul Bley: *Down Beat*, 17 January 1974
5. Charles Mingus: *Down Beat*, 26 May 1960
6. Charlie Haden: *Down Beat*, 20 July 1972
7. Archie Shepp: *Down Beat*, 14 January 1965
8. Sun Ra: *Change*, Issue I Fall 1965
9. Ekkehard Jost: *Free Jazz*, Universal Editions, Vienna 1975
10. John Handy III: *Down Beat*, 4 May 1967
11. Ravi Shankar: *Down Beat*, 7 March 1968

Chapter thirteen

1. Ornette Coleman: *Down Beat*, 22 November 1973
2. Ornette Coleman: *Down Beat*, 22 November 1973
3. Ornette Coleman: *Down Beat*, 22 November 1973
4. Charlie Haden: *Down Beat*, 20 July 1972
5. Jimmy Garrison: *Down Beat*, 6 June 1974
6. Warne Marsh: *Coda*, December 1976
7. Jackie McLean: *Down Beat*, 12 September 1963
8. John Coltrane: *Down Beat*, 29 September 1960
9. John Coltrane: *Down Beat*, 29 September 1960
10. Gunther Schuller: *Jazz Review*, November 1959
11. Cecil Taylor: *Down Beat*, 10 April 1975

Chapter fourteen

1. Sam Rivers: *Melody Maker*, 14 August 1976
2. Sam Rivers: *Newsweek*, 8 August 1977
3. Valerie Wilmer: *As Serious As Your Life*, p. 167, Allison and Busby/Quartet, London, 1977
4. Miles Davis: *Down Beat*, 3 September 1970
5. Ron Carter: *Down Beat*, 27 March 1975
6. McCoy Tyner: *Down Beat*, 6 December 1973
7. Herbie Hancock: *Down Beat*, 9 November 1972
8. John McLaughlin: *Down Beat*, 26 April 1973
9. Gato Barbieri: *Down Beat*, 20 June 1974
10. Stanley Turrentine: *Down Beat*, 6 November 1975

Index